# Healing
# Suicidal Veterans

# Healing Suicidal Veterans

Recognizing, Supporting and Answering
Their Pleas for Help

by Victor Montgomery III, MAEd., CMAC, RAS

New Horizon Press
Far Hills, New Jersey

New Horizon Press
P.O. Box 669
Far Hills, NJ 07931

Montgomery III, Victor
Healing Suicidal Veterans: *Recognizing, Supporting and Answering Their Pleas for Help*
Cover design: Wendy Bass
Interior design: Susan Sanderson

Library of Congress Control Number: 2009922795

ISBN 13: 978-0-88282-310-2
New Horizon Press

Manufactured in the U.S.A.

2013  2012  2011  2010  2009  /  5  4  3  2  1

# Author's Note

*Healing Suicidal Veterans* is based on my research and personal experiences counseling and ministering to suicidal veterans and their families and friends. It is meant to reflect my discernment, sensitivity and observations of the personalities, events and conversations as well as the steps, strategies and measures taken to bring them help and hope. I have reconstructed from my recollection and memory of interviews the rescues and, in several cases, the outcomes.

I have taken full responsibility and caution in honoring the anonymity of the veterans, families and survivors around the country who have entrusted me with their stories. In order to protect the identity and privacy of others, I have changed the names of individuals and have altered identifying characteristics.

All references to the definitions of psychological and substance-related disorders come from the American Psychiatric Association's *Diagnostic and Statistical Manual of Mental Disorders* (4th ed., Text Revision. Washington, D.C.: American Psychiatric Association, 2000).

For purposes of simplifying usage, the pronouns his/her and s/he are sometimes used interchangeably.

My opinions are based on my personal experience and do not represent those of the Department of Veterans Affairs or the United States government. This book is not intended to cure or treat injury, illness, disease or any other medical problem by the layman. The information contained herein is not meant to be a substitute for professional evaluation and therapy. Any application of the recommendations set forth in the following pages is at the reader's discretion and sole risk.

# Dedication

This book is for you, our American veterans, and your fathers, mothers, wives, husbands, sons, daughters, brothers, sisters, buddies, friends and extended family.

You have turned to this book with a purpose in mind. What are you looking for? My prayer and desire is that you are looking for HOPE. Whether you are looking at your loved one from the sidelines feeling helpless or are the one thinking of ending your own life, you are my most important person. I am writing to you and for you.

Please be aware you are not alone in this battle to understand the meaning of your life and purpose. Today your mind and heart may feel overwhelmed. Depression and suicidal feelings are signals to get help right away. There are psychological and medical treatments that will help you recover.

You served our country, went to war zones, were successful warriors and returned as veterans. All were admirable and, in many cases, heroic. But now you are unable to make a successful switch to a new phase in your life. Instead you have become one of the countless psychologically traumatized medical casualties of war.

I dedicate this volume to you, to all military personnel around the world in uniform today in Iraq and Afghanistan and to all veterans of prior years' conflicts and wars. This book is especially for those of you who have returned home from foreign soil, forever changed men and women. And for your families and close friends, who in most cases are at home feeling helpless and hopeless watching their once energetic, happy and independent sons or daughters deteriorate physically, spiritually and emotionally before their very eyes.

Through my work I have come to realize that many veterans who served and are serving in war zones around the world think about taking their own lives. An extremely high percentage of returning veterans are using alcohol and other mind-altering chemicals to self-medicate and numb the mental pain and anguish from survivor guilt, loss of a friend, haunting flashbacks, ugly memories and nightmares. I know firsthand, working as a suicide crisis hotline interventionist and addiction therapist, that combat veteran suicides have become daily events. Statistical evidence shows this tragedy is a scourge that is on the rise.

I want to acquaint you with the veterans themselves and families like you and their true stories of suffering. I also want to share with you the ways in which they have learned to hope and triumph over their anguish. For you I present the information, insights and strategies in this book as an opportunity to grow and begin to heal and live again.

I have told you these things, so that in me you may have peace. In this world you will have trouble.
But take heart! I have overcome the world.

John 16:33 (NIV)

# Contents

# Preface

As a professional suicide crisis intervention counselor working in outpatient clinics and on crisis hotlines, hour after hour I have heard the click and cylinder spin of a revolver as the shells were shuffled on a kitchen table and the rattle of a bottle of pills held near the telephone receiver with the threat of an impending overdose. Every day I witness the emotional cries of anger and rage, from the gut level, of men and women being tormented with feelings of hopelessness, abandonment and physical illnesses beyond their abilities to cope. Every day I hear despairing voices saying, "I have nothing to live for."

Veteran suicides are "steadily rising and raising alarms in both the homeless and veterans' communities." Some returning veterans can't find jobs after leaving the military, some are losing their homes because of the mortgage and credit collapse and a good percentage of them begin or continue to struggle psychologically with their war experiences. Many feel the soldiers currently returning from Iraq and Afghanistan are "just the beginning of an influx of new veterans in need."[1]

Experience and research have revealed hospital emergency room psychiatric nurses and doctors from California to New York are overrun by depressed and suicidal veterans. Veterans Administration Medical Centers are understaffed and underfunded to handle the surge of veterans seeking psychological help. Most veterans are using alcohol and other drugs to mask and suppress the physiological and psychological pain caused by a myriad of injuries, disorders and illnesses. Many are diagnosed with post-traumatic stress disorder (PTSD).

Ilona Meagher collected statistics on military suicides for her Web site, PTSD Combat. Her research reveals:

> The Marines...revealed the number of Afghan-
> istan and Iraq combat troops and veterans who took
> their own lives in 2007 had doubled from the previous
> year.[2]

The Army and VA also reported record increases in suicides for
Afghanistan and Iraq combat veterans.[2]

Among the many hotline calls received are some from Desert
Storm veterans who are suffering from the painful illness of fibromyalgia. Some believe this disease developed as a direct result of
chemical warfare. "I can't take the pain anymore" is the resounding message from these vets. So many other callers are feeling miserable from
physical wounds, such as learning to live without limbs or eyesight.
Repeatedly I hear from male and female veterans of all ages, from all wars
and foreign conflicts, struggling with the diagnosis of schizoaffective
disorder, trauma-induced bipolar disorder, schizophrenia, depression and
anxiety neuroses. These veterans tell me they are already taking prescribed medications and have been in therapy for years, yet are finding no
relief and no resolution for their suffering.

For all veterans who feel anxious, depressed and in pain, I have a
message: YOU ARE NOT ALONE! Young and old veterans from all
walks of life are coming to Veterans Administration Medical Centers,
emergency rooms, local community hospitals, treatment centers and outpatient clinics around the country, because they experience unfamiliar,
unknown pain in their hearts and minds and cannot understand or cope
with it. Many more suffer but are afraid or feel too ashamed to reach out.
Please know your pain can be treated.

A prominent clinical psychotherapist, Ed Tick, Ph.D., says in his
book, *War and the Soul*, "PTSD is not best understood or treated as a
stress disorder....Rather it is best understood as an identity disorder and
soul wound, affecting the personality at the deepest levels." [3]

In this book we'll discuss my conversations with men and women,
Iraq, Afghanistan, Persian Gulf, Lebanon, Vietnam and Korea veterans,

who call for help as last-ditch efforts to save them from their experiences of overwhelming and unbearable physical and emotional trauma. By the time I get the call, suicide looms near.

Many have seen horrific sights, such as witnessing buddies' bodies blow up into pieces around them. This reality is, I truly believe, fundamentally immoral. It goes against every fiber of humanity. After seeing and experiencing the most graphic and shocking instances of savagery and brutality, their tours finally come to an end. How can anyone ever believe we can expect our men and women in uniform to suddenly and robotically come home and simply flip a "feelings switch" on and off? The fact most American Army, Marines, Navy, Air Force, National Guard and Reserve warriors are trained in the "art of killing", schooled to be mentally tough and considered excellent combat troops by all standards does not conceal the responsibility of allowing them to process their feelings before, during and after combat. Nevertheless, help is in short supply.

Homecoming veterans are crying out for help. Otherwise, as one Afghanistan veteran told me recently (in reference to suicide), "I would not be talking about it. I would have done it."

It is not only the veterans of Iraq and Afghanistan, but also those of earlier wars who experience recurring mental pain and depression resulting from their tours of duty. In addition to recent vets, I have had a record number of calls from Korea and Vietnam veterans in distress. Many of these veterans have delayed onset symptoms from traumas experienced forty or more years before, but have learned to cope by any means necessary, mostly substance abuse and isolation. These "forgotten few" veterans of yesteryear now are emerging from the shadows of the silent disguised worlds they created in order to survive the psychological scars of combat. They are not calling for help or a handout in unreasonable or repeated ways. They are "true grit" people—proud American warriors. Many are highly decorated and battle-scarred. Generally, when they reach out for help and call a hotline, they have hit the proverbial wall: the point of no return. They are exhausted and can no longer ignore their wounded souls. For them, the clock is ticking.

In a *Boston Globe* article by Bryan Bender titled "New veterans fear repeat of Vietnam", Richard Gibson, a twenty-five-year-old former Marine corporal, comments, "I think about how the Vietnam veterans were mistreated in basically every facet of life. I don't want the same result that happened in Vietnam." Gibson is involved in a newsletter that focuses on troops' accomplishments in Iraq. In this way, returning soldiers can connect with fellow veterans and feel encouraged to speak about their experiences.[4]

A particularly eye-opening compilation from my research suggests a surprising number of first and second Gulf War generation vets have also begun to call the hotline, many in distress because of homelessness and unemployment. They are experiencing the inability, after years of service, to adjust to living once again in society. Many of these vets have never adjusted. They have hidden, have violently acted out or have just given up and now some make one last call for help while others quietly take their own lives.

News media and studies indicate suicide numbers are never recorded accurately from any war era. The government has recently been accused of covering up the "real" numbers of veteran suicides from the Iraq and Afghanistan wars. The fact is our country really does not track nor has the ability to accurately track the actual veteran suicide death toll numbers. It is suggested that 100,000+ Vietnam veterans have ended their own lives. I challenge those numbers. Based on the continuing crisis of suicide ideation encounters, both in emergency rooms and over hotlines throughout the United States, I suggest that the number of Vietnam veteran suicides is double that, more in the range of 200,000 suicides, more than three times the number of deaths (58,320) inscribed on the Vietnam Memorial Wall in Washington, D.C.

How many veterans' suicides go unrecorded? How many cars and motorcycles slam into trees at high speeds or launch off cliffs and bridges and go reported as accidental? How many drug overdoses in the emergency rooms are recorded as accidental deaths while families know better, but say nothing in order to hide family embarrassment? Perhaps those veterans' screams or silent cries for help were never heard or noticed. Perhaps they were heard and either misunderstood or ignored.

Week in and week out I receive many urgent calls for help from shut-in disabled veterans: those who are isolated and who are unable to transport themselves to and from the store for food. They express feelings of hopeless and helpless desperation. "I am at the end. No one cares about whether I live or die," one veteran said on the phone once. "I can't even call Meals On Wheels anymore."

I have talked at length with many of the government's Vet Center counselors and managers who also have answered hundreds of calls monthly for emergency services. They receive urgent calls for help from shut-in warriors, many of them amputees or in wheelchairs due to other injuries or war-related illnesses. Most of the time Purple Heart recipients hear these words: "There's no money for VA shuttle transportation. Sorry, nothing we can do." For many of these vets, suicide looms near: loneliness and abandonment are killers. There's no money for transportation to get wounded veterans to doctors' appointments or to get groceries? Yet our government gave 700 billion dollars to "bail out" the Wall Street money mongers and automakers' "executive bonus" programs? Something is truly wrong with this.

Some World War II Vets have called the hotline not necessarily to ask for rescue, but the eighty-year-old or older vets just want to talk to someone; they are feeling alone and abandoned by their families and communities; their military buddies have all died. While Afghanistan and the Middle East combat troops' suicide numbers are still small compared to Southeast Asia era's 100,000+ suicides and counting, they are steadily rising.

The true stories told in this book get to the very heart and soul of the matter of suicide and suicidal ideation. Nothing here is fabricated. The researched historical facts quoted are accurate and verified. The Jake Storm story in chapter 12, "The Tide Within", is a biographical narrative about one veteran's personal journey through Hell and back and how only a veteran friend, his sister and God's intervention saved his life, his sanity. In other chapters there are stories from courageous, war-torn warriors coming home, never to be the same again, many facing the most difficult choice and challenge of their lives.

# Introduction

*Healing Suicidal Veterans* gives straightforward, down-to-earth advice about encouragement and hope. While revitalizing the therapeutic approach used to overcome the combat veterans' immediate life-threatening darkness of depression and suicidal thoughts, I define my unique tried-and-true method of suicide crisis intervention counseling as a matter of "heart-to-heart resuscitation," as I call it. The window of opportunity to make a difference for you or someone close to you can literally be a matter of seconds, whether over a telephone hotline or face-to-face in a community hospital emergency room. Your, your loved one's or your friend's life may hang in the balance.

The process of heart-to-heart communicating is one I suggest and utilize. I believe through encouraging, motivating and mentoring, suffering veterans can be helped to find the strength, self-determination and support to get into treatment and out of danger.

My number one priority is to get suicidal veterans to safety. I say to them and you, "Oh yes, you do have a reason to live and I'll tell you why!"

1

Veterans of the Iraq and Afghanistan Wars are now living on city streets, in cars and in the nation's homeless shelters. Some are so desperate they commit crimes and are going to prison. Many struggling vets or family and friends finally end up calling hospital emergency rooms, psychiatric nurses, 911 or the VA hotline for help and advice. Many are reluctant to contact anyone.

Account after account report veterans locking themselves in their bedrooms, some actually barricading themselves in their rooms, not coming out for days at a time. When they do reach out for help to a hotline, they explain, "Asking for help is like saying I've failed my mission. Most of us cannot bring ourselves to ask for help."

If you or someone close to you is feeling depressed and has thoughts about harming yourself or others, it's important that you recognize that feeling suicidal is a serious but treatable condition. Depression is a treatable disorder as well. Certain signs and symptoms, of which I'll later get into, will tell you that you need to ask for help. Seeking help is not a sign of weakness or something to be ashamed of; it is your right to seek help.[1] "It takes the courage and strength of a warrior to ask for help" states a popular VA poster slogan. Your military buddies will be proud of your showing the courage to face the obstacles in your life.

When veterans call a clinic expressing symptoms of depressive illnesses that interfere with their everyday life functioning, they are made aware that professional medical treatment teams will be needed and should be sought. A call for help is highly recommended if you or someone you care about has thoughts of or mentions a plan or intent to harm him or her self. Even if there is no suicide ideation, you or a vet close to you may be experiencing a "crisis" of a different nature: unrelenting psychological (mental) and physiological (body) pain, the feelings of helplessness and hopelessness, substance abuse or other addictions, feeling out-of-control or in need of anger management and family counseling. If you feel trapped and see no way to escape, these are very good reasons to call for help.

Mental health clinicians around the country are seeing significant substance abuse cases, particularly alcohol dependency, among veterans.

Some veterans exposed to trauma and negative experiences in the war zones are using alcohol and other drugs at a high rate in order to "self medicate." After coming home, they seldom report, at least at the beginning, any mental health problems.

Often it is not until several months to several years after veterans settle into their lives at home and work that delayed symptoms of anxiety, panic, rage, anger, depression and trouble sleeping begin to appear or become recurrent and repetitive in their daily routines. Increasing alcohol intake and the taking of other illicit street drugs, such as marijuana, opiates, cocaine, methamphetamines and pain killers often become daily scourges. Domestic violence, marital and family disputes are other ways veterans show their pain and depression. Marriages are in jeopardy, jobs are lost or never found, financial difficulties surface and children begin to fear for their safety in their own homes.

An increasing number of veterans come home from the conflicts in Iraq and Afghanistan already diagnosed with post-traumatic stress disorder or traumatic brain injury (TBI). If you find yourself or someone close to you increasingly depressed and despondent after months and even years of experiencing tours of nighttime firefights, picking up enemy bodies, finding baby toys and articles of children's clothing on the floors of suspected terrorists' houses, you are not alone. The number of combat veterans taking antidepressants daily to control and ease the effects of lengthy and repeated tours is rapidly increasing.

*Healing Suicidal Veterans* has important information for you or someone you care about to identify recognizable signs and symptoms that may increase suicide risk, veteran-specific risk factors and signs of suicidal thinking.

In this book, I will try to answer difficult questions for you about what is happening to you or someone close to you, our veterans and why so many are dying by their own hands.

I will introduce you to the psychological wounds of war, use some terms that may be unfamiliar, including *passive and active suicidal ideation, high risk signs for suicide, suicide desire, suicide capability, suicide intent,* and put in plain words with careful description how to recognize what defines a veteran's suicidal ideation, what signs to look for and what to do when you discover them.

In the following chapters you also will find real stories of raw emotion, expressed by men and women veterans, family members and friends and callers pleading for help before it is too late.

I will move you through the poignant, uncensored personal stories shared by desperate crisis line callers and veterans coming into clinics representing many war and conflict experiences from World War II to Afghanistan. Some have already hurt themselves and are in need of immediate emergency rescue while others are confused and cannot find their ways in life. And some just want someone to listen.

Most importantly, I will try to point out the steps and strategies that help them recover and heal. Then I will do my utmost, drawing on my long experience with other veterans, to guide you on a path that will lead you and your loved ones from the darkness and anguish of pain and suffering to growth and healing.

Our journey together calls for strength and courage, but I know you have both. You or your loved one is a genuine American hero.

# PART I

# IRAQ AND AFGHANISTAN COMBAT VETERANS

# Chapter 1

# A Family in Crisis Cries Out for Help! An Iraq Vet

Family members agonize over feelings of helplessness and hopelessness as they stand by and watch their once loving fathers and mothers, husbands and wives return home from Iraq changed and different people. The family lives in constant worry and fear. It takes courage, moral support and encouragement among family members for a veteran's loved one to call for help.

Suicidal veterans feel that they are cut off from the world without the support system they need to continue through life. Al's story is about a family's determination and courageous attempt to rescue their loved one.

### Al's Story

The veteran's wife called the hotline. I picked up the call.

"I may have to hang the phone up quickly. My husband is not himself," a woman whispered, sounding jittery and upset. "I don't know him anymore. I am afraid for my safety at times when he drinks too much, but I love the man. He never was a drinker. But now I don't know what to think. I can't leave him. He says he wants to kill himself. He is so angry. What can I do?" she pleaded.

"You already have done the important first step in helping your husband: You called the hotline for help. Good work. It must have been very difficult," I responded.

She gasped slightly and uttered, "I am afraid of what he would do if he knew I made this call tonight; he loses his temper a lot lately. It has taken me several months to build up the courage to call for help. I opened this letter to my husband we received from Veteran Affairs months ago telling us about the signs of suicide to look for. My son also read it and kept asking me to make the call for his dad's sake—for our sake. I have the letter right here." She began to read it to me. I could tell she was overwrought with worry so I did not interrupt. "It says here to call… 'If you're experiencing an emotional crisis and need to talk with a trained VA professional, the National Suicide Prevention Hotline toll-free number, 1-800-273-TALK (8255), is now available 24 hours a day, 7 days a week. You will immediately be connected with a qualified and caring provider who can help. Here are some suicide warning signs. Threatening to hurt or kill yourself, looking for ways to kill yourself, seeking access to pills, weapons and other self-destructive behavior, talking about death, dying or suicide. The presence of these signs requires immediate attention. If you or a veteran you care about has been showing any of these signs, do not hesitate to call and ask for help.'"

The hotline caller paused, breathing heavily into the telephone receiver. "My husband needs help right now. He has over half of these signs it says here. I don't know which way to turn."

"What is your name?" I calmly inquired.

There was silence for a moment. She appeared to be reluctant to give me her name. I waited. Then she spoke: "Elaine."

"Elaine, you have made the right decision to call us—a very good decision. Now I need to ask you a few questions and get some additional information so that we can take good care of your veteran. Does he have a weapon?" I responded.

"I don't think so; I haven't seen one around the house," she replied.

"Has he hurt himself or anyone else?" I continued.

"No, but I'm not sure about the pills he takes for sleeping; he has them in his room. He wakes up in the middle of the night sometimes screaming words I don't understand and his legs flying around under the sheets. It scares me," the vet's wife said, sniffling into the receiver.

"Elaine, has your husband ever attempted suicide before?" I spoke inquisitively.

She sounded somewhat surprised by the question. "Him…no way," she said amused slightly. "He is Mr. Tough Guy, a real survivor, a good soldier, too. He has been decorated for combat—some commendations, I think—but he never talks much about them."

She continued sparingly, "He doesn't think that way, or at least he didn't use to…I am not sure anymore what he is thinking. He has really changed since his deployment home. It is hard for us. He won't go in for help."

"Your husband's condition is treatable, Elaine, and his mental health is not a sign of weakness by any means. He is not alone in this struggle. Many families are going through what you are experiencing right now. And I will tell you, Elaine, from my years of firsthand experience, many families in similar circumstances are restored and their veterans recover. Trust me on this. I am not saying that just to make you feel better. That is the truth. A great number of troops come home from Iraq and Afghanistan and as far back as Vietnam still suffering and struggling in psychological confusion. I will help you get him in for help, okay?"

"It's so hard to believe he is having so much trouble this long after he was over there; we have got to do something," she said with questioning sadness in her tone.

"What is your husband's name?" I continued to explore.

"Al," she quickly responded. "Specialist Al Stuart, United States Army Reserve."

"What is his date of birth?" I asked.

"June 23, 1979." Again she answered with a quick response as if she wanted the conversation to move along or end, I was not sure which.

"What is your address?" I continued.

"Wait a minute! I don't want you calling in the police! Hold on here ... Al doesn't know I called you...you are going to get me into real trouble here," her voice swelled and sounded annoyed.

"Elaine, hold on, I am not calling the police or an ambulance unless you or your husband wants an emergency rescue. If there are any signs he has taken those pills or hurt himself in anyway, we will need to call for an ambulance. We need to check it out right now. If he hasn't, we will still try and talk to him, all right?" I said, retreating a bit.

This is a real conversation and a story of hope, strength and courage; you will witness how Elaine and her son pulled together as a family during this difficult time. I guided Elaine to talk to her wounded suicidal warrior suffering with unrelenting symptoms of suicidal thoughts; learn how to stay connected and how to keep lines of communication open. Take suicidal ideation seriously.

A significant other of a suicidal veteran lives under immense pressure. Elaine told me "most of the time I try to be especially careful about my speech and behavior toward my husband and try to do whatever I can to minimize the stresses in his life so as to avoid making him angry and threatening to kill himself. I hate when he says that. I don't know when to believe him or not."

Case in point, Elaine found herself carefully monitoring not only her own actions, but also those of her son. "We can't upset your father," she often told her son. She also tried to make life easier for her husband by not pressuring him to attend certain social and family get-togethers. At first she was willing to go alone. Eventually, however, she stopped going out at all and became reclusive, like her wounded warrior. Elaine was beginning to realize just how damaging her own isolation had been to her mental health.

Even after a heightened suicidal threat has subsided and your vet appears calmer and more elevated in mood, a partner needs to be aware that suicide can occur at any time. Sometimes the veteran seems improved, but it may be because of the result of an inner decision to commit suicide at some future time and thereby terminate what he or she perceives as an intolerably painful and hopeless way of life.

My research indicates 75 percent of people who commit suicide hint that they plan to do so. Often, the veteran might say things like "You would be better off without me here" or start giving away his or her possessions. Another sign of suicidal depression includes withdrawing from normal family activities. Validate your veteran's concerns. Even if the problems may not seem big to you, they are very real to the vet in crisis. Show compassion for the pain he or she is experiencing. Tell him or her how much you care. Reinforcing the connection you share with each other is the first step to preventing the vet's suicide.

"Elaine, I sincerely suggest to you that the important essentials in helping to rescue your husband are *open channels of communication,*" I expounded.

At this point in the conversation, I guided Elaine's intervention strategy by suggesting, "You should say what you must say and do what you must do to keep the relationship between you and Al undamaged, however shaky it may be.

"In your particular situation, Elaine, the conversation with Al will be through direct dialogue face-to-face or through his closed door, right?"

"Yes, but I don't know if he will open the bedroom door and come out of his room to talk to me. He is sleeping in the spare bedroom and sometimes doesn't come out for days," she replied in a nervous and agitated manner.

"Mrs. Stuart, I believe the best thing to do in your situation, and right now, because he may have taken those pills already, would be a face-to-face conversation asking him to come to the phone and telling him that a counselor, a veteran, would like to speak with him. If he asks who made the phone call tell him the truth that you called the crisis line, because you love him and are concerned about him and how he is acting right now. Don't mention his suicidal threats. Can you try to do that, Elaine?"

Once again there was an awkward silence. "You seem upset, Elaine, and understandably so. This is a tough situation you are in, but you can do this. I know you can do this. You have already shown me your courage and determination to help Al. So, please talk to me. If you do not understand what I am suggesting for you to do, tell me, okay?" I heard her breathing on the line. I remained silent for a minute hoping and praying she would follow through and persuade her husband to pick up the phone. She said nothing. I could almost hear her mind bustling as I continued in a low, controlled voice, "I can always send a rescue team out to help you if you can't do this. But one thing I know is that I can't ignore your plea for help. In fact, Elaine, your husband is also crying out for help, these things I know. "

"I am listening, but not so sure I can do it," Elaine replied rather hesitant.

"If you fear confronting him, by all means talk to him through the door he is hiding behind. Is the door barricaded or locked from inside?" I asked.

"I don't really know. I stay away from him when he gets like this. I have heard him moving something around in there from time to time. Don't really know," she said.

At this point, I suggested again to Elaine that any conversation with her husband perhaps should not begin with reference to the fact that the veteran was threatening to kill himself and was at the moment the center of his own distress and anxiety. Rather, the talk should begin by directing the conversation in a particular way toward a particular objective, such as getting the veteran to safety; in this case the objective was to talk with me on the phone.

The rescuer, in this case Elaine, may then state how she wants to be of service to her husband in any way possible and then ask him how he thinks he can be assisted in his obvious dilemma. If the suicidal veteran draws back and refuses to respond or otherwise indicates hopelessness, Elaine must continue in offering a variety of conversational remarks in the hope of winning an acknowledgment. "Can I get you some food or something to drink?" "Would you like me to bring you something to read?" In a small way, she is engaging her husband in conversation. The part of the veteran's consciousness or psyche that desires to be rescued has begun to accept the possibility that a way out of this hopelessness can be found. The longer dialogue continues, the less the likelihood of a sudden desperate decision to harm himself and the greater the possibility of the eventual successful intervention.

"Elaine, are you ready to talk with you husband?" I coached.

"I have to, don't I?" she responded unsurely.

"No, you do not, but I highly recommend that I talk to him right now on the phone and get him the help he needs. And the only one who can get him to do that at this moment is you. Elaine, we need to do this right now. We don't know what his suicidal mind is thinking. We cannot hesitate to act at times like this. Suicidal ideation is very unpredictable. I will wait here on the phone while you go talk to Al. I will wait as long as it takes; I won't hang up," I tried to reassure her.

"Wait a minute. I am going to put the phone down and go talk to him. He is upstairs ... now wait a minute ... not sure about this. He is not going to like this ... What is your name?" she asked sounding upset.

"Vic ... Vic Montgomery."

Then silence; I put my head in my hands, elbows on the desk and massaged my temples with my forefingers round and round, pushing the tips into my hair line. I do that from time to time to relax.

The minutes went ticking by on the bevy of clocks on the wall. I adjusted my headset and waited. As I closed my eyes for a moment, I began to think about the situation Elaine was in and how I wished I was physically there to take over this intervention for her, because I have the experience and training. It was obvious she was afraid of the outcome.

A search for an alternative to suicide begins when the veteran starts to speak of his or her pain. Elaine did not have the restricted view of her suicidal husband. She could suggest to him that living was worth trying and the loss of his platoon buddy in combat was a terrible blow, but the worth of those who die perseveres in the lives and work of the survivors. Hope in the possibilities of the future was the most important concept for Elaine to put into words, since her depressed suicidal veteran thought narrowly only of a minuscule range of time in the present.

If the vet identifies with the death of a war buddy, suggest the possibility of new relationships. As an appeal to the rights of the person at risk, consider him or her not unlike other persons. Remind the vet that the suicide he proposes as a solution to this problem is, in a sense, unfair. If the veteran enforces the death sentence on themselves for failing to save the life of his friend, then, by the application of simple justice, every veteran who fails to save a life should be subject to execution. Only the most delusional veteran will miss the obvious futility of that implication.

In an attempt to reintroduce a concept of self-worth to a combat veteran whose self-image is damaged, it's essential that offered promises be simple, within the sphere of realistic possibility and consistent with the veteran's values. The self-punishing veteran perhaps can't believe he can ever again take responsibility or be dependable on account of some mistake or letdown from the past, even one that he could not have prevented. Veterans wrestle with self-blame and self-hatred. During battle, the pandemonium of war combined with physical and emotional stress can create frequent situations where even the most dedicated and accomplished combat warrior could easily have a lapse in judgment. When that mistake results in a loss of a buddy or part of his patrol, the self-blame a vet in crisis faces can be so enormous, it turns the rage he or she feels inward for the mistake he or she made. Others speak angrily to themselves for personal behavior they perceive as spineless and weak or needlessly vicious. The self-blaming warrior feels like a failure by reasonable criteria applied to anyone else the vet considers trustworthy and capable. An intervention should be aimed at countering the forces of self-contempt and the vet's likely rundown in the elimination of the hated object—the failed self. This comes into play most often with veterans suffering from survivor guilt.

I opened my eyes to the rush of healthcare staff running past my desk engaged in a rescue. The staff's primary responsibilities are to contact the callers' nearest VA suicide crisis coordinators and other locations, addresses, phone numbers, area hospitals and EMT paramedics to be dispatched to aid the desperate families in search of help for their suicidal veterans.

The phone line was still silent. Twenty minutes had gone by since my last words with Elaine. I searched for some evidence of noise in my headset. I looked in the direction of the red light emitting diodes dancing on the phone equipment signifying whether a phone line is open or closed. It was still open. I had not been cut off. I heard nothing in the background, but I felt a bit of relief. The last thing in the world I wanted was a hang-up. Disconnections are such an empty feeling when they happen. And they happen quite often on the hotline, when the fear is just too great for the caller on the other end, be they veteran or family member. The heartbreaking thing is help is only a matter of minutes away. Life and death lay in the balance. I read a news article recently that said the number of Afghanistan and Iraq combat troops and veterans who committed suicide had doubled from 2006 to 2007 and that "100,000 OEF/OIF vets have sought help for mental health issues, including 52,000 for post-traumatic stress disorder alone."[1]

As I adjusted my headset, I couldn't help but think about the possibility that Elaine's husband may have had other means with which to take his life, other than the pills she knew he had. *Now I am second-guessing myself,* I thought. *Maybe I should dispatch a rescue team, at least for a welfare check. Elaine has been away from the phone for awhile now. I am getting concerned. Should I call 911?* My mind began working overtime as thoughts raced through my mind.

Suddenly I heard Elaine's keyed up voice loud and clear coming through my headset, "He is coming … he said he would talk to you … oh, he looks terrible—" she abruptly stopped talking as if someone else came into the room. Elaine was sobbing.

The next moment, "Yeah, who's this?" a gruff, shaky voice demanded.

"Hello Al, this is Vic. We are concerned about you, buddy. Your wife and son love you and the VA cares about you, too. You are one of us. Welcome home. Thank you for serving our country. We can help you get through these tough times if you will let us, Al. Have you hurt yourself in any way?"

"Well…," he hesitated as if searching for the right words. "What's your name again?"

"Vic Montgomery, Al. I work for the crisis healthcare team," I answered.

"My wife probably already told you I thought about it. I have been feeling really down for a long time…don't know…sometimes things get fuzzy. My head won't shut down…too many memories; I still can't get a good night's sleep after all these years, Vic."

"Al, have you thought of a plan to hurt yourself?" I inquired.

"Many times…," he paused. "Are you kidding me?" he cried out suddenly. "For a long time…I have a good supply of my sleeping pills I am prescribed…maybe I shouldn't be telling you this…I thought about jumping in my car and ending it all the other day. There is a very nice cliff at the end of our street that would be perfect. And my wife would get some insurance to boot—money is tight around here." He continued, "I haven't been able to keep a steady job for years since getting back from Iraq. I get angry and upset easily. It got pretty ugly over there: thinking you're going to die every day…well, it's tough to live with, man. You gotta be there to feel it."

I interrupted him to ask, "Al, are you seeing a VA doctor about these things?"

"Hell no. I went to a civilian doc for my trouble sleeping. He is the one who gives me the pills. I don't want the VA to know any of this," he admitted.

"Al, listen to me: It takes the courage of a warrior to ask for help. I am proud of you for talking to me tonight. This alone takes backbone. I would like to get some help for you, buddy…from the things you have shared with me just now and the few concerns Elaine told me, I can see why you are having a tough time of it." I paused. Al said nothing.

"One of my jobs is to get our veterans to safety, out of harm's way. Al, I would like you to do something for me. Would you please temporarily give all your pills, car keys, any alcohol or drugs you have and anything else that may put you into harm's way right now...please give them over to your wife to hold on to. Can you do that?" I asked in a beseeching manner.

"Corporal, talk to me. I want to help you. But the only way I can help you is if you cooperate with me and allow me to make sure you and your family are safe."

"I'm listening," Al responded somewhat reluctantly.

Al was slow in responding further, but I continued to wait for more from him.

"What do you mean you can help me? What kind of help?"

"Al, there are several options that the VA provides for you. But before we discuss those options at all, would you please give those items I previously discussed over to your wife right now just to hold for you? I will wait on the line and when that is done I will explain to you what the next step is to getting you support. Can you do that?" I waited for a response. Nothing. Not even an utterance or the noise of his breath, although I was certain he didn't hang up.

"Listen to me, buddy; I understand how difficult it is for you to ask for help. Many combat warriors have thick skin and a tough constitution. You are a seasoned warrior and have learned in combat to suck it up and stuff your feelings. Your wife was bragging earlier about how you were a tough guy, a good soldier and decorated. Ooh-rah!" I empathized, accentuating the age-old Marine war cry.

All of a sudden there came a faint "ooh-rah" back at me over the receiver. It made me smile to hear him say that.

"Hear me on this, Al: Many combat veterans have finally come to realize, especially with the help and courage of their families and other loved ones, that haunting nightmares, flashbacks and depression finally begin to take their tolls. We can help you work through these nightmares, traumatic combat memories and sleepless nights; we can and we will, soldier," I said assertively.

"Right now, Al, you are scaring your wife and son by your behavior and lashing out in anger. Elaine called us, because she did not know what to do to get you the help you need. They are afraid you may hurt yourself and, as you shared with me, that is a possibility, right?"

"Yeah, I have thought about it," Al said, conceding.

"Al, your young son needs you—alive and happy again. He wants the dad he knew before you left for battle in Iraq," I said encouragingly. "I can say this with confident assurance, because I have seen rewarding outcomes when family is willing to 'step up to the plate' for their warriors."

"Okay, what are the options, Vic?" Al spoke a bit calmer.

"Al, first give Elaine those things we talked about earlier: the pills, the car keys, booze. Then we will talk about the next steps to getting you help. Will you do that?"

The receiver again was put down on a hard surface. I heard the impact; I waited. Again I cradled my head in my hands, elbows on my desk and forefingers rubbing my temples. I began looking around the hotline room, reflecting.

The Veterans National Suicide Prevention Hotline is an intense place buzzing with highly skilled individuals. It takes a special kind of dedication to work the suicide hotline call center. At any hour of the day or night, the lights burn brightly.

The hotliners work in three- to eight-hour shifts. The seventy-five-year-old, weather-beaten, red brick building in the upstate New York VA Medical Center, surrounded by green rolling lawns and flower beds in the spring, dotted with peaceful 200-year-old 100-foot-tall trees bustling with gray, bushy-tailed squirrels and singing birds, hosts a tunnel walkway to a security elevator. The peace and serenity outside the building has to be left behind, at least for the moment, as hotliners take the ominous ride on the elevator to the National Suicide Prevention Hotline Room.

The team on the incoming tour enters the "hotline room" from the elevator to relieve the outgoing shift. The telephones ring in sequence. Never will a call go unanswered, nor will a veteran or family member get a busy signal or voicemail message. A live person will always respond to a plea for help with an ear to listen. Desk fans blow to cool down the circulating air of the intense "suicide hotline" atmosphere. Hundreds of calls and messages are routed daily through these highly encrypted, confidential data and telecommunication lines from around the world.

When a rested tour team of professional hotline responders filters through the security door entrance, heads turn from high-backed padded desk chairs and welcoming arms raise waving victory signs and thumbs up. Brief words of inspiration and exhilaration are shared, as the outgoing team is exhausted and looking forward to a change in tour.

The Veteran Affairs hotline room is painted blue. The color blue is believed to "soothe illnesses and treat pain." While blue has different symbolic meanings, individual reactions to the color can vary widely.

As author Kendra Van Wagner describes in her book, *The Color of Psychology: How Color Impacts Moods, Feelings and Behaviors*, "Colors on the blue side of the spectrum are known as cool colors and include blue, purple and green. These colors are often described as calm."[2]

The blue in the hotline room makes me feel cool, weightless and spiritual. The walls are decorated with posters and positive pictures. One particular poster stands out: a picture of a combat soldier with the words, "It takes the courage and strength of a soldier to ask for help...If you are in an emotional crisis call 1-800-273-TALK."

Every variety of a veteran's life experience and socioeconomic condition call the hotline; veterans of all sizes and shapes, races and beliefs and all types of psychological disorders and physiological discomforts, from wars and conflicts ranging from World War II to the present time. Professional hotline responders listen intently, compassionately. They stay on the line. They will not abandon a caller. No matter how long it takes.

One day a forty-six-year-old sergeant who served a tour of duty in Bosnia and was diagnosed with trauma-induced bipolar affective mood disorder, called. The vet was 100 percent disabled, needing someone to talk to. He could not get around: Phobias and isolation had begun haunting him. He needed an ear to listen; someone to care. I was able to arrange for him to be picked up, taken to the Vet Center and introduced to others in the same predicament who also felt isolated and alone. To a veteran who feels trapped and helpless, it is a matter of life or death in many cases.

The top guns of the hotline are a tried and tested, dedicated group of men and women; seasoned, trained professionals with several veterans on the team as well as addiction therapists and retired specialists coming out of retirement to help vets. The suicide responders pass screens, physicals, interviews, security background checks and weeks and months of crisis intervention training. The registered nurses are the top in their fields. Many have years of experience in frontline outpatient clinics and emergency rooms. Their training and knowledge covers everything from mental illness to pharmacology. The team is always on call.

My mind continued to wander as I waited for Al to return to the phone. I looked fixedly at the collection of large, round, black and white, metal clocks hanging high on the wall across from my desk. They just kept ticking: Alaska Time, Pacific Time, Mountain Time, Central Time and Eastern Time.

As I waited for Al to come back to the phone, I knew I wanted him to be rescued immediately and taken to the nearest emergency room for a psychiatric evaluation. But I also knew that it would take some convincing to get Al into a rescue and transport situation. Al was a tough and prideful vet and would not think too keenly about being escorted by EMTs to the hospital in an ambulance. I would definitely give him the opportunity to have an emergency team rescue, but I would also give him a second option to allow me to contact the crisis prevention coordinator at the closest VA medical center in order to arrange contact for an appointment and evaluation with the treatment team.

I was beginning to worry about the time that had gone by since Al and I last talked; it had been about fifteen or twenty minutes. I was hoping that Al was cooperating and giving his wife, Elaine, all his sleep medications, car keys and any alcohol or other drugs kept in his room. Of course, this was for his protection and a paramount first step in creating a safe environment around the depressed suicidal veteran.

I began hearing commotion and noises in the background and then voices coming closer to the telephone.

"Hello...hello, are you there, Vic?" Elaine's voice announced, still sounding rattled.

"Yes, Elaine, I am here. Where is Al?" I asked inquisitively.

"My husband is in the bathroom and will be out in a minute," she replied.

"Has he given you all of the items I asked for?" I inquired.

"I have the car keys and several bottles of prescriptions, a couple bottles of whiskey are empty and he assured me he had nothing more hidden. Vic, I think he wants help...finally. I see tears in his eyes when he is talking to me about our son," Elaine spoke in a treble pitch, revealing some emotion for the first time in our conversation.

"Where is your son?" I asked.

"He is at school and will be home in another two hours," Elaine replied.

"Is Al still in the bathroom?" I asked intently.

"Yes, he is still in there...I think," she said questioning.

"Elaine, go check on him right now. Find out what is taking him so long and tell him I am asking to speak with him again...quickly, Elaine, please," I insisted.

She put down the receiver. A few seconds later I heard her voice in the far background; then silence.

Another minute or so passed, though it felt like eons. I don't like silence, especially at the moment of a possible trauma. *I have to get this vet to safety*, I thought.

Another minute later, "Hey, yo, I am back from the dead. What's next?" Al suggested boldly and in fact, sounded a bit tension free. A huge improvement from the first conversation we had earlier.

"Well, Al," I said energetically, "we have a couple of ways to go. The first way, I can call for an emergency rescue team to be there probably in less than fifteen minutes, which would include the police and the EMT ambulance unit. The police will not be there to arrest you, but simply to see that it safe for the EMTs to transport you to a local community hospital emergency room. In the meantime, I will be calling and arranging for a crisis prevention coordinator at the nearest VA hospital to make arrangements for your transportation from the community hospital to the nearest VA hospital for a psychiatric evaluation. After that you'll be assigned a treatment team and a treatment plan will be developed. The treatment plan can involve many things but the first will be determining a level of care, which will either be on an inpatient or outpatient basis, depending on your diagnosis; either way you'll be in good hands and will receive the care or treatment you deserve. Al, you are not alone any longer suffering with this inner turmoil. We are getting you the help you need if you will let us.

"Are you with me, Al?" I questioned.

"What's another option?" Al fired back.

"Well, another option would be for me to arrange for you and Elaine to meet with your closest VA Medical Center's crisis prevention coordinator. His name is Dr. Miller. He is a psychologist and specializes in the treatment of combat veterans for things such as PTSD, TBI, depression, anxiety, grief and so on. He is a seasoned professional and has several treatment modalities that have proven to be successful for the exact feelings you are experiencing, Al, like flashbacks and nightmares and grieving the loss of some of your friends killed in battle in Iraq, things like that. What do you think?" I asked.

"I can do that. When do I have to go?" Al replied quickly.

"As a matter of fact, Al, I can contact Dr. Miller right now and have him meet you at the emergency room door. You will not have to wait in the waiting room; you will go with the doctor and be evaluated and treated. Because you are a combat veteran, you will be treated with the highest priorities. You and the treatment team will then determine what the next step should be. Shall I call Dr. Miller at the VA?"

"Let's do this thing," Al sharply replied.

"Good decision, Al. Would you have Elaine come to the phone for a minute? I have your back, buddy," I added.

"Hello?" Elaine picked up the phone.

"Elaine, you probably overheard our conversation. Al is willing to go into the VA and be evaluated by one of our treatment team doctors, Dr. Miller. Do you know where the closest VA is to you?" I asked.

"I think so. Al does," she replied.

"You will need to make arrangements for your son to stay with someone. Pack up the car right now and transport Al to the VA emergency room. Dr. Miller will be there to meet with Al, understand?" I said.

"Will he stay the night?" she said whispering.

"Be prepared for anything. Pack him an overnight bag. They may want to evaluate him for a few days or not. It is solely up to the medical team and your husband. However, be assured Al will be in good hands there. You will get your old husband back, Elaine. I know this, because I could hear in his voice that he wants help and is willing to risk his pride and work to get free from the bondage holding him captive in his mind. You have a good husband and father; a good man, Elaine. And you have been a great support in making this happen in every way. What courage…I applaud you. I will call and check up on your husband at the VA over the next few days. Any questions for me?" I concluded.

"No, I don't think so. I'm pretty nervous, but happy at the same time. I want to thank you for what you have done today, Vic. You have changed our lives forever and saved my husband's life," Elaine expounded.

"He is one of ours, Elaine; I just covered his back, as we say in combat military jargon," I smiled.

"Thank you so much," she returned.

"Ooh-rah," I proclaimed as I ended our call. "You are welcome."

## Steps to Prevent a Veteran's Suicide

- Confront the veteran with the probability he has been planning suicide and has lethal means at hand. Request that he voluntarily turn over his guns, car keys, knives, beer and liquor and cache of pills to a trusted relative or friend. Encourage him to communicate and confide his fantasy of carrying out his death. Encourage the vet to talk.
- Remove lethal means and opportunity from the veteran or vice versa at the earliest possible opening.
- Ask questions to find a reason for him/her to live, feeding the warrior's heart and soul with winning encouragement and affirmations. When the veteran is stabilized, finding some glimmer of "hope of help" diminishes the suicide risk.
- Get the veteran to safety by connecting the veteran to supporting veteran resources or emergency services in the community or a VA Medical Center wherever he or she lives. The federal government, Congress, has mandated a follow-up protocol for all suicide and crisis calls: they are to be referred for a private, confidential consultation with a well-trained, professional suicide prevention coordinator at one of the more than 153 VA Medical Centers throughout the United States.

# Chapter 2

# Honoring God:
# A Vet's Story about
# Transformation

During my years in graduate school, one college professor assigned Denis Waitley's best-selling book *Seeds of Greatness* as required reading. I am forever grateful.

Dr. Waitley tells the story, "It's Still Me Inside," about a man named Larry who endured more than sixty operations. Dr. Waitley said that even after a year, it was very difficult to look his friend square in the face. Larry had been burned much more severely than Waitley had anticipated. Waitley went to the physical therapist with his friend and watched him go through the excruciating pain of having his fingers pulled, bent and massaged so he could move them properly and get the tendons stretched back in the right direction.

Waitley wrote in his book that Larry assured him he was the same person even if he looked different physically. The author goes on to say, "He told me that if you had faith and really knew yourself from 'inside-out', you wouldn't get discouraged when something unexpected came along to threaten you from the 'outside-in.'"

"Why was he not crushed or broken?" Dr. Waitley wrote. "I thought about the thousands of young people who take their lives every year because they are depressed about their inability to cope with change."

Flying back to San Diego, Waitley stared out the airplane window and tried to comprehend his friend's unbelievable attitude. He figured that if you're born in despair, it would be tough to maintain your faith. But Larry's belief was that since he had been born healthy, in America, with a strong spiritual faith, he wasn't going to let an accident discourage him. Many people feel it's easier to retreat to what feels comfortable instead of embracing change.[1]

So it was with Chuck. He knew who he was before serving in the military. He shared with me over the telephone how he was a faithful church youth group leader and believer in the word of God. In fact, he told me that he had read the Holy Bible cover to cover in his teenage years. Chuck yearned for a spiritual transformation; his story shows how to discover your spiritual condition and what to do if you are spiritually bankrupt with no will to live another day. Like many of the hotline calls, the events in Chuck's story can only be described by three words: God's amazing grace.

## Chuck's Story

"You have two minutes to convince me not to kill myself...starting now!" a voice challenged me when I picked up the hotline call.

Chuck is an Army veteran of the Iraq War who called while holding an untwisted end of a metal coat hanger to his jugular vein. He was sitting in a chair at the edge of his bed in a motel room at some unknown location at the time of his call. The vet sounded a bit loose, possibly intoxicated, but understandable.

I found out during our two hour hotline phone conversation that Chuck had been homeless since returning to the States from Iraq and living under a bridge with about fifteen other homeless Iraq and Afghanistan veterans.

Chuck had been told he had a "mild" traumatic brain injury (TBI) as a result of an improvised explosive device (IED) explosion, which the medical doctor said represents a very significant traumatic event. I uncovered that many other things happened when Chuck experienced his concussion, such as his close buddy was seriously injured, others were killed and the TBI concussion occurred while in combat with the enemy.

His medical assessment coming back from deployment indicated that such a close call on his life had led to post-traumatic stress disorder. Obviously he was depressed and feeling hopeless and helpless when he called; Chuck was giving up.

"I lost touch with Jesus," he said somewhat apologetically. "I knew better but I was angry at Him. War is a bloody place. I witnessed some tragic stuff...stuff that I can't even begin to express what it did to me. Oh yes, I had a concussion, but that was not as critical to me as seeing my buddies blow up. Vic, I just can't talk about it; it was horrible. I have just tried to put it out of my mind. The medical docs, when they checked me over for my concussion, wanted me to see a shrink, too, but I told them...hell no, I'm not weak and helpless. I can handle it." Chuck began to cry. I gave him time.

"Chuck, you are a good man with a kind heart. I can tell that just in the brief time we have talked together. You are a sensitive man, a good and faithful warrior. Welcome home, soldier. Thank you for serving our great nation. I want to help you, buddy. I want to send some help to you right now, right where you are sitting. Is there any reason why you don't want me to do that?"

There was silence on the other end. *Oh, silence can be a bad thing,* I thought. "Chuck, are you still with me, buddy? Chuck, have you hurt yourself? Talk to me, buddy; you have the courage of a warrior. Let me help you!"

His voice came back on the line. "Okay, I am ready," Chuck uttered. "You don't have to arrest me do you? Are you going to send the police?"

"Yes, the police will come, but not to arrest you. The police only have to be there to bring with them the EMTs who will transport you to the nearest community hospital emergency room, understood?"

"They aren't going to handcuff me are they? I don't want to be cuffed," Chuck said somewhat stubbornly.

"No, Chuck, they won't handcuff you. You haven't done anything wrong, have you?"

"No, I don't think so," he replied coyly.

"Good, so then I want you to put the coat hanger wire down, away from where you are sitting, out of reach. Will you do that for me, buddy?" I coached. I heard some background noise, some apparent rustling around for a minute, and then, "Okay, it is on the floor at the end of the bed."

"Good, now please open the motel door so when help arrives they can see you sitting in the chair. Your hands on your lap...okay, Chuck? I want to make sure that when they come to the door the police and emergency team will see it's safe to enter the room, alright?" I instructed.

"The door is open, I am in the chair and my hands are on my lap," Chuck responded a tad like an elementary student might behave in the classroom.

"Great! Now just relax, buddy. I am dispatching emergency services to you as we speak. We have a telecommunications locator. Because of your phone number we know your approximate location. The local police will do the rest. Sit tight, Chuck. I will remain on the phone with you until they get there. The first to arrive will be the police. When they come in, hand the phone over and tell them that I want to talk to one of them. I will make sure you are treated properly and transported to safety. Alright, buddy?"

"Vic, I feel a little uneasy about this, sitting here waiting for police to arrive," Chuck said, obviously shaken.

"You will be just fine. I am here with you. Right now the crisis team is calling the VA nearest you and arranging for a crisis prevention coordinator to meet with you tomorrow and for a mental health evaluation. You will be in good hands, Chuck," I replied trying to reassure him that help was just around the corner. I added, "Hey, this is your chance to get back into the Word [of God]. You, my friend, can begin to work on getting the help you need to deal with those haunting memories that have overwhelmed your very soul."

"That sounds good to me. I am ready. Wait...there is someone at the door," Chuck reported.

"Just hand them the phone and tell them I want to talk for a minute. I wish you the best life has to offer you, Chuck. Good work. Oh, by the way, make sure you read John 3:16 again. This is a new start for you. Goodbye, buddy."

Three months later, I called the VA where Chuck had been taken. I had talked several times with his crisis prevention coordinator over the intervening months, checking up on Chuck's progress and subsequently I was given his phone number where he was staying at a PTSD recovery center. I felt in my heart I wanted to see how he was doing. Frankly, I hoped he had made progress. I decided to call him. I care greatly about these veterans, so I made the call to Chuck, who immediately picked up the phone.

I opened up the conversation saying, "How is the world treating you, Chuck? This is Vic. Thought I would give you a call today and check up on you."

"Vic, I didn't know how to get in touch with you. Man, it is good to hear from you. I want to thank you for what you did for me. You gave me hope, Vic. You encouraged me. And God did the rest. You wouldn't believe what I am doing." I could tell Chuck was building up steam in this conversation. I couldn't believe my ears. *This is a new man,* I thought.

It turned out that Chuck went back to church and renewed his commitment to God. He began praying for a renewed spirit to serve. He started gathering donated Bibles from churches in the community and passed them out to his buddies under the bridge where not so many months prior he had called home. He began a Bible study under the bridge and other homeless veterans and non-vets started to gather together reading and studying the Word of God. Chuck told me he taught mostly from the Book of John found in the New Testament. "It is a book that explains in great detail about the truth and life of Jesus Christ. I found an unconditional love that healed my mind and body and transformed me."

Later I thought about the amazing transformation Chuck had experienced. Chuck had lost all hope of living. He was haunted day and night by the heartfelt scars of losing his buddies in battle. At times he felt guilty for surviving the bomb blast.

The fact that he chose to seek professional help and get out of his depressed stupor was absolutely uplifting. The great work his treatment team at the VA and PTSD center did illustrates the dedication of the men and women on staff. *This is what I come to work hoping to accomplish each and every day,* I mused thoughtfully. *This is what makes me eager to get started when my feet hit the floor each morning. But I know deep inside the transformation I witnessed that it was not me who made the difference in Chuck's life, but his belief and faith in a power greater than himself. Chuck is a Christian believer, a combat veteran who lost his way and now has found it once again.*

Rick Warren, author of *The Purpose-Driven Life* and founding pastor of one of the largest and most well-known churches in California, writes: "You are not an accident. Even before the universe was created, God had you in mind, and he planned you for his purposes. These purposes will extend far beyond the few years you will spend on earth."[2]

So it is for Chuck. He found his purpose. He was led to spread the Word and inspiration of God to the lost and forsaken few; in his case, these were the homeless veterans and others living under the bridge in his town.

### Inspirational Encouragement

Religious counselors frequently carry the burden of grief resolution. Many priests, ministers and rabbis are experienced and comfortable in the role of bereavement counselor. When acceptable and solicited, the implications of the existence of an all-forgiving, all-knowing, loving God who is the ultimate spiritual resource may offer security and hope as well as strength to tolerate the painful effects that afflict the veteran survivors of traumatic combat experiences.

In a magnificent book I read when I was younger, *The Greatest Salesman in the World*, Og Mandino writes:

> Can I call back yesterday's wounds and make them
> whole? Can I become younger than yesterday? Can I
> take back the evil that was spoken, the blows that

were struck, and the pain that was caused? No.
Yesterday is buried forever and I will think of it no
more. I will live this day as if it is my last.[3]

Many years ago, when I was going through some difficult times in
my own life, I was given an inspiring book by Spencer Johnson, M.D.,
titled *The Precious Present*, in which Johnson writes that the present is
precious, even if the reasons are unclear or unknown:

It is already just the way it is supposed to be....The
present moment is the only reality I ever experience.
As long as I continue to stay in the present, I am
happy forever....The present is simply who I am just
the way I am....For I am precious. I am the precious
present.[4]

I hope these two messages inspire you as they have me.

# Chapter 3

# One Combat Pilot's Struggle: The Iraq War

It is my experience as a primary therapist and professional hotline responder that veterans from all past and present wars and conflicts are coming forward in increased numbers with symptoms they have been living with for years, even decades. Delayed post-traumatic stress disorder problems often occur unexpectedly. Flashbacks or a sense of reliving the experiences, feelings of extreme distress when reminded of the trauma and physiological stress responses to reminders of the incidents (throbbing heart, quickness in breathing, stomach queasiness, muscle tension or sweating) all are disturbing memories of and reactions to the traumatic event, resulting in bad dreams about the insidious encounter.

These distressing symptoms can emerge at any time, anywhere—sometimes ostensibly out of the blue. At other times they are triggered by something that reminds the veteran of the original traumatic event: a noise, an image, certain words or even a smell.

Hanna's story presents suggested methods for overcoming these haunting feelings of fear and guilt.

## Hanna's Story

Hanna was an Air Force combat pilot, living with a 100 percent service-connected disability: post-traumatic stress disorder. To perpetuate her disability further, she felt guilty for contributing to the deaths of so many innocent Iraqi civilians. She called the clinic sobbing heavily; her forced breathing noisily affected the handset. The veteran was difficult to understand. Her whimpering voice began, "I am shaking and wrapped around holding my best friend in the world," she sniffled, "my dog."

The combat veteran went on to say the fireworks were too much for her. She was on prescribed medication every day, but during times of storms, sonic booms from the F-14 jets at the nearby Air Force Base and most anything noisy and sudden startled her. The Independence Day fireworks' loud bangs and whistles over and near her house triggered too much of her past experiences as a bomber pilot.

"Too many memories and flashbacks," she said and began to cry.

Post-traumatic stress disorder (PTSD) has become a significant disabling wound that began to be identified and renamed during and after the Vietnam War. Today, PTSD continues to affect approximately 30 percent of the veterans who served in Desert Shield/Storm and the Iraq and Afghanistan Wars. Research has found that trauma, as the result of deliberate intent, such as military combat, produces a profound sense of alienation and alarm and threatens basic life assumptions that one's environment is physically and psychologically safe.

Hanna did not feel safe. In fact, she could not keep the lights off in her house when she slept. "I am dreadfully afraid of thunder and lightning when the summer storms come. I cannot fly in airplanes anymore. My life is over. Give me two reasons why I should live. I find myself avoiding all social activity and most of the time recently I feel numb and nervous; I think I am depressed. I cry often; sometimes daily. If it weren't for my fifteen-year-old dog, I wouldn't be here today talking to you. I know how to kill myself. I am an American combat pilot," Hanna proclaimed.

As I began to talk to Hanna and reassure her that I was there to support her, not judge her, she began to open up and stop crying.

My caller shared she was a combat bomber pilot at the beginning of Operation Desert Storm, an offensive campaign that was originally designed to enforce the United Nation's resolutions that Iraq must cease its rape and pillage of its weaker neighbor Kuwait and withdraw its forces from the small country. The veteran remembered a message delivered to the command on January 16, 1991, by General H. Norman Schwarzkopf, Commander in Chief of U.S. Central Command. Hanna said she memorized his short message:

My confidence in you is total. Our cause is just! Now you must be the thunder and lightning of Desert Storm. May God be with you, your loved ones at home, and our country.

Hanna continued to reveal to me and remember the beginning of her experiences in the war. She recalled that the day after the general's opening message, on January 17, Desert Storm began with a coordinated attack that included Tomahawk land attack missiles launched from cruisers, destroyers and battleships in the Persian Gulf and Red Sea. The missile launches opened a carefully crafted joint strategic air campaign. The initial barrage of over 100 missiles took out heavily defended targets in the vicinity of Baghdad and made a critical contribution to eliminating Iraqi air defenses and command and control capabilities.

During those early hours of the war, Hanna recalled, "I contributed to the destruction of Iraq's air and naval forces, anti-air defenses, ballistic missile launchers, communications networks, electrical power and more. I joined the joint and allied partners in inflicting violent military losses with precision bombing from our high-tech aerial weaponry. As full partners in that campaign, we as Navy and Marine Corps aviators flew from carriers and amphibious ships in the Red Sea and Persian Gulf and from bases ashore, from the day hostilities began until the cease-fire was ordered."

Hanna paused; the phone went silent. I waited. Faintly over the telephone receiver I heard some shuffling and background noise. I know about post-traumatic stress disorder. Avoidance through emotional numbing, anxiety and depression is most common. The signs were all there. I waited. Then she began speaking again. "Umm…from 'H-hour' when the air campaign began," she whispered, "until the end of offensive combat operations forty-three days later, I helped obliterate key targets and helped ensure the United States military and its coalition partners owned the skies over Iraq and Kuwait."

The former combat pilot continued. "I have had to learn to live with this painful memory and the thought I could be responsible for the deaths of innocent people; women and children. My thoughts are intense at times. I feel irritable and I can't concentrate. I experience life-like daydreams of certain scary experiences that return repeatedly and haunt me; and oh my…the nightmares. I can't take this anymore. I don't want to wake up tomorrow," she said poignantly.

I listened intently. I marveled how specific she was, every detail, yet I felt a broken heart. A wave of helplessness brushed through me. My stomach tightened and my heart began to pound. *A suicide is about to take place if I don't act now! I have been here before. It isn't that I don't know what to do. I am a professional interventionist. It just hurts the very essence of my being to witness such a good person go through such agony,* I thought, respecting her situation. *This is a good woman, a fine veteran pilot desperate to be forgiven for her deeds.*

I felt Hanna was going through the feelings of seeing her life as an unconnected, distinct separation of emotions. I heard it in her words. Clinically, I would say these symptoms are the separation of a group of usually connected mental processes, such as emotion and understanding, from the rest of her mind. In translation, she was reliving the trauma of combat through dissociation. At that moment, she felt the only way to separate her from all that misery was by ending her life. She saw no other way to relieve the mental anguish inside of her.

Dissociation is a normal response to trauma and allows the mind to distance itself from experiences that are too much for the psyche to process at that time. Dissociative disruptions can affect any aspect of a person's functioning.

"Hanna, will you let me help you?" I offered after she stopped speaking. There was nothing but silence.

"Hello, Hanna…are you there?" I waited; still no response. She had not hung up. I heard no disconnect; I waited. I knew from experience this would be a long night. I was beginning to think I needed to get emergency vehicles out to her immediately. "Hanna…I am here. I will not leave you. We are in this together. I care about what happens to you. We can get you the help you need. I will see to it. Oh yes, you do have a reason to live and I will give you more than two reasons if you will let me!" I paused again, but at the same time thinking I had to send for a rescue. She may have harmed herself already.

"Hanna, I know you are still on the line. Please talk to me," I said empathetically. "Have you done anything to hurt yourself?" I pleaded for a response. *I know Hanna is crying out for help, because she made the hotline call; but if she made the call after taking some pills or cutting herself, this could be tragic.*

"I am so hurt," she quietly began talking again. "I am not a killer. I had no idea I would feel this way. I am guilty of slaughtering innocent women and children. I can't sleep in my own house. I can't work. I already see doctors. I am on medications every day. What else is there? I feel hopeless. What is there to live for?"

I had to act swiftly. I signaled my health technicians sitting across from me that I needed an emergency rescue—now! They began trying to locate the caller by tracing her phone number from the caller ID and pursued calling the police in Hanna's town. We had no time to lose.

"Hanna, have you hurt yourself? Please talk to me," I said insistently. "I want to get you some help but I need to know where you live so we can come to you right now."

The distinguished college professor and medical doctor Victor M. Victoroff, M.D., wrote in his book *The Suicidal Patient* that people are depressed if they feel trapped or confined by events in life and emotions and cannot glimpse any possible solution except suicide.

He states, "The expression of hopelessness is a sensitive indicator of suicidal intent."[1]

Hanna needed help and quickly! The police and fire department had been alerted and were en route. They had located her home. Now I waited. Hanna was not responding on the phone. My responsibility was to get her to safety. My thoughts raced, *I hope and pray we will get to her in time to save this faithful American combat pilot. These are the toughest moments of my job.*

## Identifying Suicidal Signs and Symptoms

It is of the utmost importance to know some of the warning signs, "silent" signals and personality characteristics if you or a veteran close to you suggests life is too tough to face. Here is a checklist.

*Signs and Red Flags*
- Feelings of not belonging; a difficult time connecting in relationships and bonding with others
- Social isolation: not participating in the social community
- Continually expressing feelings of helplessness, worthlessness, hopelessness
- Survivor's guilt: "It should have been me" or "It is my fault my buddy died"
- Feelings of being trapped
- Not taking prescribed medications for psychiatric disorders such as anxiety and depression
- Physical pain that is unbearable with little hope of relief
- Family history of suicide or depression; a fellow veteran's suicide
- Prior suicide attempts
- Untreated medical problems, such as PTSD and TBI, that go undetected or unreported
- Covered up rage that is acted upon from time to time
- Living with a constant negative attitude: everything past, present and future is bleak
- Possessing the lethal means to follow through with suicide
- Pre-existing conditions of major disorders, such as PTSD, TBI, depression, alcohol or drug abuse, schizophrenia and paranoid personality disorder

Some disorders can trigger a veteran's suicide even if medications, under treatment, are being taken. Research and media reports indicate that a significant number of veteran suicides happen while under doctor's care.

Such signs and red flags can occur even when veterans, who have gone in for counseling and therapy, have themselves realized the impossibility of forgetting their combat experiences and have recognized their hopeless and debilitating characteristics.

I usually advise my clients that for now they should attempt to banish all thoughts of war from their minds. In most cases, all conversation between clinic vets about the war is strictly forbidden and my combat-hardened warriors are instructed and counseled to begin guiding their thoughts to other topics, to beautiful surroundings and to other pleasant aspects of their life experiences. They should look forward, not behind.

I firmly believe in heart-to-heart resuscitation: a genuine, caring and spiritually loving attitude toward every veteran; encouraging, motivating and coaching traumatized combat veterans to visualize pleasant thoughts far, far away from the combat zones. As many veterans know, "Living with a chronic illness, physical, mental or both, adds to the normal pressure of everyday life. This can lead to feelings of anxiety or stress."[2] It is important that veterans are taught basic techniques to help them manage their feelings and anxious situations and to avoid additional stress and negative health effects.

Remember, your VA doctor or healthcare provider is the single best source of information regarding you and your health. Please consult your doctor or healthcare treatment team if you have any questions about your health or any of your medications.

Next, let's focus on some helpful strategies for getting beyond troubling symptoms and relieving stress, depression and anxiety. The most common ways to relieve stress and anxiety are breathing exercises and muscle relaxation; other techniques include visualization, total desensitization, positive thinking, storytelling and spirituality. Here is a brief summary of suggested techniques.[3]

## Breathing Exercises

Begin by sitting or lying in a comfortable position. Then take a deep breath, feeling your abdomen expand. Exhale by drawing your lips together at the sides to form a circle. This allows you to prolong and regulate the breath. As you exhale, feel your abdomen deflate and your shoulders relax. Take two or three deep breaths in this method. Once you become proficient, begin using this breathing technique when you experience stressful situations and practice daily to relieve everyday stress.

## Muscle Relaxation

Tense, strained muscles are a common effect of stress. To relax your muscles, begin by sitting or lying in a comfortable position. Take a deep breath and slowly tighten and relax muscle groups—hands, feet, arms, legs, chest, shoulders and abdomen—in succession. Exhale before relaxing each group.

## Visualization

This technique has you assign mental representations to your negative feelings and then change those images into positives. For example, try adding music and artwork to enhance the relaxation benefits of visualization.

## Total Desensitization

In counseling, combat veterans are often asked to prioritize a list of stress-producing events such as exercise, travel, mixing with family, etc. Create your own list. Beginning with the least stressful activity on your list, "Concentrate on it during a state of relaxation until you feel mentally comfortable with it." Once you attain a comfortable feeling with it, repeat the process with the next item on your list. Continue in this manner until you feel comfortable with all of the items.

## Positive Thinking

This technique is similar to visualization. However, instead of images, it focuses on changing negative thoughts to positive ones. Take a moment to reflect on negative thoughts you've had recently or recurring negative thoughts you have. Once you identify these thoughts, you'll also begin to identify negative thoughts as you have them. Take time to address these negative thoughts and turn them into positive ones.

## Storytelling

Deena Metzger, author of several books about healing, identifies story-telling as a "map for the soul." Metzger says, "One person can not teach another person how to heal but we can tell stories."[4] Psychotherapist Dr. Ed Tick writes:

> Survivors need facilitators (counselors) who...encourage diving deep into the story. Otherwise, a survivor might endlessly repeat details of an event but not experience the release of related emotions, the accurate recording of history, or the making of meaning— all of which are essential in the recovery from post traumatic stress.[5]

## A Spiritual Journey

You and I are spiritual beings. We have souls as well as flesh and bones. We all are special in the eyes of God. The Bible says we are made in the image of God. How amazing is that! Whatever your belief is right now, a power greater than us all must be sought after. And learning to pray is where the discovery can begin.

It is here where life begins again for my distressed combat veterans with wounded souls. Right here the suffering, tormented soul can find relief and a reason to live. My technique of heart-to-heart resuscitation provides a safe environment that lays these important foundations and helps you prepare for a renewed spirit wanting to embrace life once again. Expect a miracle.

Eugene Peterson's *The Message* expresses and paraphrases a passage from the New Testament scripture Ephesians 1:11-12: "It's in Christ that we find out who we are and what we are living for. Long before we first heard of Christ…he had his eye on us, had designs on us for glorious living, part of the overall purpose he is working out in everything and everyone."[6]

All crisis responders who have answered the ringtone of a hotline encounter cases of combat mania and especially the form of neurosis dependent on anxiety. Responders are faced by the problem of what advice to give concerning the attitude the caller should adopt towards his or her war experience.

Generally, the primary goals of all crisis hotline intervention therapists, nurses, counselors and clinical social workers are not to provide callers with over-the-telephone therapy or tele-psychiatry. A hotliner's mission is to get the veterans to safety. In fact, each and every crisis call should be handled with extreme priority that includes immediate intervention advice and heart-to-heart interviewing and assessment. The caller must then be stabilized and/or rescued by the police and emergency medical team and in many cases, with an emergency room stay for psychiatric evaluation and consultative follow-up. The most chronic cases will require immediate hospitalization and an assigned behavioral health treatment team.

And so it was with Hanna at that point. I was waiting for the report of her condition by the on-site emergency team that is always instructed to call the VA hotline back with updated information in order for us to make VA Medical Center arrangements with the crisis prevention coordinator at the nearest hospital. Still no word. Hotliners go temporarily "off-line" in the hotline room and take no other callers until the veteran in crisis has been reached and is on the way to the hospital or other arrangements have been made.

"Hello? Hello, this is Sergeant Bill Williams," came the voice barreling over my hotline. I had not hung up the phone line. I held Hanna's hotline open all that time. I promised her I would never leave her.

"Hello, Sergeant Williams, this is the Veteran's National Suicide Prevention Hotline in upstate New York. How is our veteran Hanna doing?" I asked, worried about her welfare.

"What is your name?" the sergeant asked, questioning my authority to be involved.

"Vic Montgomery. I work as a therapist for the VA suicide hotline...Hanna is one of our vets. Please handle her with care, officer, she is a war veteran, and please see to it she gets to the nearest Veteran Affairs Medical Center for her medical needs and psychiatric evaluation. Will you do that for me?"

"It is being done as we speak," the police officer replied. "The EMTs are here already and attending to her. It appears she is unconscious sitting in a chair with the telephone in her lap. Her vital signs are irregular, but the paramedics say she will be alright—pill overdose they think. We got here just in time," he reported. I found out later the police had to break a window to enter the home and found Hanna slumped in the chair by the phone.

After finding out Hanna was safe, I put my headset down on my desk and walked briskly down the hall. As I made my way, I said a prayer of thanks for the help God had given me to get this vet to safety.

Hanna needed to find out how to administer self-care and learn how to forgive and let go. This courageous combat pilot had to learn how to heal her feelings of having done wrong and realize the purpose for which she served was courageous and meaningful for her country.

Hanna received specialized care for her condition. Many of the 153 VA Medical Centers that operate PTSD clinics are listed by region in appendix A of this book.

# Chapter 4

# "I am a Monster": Two Tours in Al-Fallujah, Iraq

Several military media reports, along with my medical research, suggest that about 30 percent of veteran warriors who have returned home from combat have shown signs of post-traumatic stress disorder (PTSD) and/or traumatic brain injury (TBI). Suicide ideation as a result of PTSD and TBI continues to be a growing concern. It is crystal clear to me, after hearing the frantic, crisis-induced phone calls from hundreds of family members, friends and the vets themselves returning home from multiple tours of combat, that the unrelenting direct orders to deploy a second, third and, in some cases, fourth tour to Iraq and Afghanistan is unconscionable. Numerous medical studies already indicate the incidents and severity of post-traumatic stress disorder and the onset of suicide ideation are increased with each added tour.

An article on the Web site for the Pennsylvania-based NBC affiliate, WJAC-TV, quotes Gordon Mathers of the VA Medical Center as saying, "When they come back to the U.S., there's no switch there to just say that it's all over. 'I don't miss the combat, but I miss being up and ready.'"[1] The rush is similar to a drug addiction.

Conquering the addiction of a warrior's adrenaline rush and discovering how to recognize alcohol and substance dependency are important steps for a veteran's healing.

## Burt's Story

The caller blurted out these words almost immediately: "I can't share anything with my family and friends. I don't want them to think I am a monster," he said, slurring his speech. "I began to love the smell of death and burned powder. The command ordered 'everyone needs to be eliminated.'" The caller wanted to remain anonymous, but after I told him my name, he told me his first one, Burt, but withheld his last name. No location given but I could see by his area code from my caller ID line the state from which he was calling.

Burt's story is an emotional and painful one. He is a former combat Marine stationed in 2004 within the combat zone in the Iraqi city of Al-Fallujah, described by the Web site Global Security (www.globalsecurity.org) as "a large town forty miles west of Baghdad. Fallujah is the most violence prone area in Iraq and since early April 2003 they have experienced violent crowd control incidents, murders and bombings."[2] As our phone call continued, he blurted out in fits and starts that he was only thirty-three years old, his wife had left him for another man and his best friend had committed suicide.

"I am listening," I said, not knowing what to expect next with this caller's volatile message.

Burt continued, "I continually see bodies and their lifeless eyes in my dreams. I wake up soaked in sweat. I can't sleep. I began to love seeing the dead bodies of the enemy in front of me," he paused and sniffled. "I'm tired of hearing about the war. I don't know who I am anymore." He then lowered his gruff voice and mournfully said, "We came back home from Iraq and after four months my Marine buddy blew his brains out." He paused. "I have a weapon. I can't get any rest. I have nothing to live for…no one left…my buddies are gone…and other friends…dead. I wrestle and toss and turn at night…I can't sleep, man…I see their lifeless eyes in my dreams." He paused again, sounding like he took a sip of something. The noise of a glass was being rattled near the receiver.

After two tours in Al-Fallujah, Iraq, this veteran had lost his identity. Burt saw himself as a monster. He drank a fifth of whiskey a day to help suppress the inner turmoil. Burt was discouraged and felt trapped. He was a suicidal, depressed warrior. He had lost his way; hence, the battle for personal survival was on. A cleansing of the mind often occurs through a careful process of bringing to the surface withdrawn, covered-up emotions and feelings in an effort to identify and relieve them. Burt needed help and guidance to learn how to release the combat adrenaline rush he still felt and to disown the addiction to that rush he developed during his battle and bloodshed experiences.

I hesitated to say anything, because I felt as if this Marine needed to vent at that point, needed someone to listen to his obviously pent-up emotions. So I just listened. I adjusted my headset, leaned forward, elbows on my desk. I looked up briefly at the clocks on the wall. The night was relatively calm for a Saturday.

I heard Burt breathing into the receiver on the other end of the line. Then he continued. "Hey!…are you there or did I scare you away?" he said with mockery in his tone.

"No, Burt, I am still here, buddy. I will not leave you. I am listening to you," I responded calmly, trying to defuse the emotional ranting.

Burt began speaking again. "I can still smell the decay of death…I will always remember…my mind repeats the same scenes. I am trapped in this insanity. It's over man…it's over…I am going to hang up now… goodbye!"

I responded instinctually, "Wait, Marine, don't hang up…give me another minute to talk with you. Oh yes, you do have a reason to live and I will tell you why! For one, I care, Burt…*Semper Fi*! I care that you served our country with honor. Thank you for serving! Welcome home, Burt. Many people care whether you live or die. You have family who love you. They might not understand exactly what you are going through right now, but that can change if you will let me help you. I have your back,

Burt. Listen to me, buddy, you are not alone in this battle…let me help you right now…I can have help to you in five minutes and get you to the VA if you will let me. You will be safe there and they will help you work through this." There was a ghostly silence. "Talk to me, Burt…don't hang up, buddy—" Click…dial tone.

When he hung up the phone, my heart sank. A feeling of nausea came over me. My head dropped to the desk in fatigue and dejection. *I couldn't help this Marine tonight*, I thought. I began questioning my own abilities and conversation with Burt. *What could I have said differently?* I took my headset off and slung it on my desk while kicking the trash can. I looked distraughtly in the direction of the support technicians. Their eyes were wide open with a look of expectation on their faces; they knew something was coming down. I called out at full volume, "Find where this call on line six was coming from. We have a Marine with a weapon and a plan to kill himself! We need a rescue here…now! He hung up on me…"

I got up from my desk and took a walk down the long, shiny, waxed and buffed hallway, my hands resting on the top of my head, fingers clasped and elbows in the air. I kicked open the outer door to the outside deck to get some fresh air. Thinking carefully, I continued to replay the conversation with Burt in my mind. At that moment, I was discouraged and saddened that I failed to bring a troubled warrior to safety. This is my job. It never gets routine or easy. Hotliners have to shake it off and get back on the line for the next caller.

Meanwhile, in the hotline room, the health tech team was feverously trying to locate Burt. The health technician support teams are there to back up and support the hotline responder in all efforts to locate and get emergency services to suicidal veterans. The technicians have their own set of telecommunications, data equipment and separate phone lines to work parallel to us in locating and contacting law enforcement agencies and emergency services, fire departments and ambulance services in the area code of the identified telephone number of the suicidal veteran. This is no easy task. Yet it is so important in cases like this one where the veteran does not give an address, full name or the name of the place from which he is calling. Another monumental roadblock in finding the embattled warrior is if the phone number happens to be a cell phone. It makes the task of getting help to the veteran even more difficult, because there are no ways to find out where the veteran is calling from except through the cell phone company and that takes precious time—time we don't have especially if the caller is roaming out of his original area code. Sometimes it becomes a high stakes guessing game.

A few minutes had passed as I was taking my break. I heard a shout coming down the corridor from a colleague. "Phone call, Vic. Someone asking to speak only to you by name." I hurriedly made my way back to my desk and picked up the line. It was Burt.

It is natural to push aside agonizing memories just as it is instinctive to avoid dangerous or unspeakable scenes in actuality. This natural tendency to cast out the stressful or the dreadful is especially well-defined in veterans, whose powers of resistance have been reduced by the long-continued strains of combat firefights, second and third tours or other catastrophes of war incidents. Even if Burt was left to his own devices, most vets would naturally strive to forget distressing memories and thoughts. He was, however, very far from being left to himself. The natural tendency is to repress feelings. In Burt's case, he was isolating and drinking heavily to numb the daily struggles and stressors of the day as well as the trauma of unfamiliar feelings of suicidal ideation.

I adjusted my headset and dug in for the call. "Burt…buddy, you had me worried. What's up…what's going on with you right now? Talk to me," I said, engaging him caringly. Burt began to speak a bit calmer than before. I felt as if he was testing me to see if he could trust me with this unbelievably private, raw information; possibly some fear hovered nearby.

"I can't talk to nobody about this stuff. How do you describe to family or friends or even a shrink what it was like to pull the trigger and watch your first kill crumple to the ground before you? How do I talk about the short bursts of bullets buzzing over my head and the fear and adrenaline rush inside of me? These people don't know anything. How can they understand what I feel inside my head and my heart? Man…this talking to you is no use. What can you do for me?" I continued to listen. "I approached the insurgent. He was just laying there, eyes and mouth wide open—just a kid. The thick blood was pooling around his head." Burt paused abruptly as if checking himself. I heard a bit of a frog in his throat.

"Burt, I am listening and we can get you the help you need to work through these memories. And you aren't a monster, buddy. You were sent into battle. You are a Marine…ooh-rah, you did what you had to do," I said with sensitivity.

"Are you a veteran?" Burt said inquisitively.

"Is that important to you…whether I am a veteran or not?" I responded.

"Yeah, kinda," Burt retreated.

"What about my being a veteran would make you feel more comfortable?" I questioned.

"Oh, I don't know, just wondered I guess. I feel like I can talk to you," he slurred.

"Burt, I want to get you to the hospital as soon as possible," I pleaded. "Would you agree to that? So we can get you to where you are safe and out of harm's way. Burt, you have a weapon and that concerns me, buddy. You have already told me you want to end your life. At the VA, there they can evaluate you to see what the docs suggest for you to do with all of these nightmares, depression, built-up emotions and your drinking."

Burt began to ramble. I felt the booze was beginning to affect him. "When my wife and I were together, she worried. She couldn't understand why I repeatedly jumped out of bed in the middle of the night screaming war cries. I don't blame her for leaving me. I am some kind of monster." Burt slurred his words. "But I miss her and can't take this being alone any longer, day in and day out…I feel hopeless, man…just sitting and staring at the walls with my whiskey bottle between my legs."

"Marine, listen to me. I can get you some help." There was silence. "Where is your weapon?" I requested an answer.

Burt replied, "My pistol is on the couch right next to me, friend...fully loaded," he paused. "But all I need is one bullet...haw." He spun what sounded like the cylinder near the handset. I felt helpless. I knew the more he drank, the more drunk he would get and the greater the possibility of suicide.

With the wave of my free hand I signaled my health technicians to come over to me. I began writing on the yellow pad in front of me: "He has a loaded gun on the couch next to him!" The techs leaned over to see my note and whispered to me they had found his location and the police were working on the address. I wrote on the pad: "Hurry!"

Burt was on the edge. He needed a reason to live; he was calling for help. Sometimes it just takes someone showing he or she cares whether a person lives or dies. When veterans begin drinking heavily they become abusive, mostly to themselves, and at times, lash out at others. But there is no question suicide becomes a real alternative to them especially if they "become sick and tired of being sick and tired." Over a longer period of time drinking and building up a tolerance, needing more alcohol or drugs to reach the same effect, the vet may become dependent on the substance. This becomes a serious health disorder and requires immediate professional help. The VA has alcohol and drug rehabilitation units all over the country. It was my task to get Burt out of suicide danger, to a safe place and assessed for alcohol abuse or dependency treatment at the nearest VA Medical Center.

"Burt, would you do me a favor, buddy?" I asked. "Take the bullets out of the chamber and cylinder of your weapon while you have me on the phone and put them somewhere in your place away from you...so we can talk this over? I can't carry on a conversation with you knowing you have a pistol cylinder loaded with bullets, spinning it in my ear. Agreed?"

Burt was slow to answer. I could tell he was thinking my question over; I have been here before. The important task at this point is to disarm the warrior and talk him down from harming himself before the police and paramedics get there.

As I was waiting for Burt's response, one of the health techs reached over to me with a note: "Help is on the way. Sheriff will be there with EMTs in seven minutes."

"Burt, will you unload your weapon for me?" I asked with urgency as I needed to disarm him before the sheriff got to the location. Not that there would be a shoot-out or that Burt was in trouble for having a gun, but law enforcement won't let EMTs in to help vets with a potential suicide intervention unless it is a safe place, which certainly makes sense. This way, the sheriff will call and ask what the conditions are before the emergency team makes an approach to rescue the vet.

"Burt, talk to me. Do you hear what I am asking you, soldier?" I said insistently.

"Yeah," he muttered. "Okay, I will drop the bullets into my hand and put them in my drawer in the kitchen...is that good enough for you?"

"Yes, Burt, that is good enough. Let me hear the loose bullets in your hand, okay?"

"Wow, you sure are picky, picky...don't you trust me?" he blurted out.

"I am listening. I want to make sure you are safe, Burt. I really do care that you get the help you need, alright?" I asked. He said nothing. Then I heard him rustle around and some background noise. It sounded like there were bullets in his hand. He left the phone for a minute. I waited. I stared at the clock on the wall. I had been tracking the time. *Seven minutes*, I thought. *Estimated time of arrival for the sheriff and emergency team is two minutes away.*

At that moment one of the health technicians leaned toward me as if to say something. I slid my headset off my right ear and heard him report, "The sheriff is outside of the veteran's house. They just pulled up with an ambulance for transport to the VA. They are asking what the status is inside; I have them on my line waiting for an update."

"Tell them to wait outside. I am still in conversation with the veteran. There is a weapon inside, but the bullets are out of the gun," I replied to the technician.

"Burt, can you hear me?" I said into my headset and waited for some sign that Burt was there; nothing. I wasn't sure what was happening. *Where is he? I thought. What could be happening? The phone has not disconnected. I heard no disconnect and the light signal on my telephone equipment is still lit in the connect mode.*

"Burt, Marine, talk to me!" I said rather excitedly. Then I heard movement near the phone.

"Hello...you still there?" Burt belted out in his handset into my ear.

"Yes, Burt, I will not leave you, buddy. I want you to get some help. Will you go to the VA tonight? I'm concerned for your safety. I don't want to leave you alone tonight. Do you hear me, Burt? I have your back, Marine. I have sent for some emergency transportation for you," I confided.

"What do you mean some transportation?" he inquired, sounding somewhat puzzled.

I responded, "I have sent for a rescue, Burt. The sheriff's vehicle and an ambulance are outside of your house right now. Buddy, I need to get you to safety. You are not in any condition to be alone, Burt. You have threatened suicide. You have a gun at your fingertips. You called the hotline. We take these calls very seriously. You appear to be intoxicated. Burt, I am answering your plea for help."

"Haw...intoxicated, you bet, I am always intoxicated...so what, who cares...my wife is gone with another dude, my best friend and combat buddy blew his brains out...I can't sleep without drinking myself to pass out...the nightmares and flashbacks are too much...what a life... haw! I am going to hang up now. There is no more talk," he said hopelessly. Click, dial tone.

My mind raced with thoughts of self-doubt: *What was he thinking? Should I send the police in?* I'm very much aware of "adrenaline rush" experiences by combat troops. This was a real possibility with Burt. He had already told me at the beginning of our conversation how he began to like the smell of death and burned powder. Did he want to die by a police confrontation?

Jill Carroll's article, "When the war comes back home", in the *Christian Science Monitor* immediately came to mind while talking with Burt. She describes the arrests, instances of domestic violence, fist-fights and car chases participated in "often with drugs or alcohol involved seeking to replicate the adrenaline rush of combat or to commit suicide by motorcycle or police bullets."[3]

I signaled for the health technicians to give me the direct phone line with the sheriff at Burt's location. I needed to talk with him and tell him the turn of events.

A short time after I updated the sheriff, I received the report that the sheriff deputy went to the door. And, after some conversation, Burt let him in the house. Burt agreed to go with the EMTs to the local emergency department for a psychiatric evaluation and then arrangements were made to transport him to the nearest VA Medical Center where the VA's crisis prevention coordinator was to meet him.

Later in the week I made contact with the CPC at the VA hospital and was told Burt had been admitted for a medical detoxification, mental health evaluation and referral to a long-term chemical dependency rehabilitation program.

If you are wondering whether or not you or someone close to you may have a substance abuse or chemical dependency problem, I have included this checklist to guide and assist you in helping both determine and justify looking into treatment at your local VA. Remember, it takes the courage of a warrior to ask for help!

### Self-Examination for a Courageous Veteran

*Mind-Altering Chemical Substance Use (Alcohol, Marijuana, Cocaine, Hallucinogens, Methamphetamines, Depressants and Opiates)*
This examination is designed as a self-help tool; however, it is not to diagnose you, but to assist you or someone close to you in determining or justifying immediate treatment for chemical dependency or substance

abuse. Treatment may include inpatient or outpatient services. Mind-altering chemical substances are reported to be a leading factor contributing to veteran suicides. The following diagnostic criteria are based on material from the *Diagnostic and Statistical Manual of Mental Disorders*; for more information, please refer to the complete book.[4]

## Chemical Dependence

Check all that apply for occurring at any time in the same twelve-month period:

☐ You find a need for noticeably increased amounts of alcohol or other drugs in order to reach a desired outcome, that is getting high, zoning, buzzed or intoxicated, and/or you find that using the same amount of the substance results in a diminished effect. If that is an honest assessment of your condition, then I suggest you may have built a *tolerance* to the substance. If tolerance is present, you are most likely increasing the amount you use to get the same effect.

   The fact that you have developed a tolerance for your drug of choice highly suggests that you may have a chemical dependency problem and your condition should be evaluated by the proper healthcare treatment team.

☐ Another indictor of a chemical dependency problem is *withdrawal*. You use to avoid being sick and/or use the same or similar substance to avoid these withdrawal symptoms:

   - Shakes
   - Seizures
   - Cramping

   If you have already attempted to stop using the drug of choice and you experience some or all of these symptoms, then there is a strong possibility that you are chemically dependent and in need of medically supervised detoxification.

Additional areas for concern:

☐ The drug of choice is taken in larger amounts or over a longer period of time than was intended.

☐ There is a constant desire or failed efforts to reduce usage or control substance abuse.

☐    Constant preoccupation and significant time spent in purchasing or "picking up" the drugs of choice as well as considerable time spent using the substance or recovering from the effects of the substance.
☐    Significant interruption and non-participation in social, occupational or recreational activities because of the use of the drug.
☐    Using the drug of choice is continued regardless of your awareness of having continuing or repeated physical, emotional or legal problems that have been caused or made worse by the substance.

Total number of checkmarks _____

If you have checked three or more issues in this section, this indicates chemical dependency requiring intensive treatment; possible inpatient detoxification and residential treatment may be necessary or, at the bare-minimum, intensive outpatient. Important note: Always check with your primary healthcare professional and get another opinion. Ask for an evaluation to help determine a level of care and clinical diagnosis.

## Substance Abuse

Substance abuse is a tricky and many times deceptive pattern of behavior. The substance, alcohol or other drug can sneak up on you and turn on you unsuspectingly. You may have started out experimenting or using the drugs recreationally and socially at an early age. Many military men and women are exposed to drinking almost immediately upon finishing boot camp. If you happen to be one of those warriors who has a predisposition to addictive behaviors or are genetically connected to a generation of alcoholics or drug addicts, then you must be more keenly aware of troubles that await you if you continue to use.

The following are a few signs that may indicate you have or are developing significant impairment or suffering because of the destructive behavior associated with substance abuse. If you are willing to take a serious and honest look at yourself and if any one of these abusive patterns has occurred during the past twelve months then I highly recommend you go to your healthcare provider for a clinical evaluation and screening.

☐ Continual substance use resulting in a disappointment to perform major commitments and obligations at home, work or school.

☐ Repeated substance use in situations where it is physically dangerous.

☐ Recurrent substance related legal problems (e.g. DWI, domestic violence, financial).

☐ Continued substance use despite having constant or repeated social or interpersonal problems caused or exacerbated by the effects of your drug of choice.

Total number of checkmarks _____

If you have checked one or more issues, it indicates substance abuse. This is a treatable condition and recovery can be supervised in an outpatient, non-intensive setting. Important note: Always check with your primary healthcare professional and get a second opinion. Ask for an evaluation to help determine what would be the best level of care and for a clinical diagnosis.

# Chapter 5

# Women in the Iraqi War Zones

Sexual trauma is another form of trauma that can lead to psychological complications and suicide ideation. Compounding the issue is that sexual aggressors are often military comrades.

Once a victim of sexual assault is deemed physically safe, the trauma is not over. Sexual trauma's mental health impact is a serious problem for veterans coming home from war zones. The National Online Resource Center on Violence Against Women explains the different responses victims have to sexual trauma. According to their guidelines, reactions range in severity, timing, duration and type. Many times they also inhabit mental health issues other than PTSD, including alcoholism, depression, eating disorders such as bulimia and anorexia, sexual dysfunction and drug abuse.[1]

In addition, recent studies of veteran sexual trauma survivors suggest that these veterans experience symptoms of not only PTSD but also borderline personality disorder. Borderline personality disorder "is associated with experiencing an interpersonal stressor and symptoms related to mood swings, changes in states of consciousness, physical symptoms without a medical diagnosis, an altered sense of self and others." Many clinicians are now supporting diagnoses of Complex PTSD, which includes both PTSD and borderline personality disorder, as a way of better understanding and treating sexual trauma survivors.[2]

### Jan's Story

The hotline rang; I answered with my customary acknowledgment, "Hello, my name is Vic. How can I help you today?" I paused a few seconds and repeated my greeting, "How may I help?…hello?" I hesitated. I heard nothing but air swishing in the line. I waited. I have developed a keen sense when someone is on the other end of the line, but just holding the handset at a distance, not saying a word or even breathing into the receiver. This is not a new experience for me. Many callers have a difficult time beginning to speak into the phone. It must seem like getting ready to talk into a dark abyss—not knowing who is going to answer and questioning in their minds *Will they understand me? Will they judge me?* The fear must be enormous. In many cases, the caller's emotions are raw and untested. The internal pain is just too much and the fear of sharing a personal tragedy, their stories, with anyone appears to be a gigantic feat.

The overwhelming feeling of this caller's isolation was so apparent and powerful I felt the enormity of the moment pushing its way over the phone line into my ear, then into my heart. Slowly I began to distinguish a female's voice crying, softly weeping. I felt her pain. *How could you not feel the suffering?* Even the silence was filled with anguish and intensity, which I sensed.

"Take as much time as you need," I gently responded to her silent cry for help. "Thank you for calling. How may I help you?" I paused and listened for the slightest sign of life on the other end.

She continued crying quietly for several minutes before she began to speak. It seemed like an eternity before she said a word. "It is hard for people outside the war zone to understand how living in high stress, primitive conditions can affect your ability to make decisions," she declared, her voice quivering. "I didn't report the sexual harassment and attack immediately, because I felt an obligation to continue the mission and not burden others." She explained that she also wondered how the mostly male upper command would perceive the report. "What would it do to my career and promotions?...the Army was my life," she shared, still questioning her judgment.

Jan's story reveals the secrecy and moral burden of sexual trauma. This honorable and dedicated military nurse perceived she was at the end of all possible hope for relief from the psychological demons that haunted her. Her life seemed to be over and she saw no way out.

It took this once confident veteran nurse several months to call the hotline after she was honorably discharged and separated from the service.

She told me, "I was sexually and emotionally abused, harassed and raped by a fellow Army National Guard soldier while on duty in Iraq. When I deployed home, I felt I could not share this information with my family or anyone else, for that matter. I felt disconnected from my family. I began to isolate myself and am pretty much a loner today. I feel I have lost everything...my dignity and honor. And so I decided to leave the service after eight years; I couldn't continue wearing the uniform. I felt dirty...I was and still am angry...disgusted at myself. I just can't find anything to be happy about...I don't smile, Vic. I always had a smile on my face. It's like it is painted over with a brushstroke...a blank face, nothing there. I look in the mirror in the morning and don't know who I am anymore. I'm ugly. I was a happy person, Vic." She began to cry.

"Take your time, I will stay with you. What is your name?" I requested.

"Janice...I am called Jan," she replied, sniffling between words.

"Keep talking, Jan; I am listening to you. I really care about what you are going through right now. I am so glad you called today. I will see to it that you get the help you need...okay?" I tried to encourage her. She had no response.

I could hear her labored breathing as she continued. "I had a lot of friends. I enjoyed being around people. I have no desire to have a relationship. He hurt me, Vic. I hurt all over. I will never be the same again. What's the use of living? I have nothing to look forward to but this same miserable life I live day in and day out. I go to work and come home and sit like a zombie. I have difficulty sleeping many nights." She shared with me how she felt her life was slowly fading away. It had been several years since the horrid experience. She told me how she was having continuing nightmares and flashbacks bringing back the memory of the attack and the distorted face of the unshaven rapist, an assumed American comrade in arms in the war zone of Iraq. She described the smell of his breath as "raunchy, filled with the rancid odor of alcohol and cigarettes." She paused for a moment as if to collect her thoughts and control her emotions. I heard her take some deep breaths. I remained silent and listened for more of the story, but was ready to jump in and offer her kindhearted support.

Jan recalled, "The attacker was so angry he could not hold an erection or penetrate me, so he used his fingers, viciously saying, 'You like that, c—, huh? You want more, sweetie pie?' as he pinned me down with his forearm pushing against my throat. I remember closing my eyes to escape; I went numb. Then he was gone. Vic, I have never shared this with anyone, let alone a man. I don't know why I am saying this now, to you. I feel ashamed and embarrassed beyond belief." She paused. "I feel like hanging up. I am having a hard time holding this stuff in…can't hold this inside any longer…I am going nuts."

"Jan, please don't hang up…you are doing the right thing. May I ask you a few questions so I can get you the help you deserve?" I wanted to move this intense, graphic conversation to another topic and ease the emotion that was building up the more she talked about the event, understandably so. *My word, what a burden to carry around for so long,* I thought.

My experience and therapeutic training suggests that Jan's story needs to be told in a way that transfers the moral burden of the sexual attacks in the war zone from the veteran to the community she served.

Storytelling is a very successful heart-to-heart resuscitation model for treatment.

Sexual trauma survivors need to talk to active, sincere and 'in-the-present' listeners, people they can learn to trust and who encourage them to dive headlong into the stories with no hesitation and no holding back. Otherwise, the sexual trauma survivors might continuously repeat details of the event without experiencing the release of interrelated emotions, the precise memories of the past or the concept of consequence—all of which are indispensable in the recovery from a traumatic experience that may result in a therapeutic diagnosis of post-traumatic stress, depression or anxiety disorders. I cannot reiterate enough that these are all treatable conditions; treatable, in many cases, without a medication regiment or deeply invasive psychoanalysis.

A professional counselor or other referral from your medical doctor is a wise decision; however, if fear exists to the extreme, causing the veteran not to seek help or treatment, then certainly a family member or good friend can be the trusted listener.

Getting the right help is so vital. These experiences Jan was going through are fragile. She needed to be handled with heart-to-heart caring and compassion. Jan needed to tell her story face-to-face with someone she could trust with the information, preferably a therapist familiar with combat trauma PTSD. The phone is not the place for this kind of conversation.

The National Center for PTSD explains, "Trying to avoid thinking about the trauma and avoiding treatment for trauma-related problems may keep a person from feeling upset in the short term, but avoiding treatment means that in the long term, trauma symptoms will persist."[3]

The center goes on to explain what experiencing "life-like" symptoms means:

> [They] are a sign that the body and mind are actively struggling to cope with the traumatic experience.
> These symptoms are automatic, learned responses to trauma reminders. The trauma has become associated with many things so that when the person experiences

these things, he or she is reminded of the trauma and feels that he or she is in danger again. It is also possible that re-experiencing symptoms are actually a part of the mind's attempt to make sense of what has happened.[4]

Here are some signs and symptoms of post-traumatic stress for you or someone close to you to look out for:
- Re-experiencing of the traumatic event(s)
- Stressful recollections
- Difficulty sleeping
- Flashbacks (feeling as if you are going though the sexual trauma experience again)
- Nightmares (frequent recurrent images of the sexual trauma while asleep)
- Feeling disconnected from the world around you and things that happen to you
- Restricting your emotions; "stuffing or self-medicating"
- Trouble remembering important parts of what happened during the trauma
- Shutting down (feeling emotionally and/or physically numb)
- Feeling anxious or fearful (as if you're back in that fearful place in time)
- Drawing inward or becoming emotionally numb
- Active avoidance of activities, places, thoughts, feelings, memories, people or conversations related to or that remind you of your experience
- Loss of interest
- Feeling detached from others (finding it hard to have loving feelings or experiencing any strong emotions or bonding relationships)[5]

I began with questions. "Jan, are you thinking about suicide?"
"I have thought about it…especially lately," she replied forlornly.

"What have you thought about?" I continued to probe.

"Cutting my wrists with a razor...and going to sleep, hopefully escaping from these hopeless feelings. I am tired. Some days are worse than others," Jan responded despondently.

"Have you done anything to hurt yourself?" I asked.

"Oh, it seems I always hurt myself in one way or another. I cut myself on my legs when I am feeling badly. It kind of relieves the tension and takes the edge off. I got therapy when I was a teenager, for cutting. I never have been one for using drugs or alcohol. My father was a drunk and I swore I would never be like him. I hated my mother for living with him and putting up with all his abuse. So I found I would get what relief I needed when I cut myself. The feeling is...well, I don't really want to go into it right now," she concluded abruptly.

Clinical studies indicate those who cut themselves do so to obtain the same euphoric level or release of emotional pressure as does the drug addict shooting up a syringe of heroin, the marijuana smoker smoking a joint or the alcoholic polishing off a fifth of whiskey. These are all acts of self-medication and pleasure-seeking behavior. The serious and sad nature of these actions many times ends with an overdose and subsequently the death of the user. This is a matter of life and death at every turn.

"Jan, have you cut yourself today?" I begged for the answer.

"Well, some," she eked out.

I knew by that answer I had a "high risk for suicide" vet on the phone. I quickly signaled to my health technicians; "We need a rescue now!" my hand motions indicated. The team sprung into action, retrieving information from my notes and began to make calls.

"Jan, where do you live? May I have your address and full name please? I want to send you an ambulance; I want to get you in to the VA for the mental health help you need right now. Are you willing to help me help you?" I pleaded.

The haunting momentary silence permeated my surroundings. *Come on, Jan, answer me,* I reflected.

"I need something," she whimpered.

In the minutes following I was able to get her full name, address, date of birth and social security number. She agreed she needed help. She had cut her leg more than superficially this time. The wound had been bleeding since she made the call. We had no time to spare. The tech team dispatched the police and EMTs to her apartment.

"Jan, I have help on the way. Please unlock and open your door to let the paramedics in, okay?" I asked, concerned.

"I am getting weak, Vic; I am on the toilet in my bathroom. I will try and get to the front door," she replied, sounding even weaker than before. Her voice was faint.

I heard some commotion in the background. It sounded like a door opening and then she got back on the phone.

"Alright the door is open," she said a bit out of breath, as if it was a physical struggle to get to the door.

"Good job, Jan. When the emergency team arrives, have the police officer or EMT talk to me on the phone for a minute. Jan, keep this line open; I will stay with you until help arrives and you are safe and attended to, okay?" I stated decisively.

"I am not going anywhere." Jan added, "The blood has soaked though the bath towel I wrapped around my leg…I feel nothing in my leg right now, Vic. I think I am dying," Jan said ardently.

I spun around in my chair, slipped my headset down around my neck and shouted across the room to the techs, "Where is my ambulance?! I need those EMTs! Get on the horn and talk to the police—this has turned into a life and death situation. Let's make this rescue."

"Jan, are you there?….Jan!" I called into the headset.

"How can I not keep from staying awake with all the yelling and chatter you are doing, Vic…hey, you really care about me, don't you?" Jan asked bashfully. There was a brief moment of levity in the trying moment.

"Yes, I do and so do a lot of other people, Jan. I know you are not feeling much love right now but with the proper therapy you will see a big difference in your outlook on life. I know this to be true, kid."

"Kid!" Jan's response jumped through my headset. "Kid! Are you kidding me? How old are you, Vic? Hmmm ..."

Just then a health tech slipped a note in front of me saying the fire department had dispatched their paramedics, because they were closer to the address and the police had arrived on the scene ready to go to the apartment on the second floor.

"Jan, the paramedics are coming up the stairs to your place as we speak. Remember to hand the phone over to the first person in the door, understood?" I instructed.

"Okay, here they are," Jan replied and handed over the telephone.

I always introduce the veteran to the emergency responders. "You have one of our Iraq veterans. Her name is Jan and she has cut herself. Please take good care of her and see to it she gets to a VA Medical Center nearest your location for a psychological evaluation and medical attention as soon as possible. Will you do that for her?" I requested.

"We will take good care of her," the officer replied. "The EMTs are checking out her vitals and putting pressure bandages over the leg wound. The leg wound looked very raspy. The veteran looks rattled but we will see to it she gets the help she needs."

Jan was taken to meet with a crisis prevention coordinator, one of the members of her treatment team, at the nearest VA and given the proper support she required to help her get back on her feet again.

Later, she was referred to a PTSD clinic and I found she was doing well. She had several visits from her family and a few friends from her college days in nursing. I believe Jan simply forgot she had so much love and support around her. The impact the sexual trauma experience had on this Iraq war zone veteran, the isolation and self-abuse it caused, forced her into such mental confusion that, for Jan, it seemed like suicide was the only alternative.

Jan lost her love for life. It was stolen from her and not necessarily by wounds of combat but by the cruelty of a man with no conscious: a soldier with no scruples, a drunken combat coward who had lost his way, a byproduct from the war zone.

Jan was hiding out for years not knowing how to heal her wounded soul. She stuffed the agony while remaining in the military ranks for fear of dismantling her unit's mission and those of her comrades.

Jan's traumatic rape experience is not an isolated incident. Of the female veterans returning from OIF/OEF, approximately 23 to 33 percent have experienced military sexual trauma (MST).

Matthew Tull, Ph.D., a former clinician at the National Center for PTSD at the Boston Veterans Affairs Healthcare System, acknowledges that while many women keep their instances of victimization a secret fearing reprecussions, this rate is still shockingly high.[6]

Research indicates that more than 150,000 women have deployed to Iraq and Afghanistan since 2003; more than 400 have been wounded and over 70 killed. But these statistics are only part of the story. The Veterans Affairs Long Beach Healthcare System in Long Beach, California, researched MST and its consequences on a small group of OIF/OEF women veterans. According to their findings, half the women in the study admitted they were victims of MST. Sexual harassment was the most common complaint.

"However, a third said they also experienced unwanted physical advances," the research goes on to explain. "And a fifth of them said that they had been sexually assaulted or raped."[7]

Dr. Tull reports that one study found that approximately 42 percent of women who had experienced a MST also had PTSD as a result of the MST."[8]

These female warriors are our brave and noble ladies in uniform. They are wives, mothers, girlfriends and sisters stepping up to serve our great nation. An outstanding read about women in the war zone is *Band of Sisters* written by Kirsten Holmstedt (Stackpole Books, 2007). In her book, she reveals the stories of nurses struggling to save lives, including their own, pilots, turret gunners defending convoys and women

Marines in firefights. As one female service member put it, "We love our country as much as any man and we have made the same sacrifices as our brothers in arms."

The key ingredients I have found for successful outcomes with suicidal veterans are not only the recognition by the vets that they want help and the ability to accept help when given (not always easy for a combat veteran), but also the awareness to seek help from outside sources. Many times it takes the courage and support of the family and friends to help sound the alarm for an intervention before it is too late.

More often than not, a suicide attempt indicates that a veteran is under extreme duress and in a state of acute crisis rather than primarily exhibiting attention-seeking behavior. Beyond depression and substance abuse related issues, there are a number of other precipitating factors that should be considered. These include suicidal veterans with severe health problems, vets with chronic self-destructive behaviors, veterans with a history of depression or suicide attempts and veterans with a family history of suicide.

Although having an awareness of risk factors can help with any initial assessment, the recognition of actual warning signs is equally critical from a prevention-based point of view. This is because there is often a gradual build-up before an actual attempt.

## Risk Factors
The following risk factors may represent not only the presence of depression, but also the beginning of a downward emotional spiral leading to suicidal gestures.
- Changes in appetite
- Sleep disturbances
- Excessive irritability
- Angry outbursts of rage
- Apathy
- Frequent isolation

## Treatments

Several types of therapy exist that are effective for treating veterans' depression after sexual trauma. One therapy alone is usually sufficient for treating mild to moderate depression. However, treating severe depression often requires a combination of therapy and medication:

- **Cognitive behavioral therapy (CBT):** Veterans unlearn the behavioral patterns that contribute to their depression and change the negative thinking and unsatisfying behaviors.
- **Interpersonal therapy (IPT):** Veterans work on improving troubled relationships that may have been a reflection of depression and on adapting to new life roles.[9]
- **Dialectical behavior therapy (DBT):** Often used to treat borderline personality disorder, it is also used to treat substance abuse, post-traumatic stress disorder, anxiety and obsessive-compulsive disorder. DBT takes into account clients' needs for validation and coping skills and "involves trying to create synthesis or balance between opposing ideas." DBT "recognizes the all-or-nothing, black-or-white attitude that drives the thoughts and behaviors of patients with borderline personality disorder." DBT uses the combination of three treatment modalities: individual psychotherapy, group skills training and telephone consultation.[10]
- **Service dogs (SD):** Psychiatric service dogs "are trained to know when their owners are depressed or having a panic attack" and can ease the symptoms by calming their owners. The number of veterans using psychiatric service dogs is quickly increasing. A CNN article, "Dogs chase nightmares of war away," quotes a former Army medic who is no longer on medication as saying his dog helped improve his PTSD symptoms more successfully than any prescription. The dogs can help people who have a variety of mental illnesses, including PTSD, anxiety and bipolar disorder.[11]
- **Art therapy:** Painting, drawing and other forms of art can be effective techniques for expressing emotion. For example, Vietnam veteran Gregory Van Maanen began painting after returning home,

"largely as a way of exorcising the demons he brought home from the war....He remains a firm believer in the healing power of art for veterans and non-veterans alike."[12]

Treatment of depression and sexual trauma may take time. Don't be afraid to seek advice from several different counselors and therapists or to try different treatment methods.

Jan's story is about courage: The courage to make a difficult phone call and ask for help. She was close to death: spiritually, psychologically and physically. If you or someone close to you is struggling with any symptoms or signs of PTSD, depression or suicide ideation, please don't delay and call the hotline. Getting the available help is often just a phone call away.

# Chapter 6

# Extreme Mental Hardship: Three Tours in Afghanistan

Most people can identify with someone who is sad or mildly depressed, because everyone has experienced these feelings before. PTSD depression, on the other hand, is a serious illness that involves a much deeper and more persistent depression with which few people can empathize. While someone who is sad may be cheered by a joke or able to "shake it off", this is not so with depression. A person suffering from major depression cannot will or wish it away. An article titled "Understanding Depression" by Harvard Health Publications explains that depression is not correlated with personal strength or weakness, but rather how "changes in nerve pathways and brain chemicals...can affect your moods and thoughts." In addition, "a combination of genetic variations may heighten vulnerability."[1]

Suicide is a frequent and sometimes lethal complication of depressive illness. Crisis intervention by trained interventionists or direct hospitalization should be sought immediately if the depressed veteran worsens or if the vet continues to talk about suicide thoughts or threats of self-destruction.

Seek professional help or call the VA's suicide hotline at 1-800-273-TALK if the means of suicide are explicitly stated, if the veteran has lost his or her judgment to a point that he or she demonstrates a false sense of reality, if there is an obvious, even weak, nonlethal suicide attempt or if the veteran's support system of family and friends is weak or unavailable.

## Pete's Story

Pete, a three tour Army veteran of the war in Afghanistan, struggled with flashbacks and depression: "Asking for help is like letting my buddies down—very hard for me to do." So, as a last resort before suicide and with Pete's emotions beginning to erupt like an active volcano, I got his call.

"I don't know what to do. My family is afraid of me and can't understand me. My best friends say I have changed. They don't come around to see me anymore. I can't face another day. I'm wasted."

"Pete, what do you mean 'wasted'? Have you done anything to hurt yourself, buddy?" I questioned immediately.

His shaky voice continued, "You know…I spent so much time in Afghanistan, when I go out in my own backyard I keep thinking someone is going to jump out from behind the bushes…and zip me. I can't live like this…this is no way for a man to live: in fear. I am always looking over my shoulder, even walking down the street in my town. I'm wasted, man…burnt up!"

"Pete, are you thinking about suicide?" I asked directly.

Then suddenly a loud voice began yelling in the background. It sounded like a woman's voice. She was talking so quickly the words were hard to make out. I heard, "Get help, Peter…you need help…tell him," as the voice came closer to the phone. I heard a rustling of the handset then the voice of the woman became clearer. "Here, give me the phone," I could make out amidst the commotion. "If you won't tell them, I will…give me the phone, Peter…Hello, I am Peter's wife, Marsha…is this the VA?" she said dramatically and out of breath.

"Yes ma'am, my name is Vic. I am a therapist. How can I help?"

"Sir, my husband is having trouble…keeps telling me he doesn't want to live…thinking about killing himself. He says, 'I'm going to waste myself and save you and the kids all the trouble and headaches of having to live with this madman.' I keep telling him to go to the VA and talk to a doctor, but he is stubborn as a rock and just won't do it. He says he can tough it out. He doesn't want to see any head doctors. I don't know which way to turn. Our kids are staying over at my sister's. I don't want to call the police."

Marsha went on emotionally, "He has not had a day of peace since he returned home from that godforsaken place. You know…I don't know if he told you he went over there three times—three times! I say God Bless America, but you'd think the military doesn't even care about our men; three tours…just too much…too much for our boys. Each time he came back for a short time, it was like he was never here. And it seemed to get worse each time he came back. He mumbles under his breath about things I don't understand…just the other day he started crying, sitting alone. I love him, but I feel helpless. Our marriage is crumbling around us; he gets real angry sometimes, throwing things. He put his fist through the closet door last week when he couldn't find something and accused me of hiding his camouflage jacket. He was drunk. He scares me even more when he drinks.

"I don't know what to do or how to act around him," she continued, unloading pent-up emotion as I listened. But I was wondering, *What is Pete doing? Where is he? Is he nearby listening to his wife fume?*

"And another thing," she said still frantic. "What can I do? Where can I go for help? I don't know how to help my husband. He is slowly dying here, right here at home." She started crying.

"Marsha, we can help you and Pete—" Just then Pete came back on the line.

"Hey…I heard what she said. It don't mean nothin'. She's all emotional right now. It isn't that bad around here; I'm okay, man. I just called you for a friend," Pete said fearlessly.

*But I'm not buying that,* I thought.

"Pete, you never did answer me—are you thinking about suicide?" I asked and then paused for the answer. *Yes or no, Pete*, I gripped the phone tighter.

Pete apparently tried to put his hand over the phone mouthpiece, but I could still hear him say, "Marsha, go into the other room and shut the door. I want to talk to this guy...alone! Please, trust me, I will handle this." Faintly in the background, I heard a door slam. A brief moment passed. I waited.

"Okay, I have had those thoughts...killin' myself, getting it over with. I have this letter from the VA so I thought I would just call the number to find out what it was about." He paused.

"If you can, Pete, tell me what you are thinking about, buddy. What has led you to thinking of ending your life? Was your wife right about the things she said? Was that accurate?" I asked worried, hoping he would give me more information about his suicidal ideation.

"Oh, she overreacts some, but some of it is true. It has been hard for me and hard on them," his voice yielded. "I have these thoughts, you see...they don't seem to go away. I have nightmares about the battles with the Taliban, the insurgents; the noise of the AK-47s and rocket-propelled grenade launchers won't leave my head. And the faces of the Taliban fighters just keep coming and coming at me in my dreams," Pete said.

"And the bodies, the blood squirting out of wound holes, the shuttering and jerking legs of the dead...it got so I lost all feelings. I just stuck to our mission, took care of business. I am a good soldier, lots of medals on my chest...good at what I did. It hardens a man, you know; especially the last tour. A good buddy of mine died. He was on my team. I saw him hit, but couldn't get to him. I had his cover but there were too many of them," he said sadly. "My wife doesn't understand...she can't." Pete paused as if slipping into a zone. "Nobody can, unless you know what it is like having bullets flying by your head...or are pulling the trigger or throwing the grenades. I don't want to talk anymore!" He abruptly stopped speaking.

"Pete, I can get you and your family the help you need. There are Vet Centers and counseling for your family. The VA Medical Centers have treatment teams that will take care of you, Pete, outpatient or inpatient services. There are PTSD and TBI clinics. The VA has chemical dependency programs to help combat veterans overcome alcohol and other drug abuses. Pete, depression and anxiety are treatable conditions. PTSD is treatable, successfully!" I explained.

I felt Pete was still listening on the line, but he said nothing. Hoping I had his attention, I continued.

"The Veteran Affairs medical and mental health teams today are the best combat trauma-trained experts ever assembled. The hotline you called has been started for you, Pete, veterans like you and your family trying to reach out for help, but not knowing how to go about it.

"Pete, will you let me help you and Marsha and the kids?" I pleaded.

"Well, I see no harm in looking into it. What do I have to do?" he asked agreeably.

Soon Marsha and Pete drove to their local VA to meet with the crisis prevention coordinator. I had called ahead and arranged the appointment. The CPC's primary responsibility is to facilitate a "fast track" to get the suicidal veteran evaluated immediately, a level of care and treatment plan determined and an initial treatment team assigned. Marsha was referred to the local Vet Center for family counseling that would help her better understand Pete's difficult readjustment to civilian life and how she could be supportive in their efforts to get their happy family life back to the way it was before Pete ever set foot in the dust and dirt of the war zones of Afghanistan.

Col. Elspeth Ritchie, a U.S. Army psychologist, was quoted in the news as saying, "Our research supports the more deployments that [a combat veteran has], the higher the likelihood of anxiety, depression and post-traumatic stress disorder."[2] Pete had three tours in the mountains and rugged terrain of Afghanistan. His story shows how families are important resources for depressed returning veterans with PTSD. Family support can help prevent mental health problems. When problems do occur, it is often the family that recognizes something is wrong and helps the veteran to get care. Family and close friends often are the most pivotal advocates and can influence the veteran in getting to safety. It is family members who are important in helping veterans stay in treatment.

## Family Resources

### *Seeking Help*

The National Center for PTSD offers these reasons to seek help for PTSD:

- **Early treatment is better.**
  Symptoms of PTSD may get worse. Dealing with them now might help stop them from getting worse in the future. ...
- **PTSD symptoms can change family life.**
  You may find that you pull away from loved ones, are not able to get along with people or that you are angry or even violent. Getting help for your PTSD can help improve your family life.
- **PTSD can be related to other health problems.**
  For example, a few studies have shown a relationship between PTSD and heart trouble. By getting help for your PTSD you could also improve your physical health.[3]

## The Vet Centers

Congress established the Vet Center Program in 1979 in an effort to help returning veterans readjust. The Department of Veteran Affairs maintains a Web site for families of veterans with PTSD and Vet Center resources, which explains:

> Vet Centers are community based and part of the U.S. Department of Veterans Affairs....The goal of the Vet Center program is to provide a broad range of counseling, outreach and referral services to eligible veterans in order to help them make a satisfying post-war readjustment to civilian life.[4]

Family members of all eligible veterans are also entitled to Vet Center services, including bereavement counseling.

## Vet Center Services

The Vet Center offers readjustment counseling to veterans and family members of veterans who served in any combat zone and received a military campaign ribbon (Vietnam, Southwest Asia, OEF, OIF, etc.).

The Vet Center defines readjustment counseling as a "wide range of services provided to combat veterans in the effort to make a satisfying transition from military to civilian life." Among the services included are "individual counseling, group counseling, marital and family counseling, bereavement counseling, medical referrals, assistance in applying for VA Benefits, employment counseling, guidance and referral, alcohol/drug assessments, information and referral to community resources, military sexual trauma counseling & referral, outreach and community education."

Readjustment counseling and other services are offered at Vet Centers for no cost. The Vet Center Directory is available on the Vet Center's Web site (http://www.vetcenter.va.gov/) or you can locate a Vet Center near you by looking in your local blue pages. Vet Center staff are available toll free during normal business hours at 1-800-905-4675 (Eastern) and 1-866-496-8838 (Pacific).[5]

## Supporting Your Veteran

Melinda Smith, MA, Robert Segal, Ph.D., and Jeanne Segal, Ph.D., provide information for helping your veteran:

- **Be patient and understanding.**...A person with PTSD may need to talk about the traumatic event over and over again. This is part of the healing process, so avoid the temptation to tell your loved one to stop rehashing the past and move on.
- **Try to anticipate and prepare for PTSD triggers.**...
- **Don't take the symptoms of PTSD personally.**...If your loved one seems distant, irritable or closed off, remember that this may not have anything to do with you or your relationship.
- **Don't pressure your veteran into talking.** It is very difficult for people with PTSD to talk about their traumatic experiences. For some, it can even make things worse.[6]

## Understanding Flashbacks and Triggers

Flashbacks can be equally as sudden, violent and debilitating as epileptic seizures. The veteran you care about may have experienced in the past or may be currently experiencing flashbacks and/or leg-thrashing nightmares that may cause him or her to sit up abruptly or leap out of bed.

Loved ones of veterans need to be careful not to trigger a flashback by mistake. Two important ways you can help with flashbacks are knowing whether your vet has them and learning whether your vet finds comfort in your presence during them.

Frank Ochburg, M.D., offers advice for dealing with a loved one's flashbacks in his article "Partners with PTSD":

> Don't ask about the details of a flashback, since that might bring one on. Do ask if you have ever been particularly helpful in preventing or minimizing flashback effects.

Dr. Ochburg explains the ways by which to use your existing relationship with your partner to guide you and your attempts to be supportive. Different people will want various support—physical or no physical embraces, not talking or repeating details—and you must be patient. He believes that if you find, while listening to your partner, you become too enraged on behalf of your spouse, let him or her know gently. Explore other ways that you can still be an effective listener and supportive of your partner if this is the case.[7]

Veterans appreciate knowing that their loved ones are working to understand and cope with their PTSD, flashbacks and other symptoms. Therapy is helpful for both the veterans and their family members, but it may take several attempts to find a good therapist to match the veteran's needs. Don't hesitate to change therapists if the veteran does not seem to be making progress, especially with overcoming flashbacks. If flashbacks are persistent, consider a mental health worker who uses re-exposure therapy. This technique guides the veteran through his or her traumatic memories and flashbacks in a controlled setting. Together, the mental health worker and veteran work through each memory to the end, eventually allowing the veteran to reconfigure his or her brain and develop the ability to remember at will.

Trigger events are certain people, places, anniversary dates, smells or sounds that trigger reactions in veterans. These reminders are more sensations rather than memories. Mental images and sweaty palms are common reactions to trigger events. Talk calmly with your veteran about what his or her trigger events might be so both of you can identify situations that could be uncomfortable for your vet. Find out what triggers your veteran wants to avoid and help your vet do so without belittling him or her. Should your veteran choose to participate in a situation that possibly contains a trigger, make a plan together for removing the vet from the situation and trigger. Make sure the vet is involved in the process of planning an "escape"; having input in the process helps the veteran better manage triggers and feel more in control.

Partners of veterans with PTSD wonder how they can support their loved ones when their veterans show little or no emotion; they seem emotionally numb and avoid being intimate. Many partners wonder if their veterans even still love them. Veterans need time to heal and cannot be rushed into emotions or intimacy. Continue to support your veteran and never blame him or her for the PTSD. Find out if you can accompany your veteran in therapy sessions or schedule sessions with the veteran's therapist for yourself. Your veteran will appreciate your support even if he or she is unable to express it to you.

Working in the field of crisis intervention and combat trauma, I often hear the question, "When is he or she going to get over it?" This is a natural and appropriate question, but one that rarely has a definite answer. Your veteran's therapist should be able to explain what is going well, what will take more time and the expected rate of recovery. Remember, it is not easy to overcome the emotional traumas of war and the timeframe for recovery and healing will differ for each veteran. [8]

# PART II

# GULF WARS AND BEIRUT VETERANS

# Chapter 7

# Casualties of
# the Gulf Wars

Sometimes the immediate intervention and treatment of a veteran is critical. Veterans need guidance in order to learn how to connect with other veterans coping with the same or similar disabilities. Another vet can provide the encouragement and support a suicidal veteran needs in order to begin the process of overcoming obstacles and healing. To help you in the quest to connect, a list of VA resources is provided in appendix A.

## Rick's Story

As soon as I heard his voice I knew he was troubled and quickly responded. "Rick, I am glad you called the hotline today, buddy; thanks for serving our country. Welcome home. How may I help you?" I asked.

"Welcome home, my ass! I have no home! No reason to live," Rick agonized loudly, spitting the words into the telephone receiver. "I have no money and no gas to get out of this stinking trailer park parking lot; no one will hire me; I have no food; I am living in my truck. I am tired of all this f—in' shit. I served my time for this country! No one cares about what happens to me."

Rick, a Gulf War vet, was 100 percent disabled and needed someone to talk to, someone to reach out to or, more importantly, he needed someone to reach out to him. At the moment of the telephone call, Rick apparently was not aware of his vulnerability of being seduced by suicide ideation. He had isolated himself from his family and friends and seldom went out into the community. He was on prescription medication for bipolar disorder. Rick suffered from a combat- and alcohol-induced mood disorder in addition to mood swings from mania. This may show up as exaggerated feelings of well-being or stimulation. In such moods a vet can lose touch with reality and feel acute depression, which Rick described as "engulfing me with overwhelming feelings of sadness and anxiety."

"Are you thinking about suicide, Rick?" I questioned.

"Maybe…just need help…someone to talk to. I'm sitting here in my truck and I'm tired of living like this," he said, sounding a bit more approachable.

"What led you to call this suicide hotline?" I asked. *I need to know the reason Rick dialed this number today*, I thought, waiting for his response.

"I get pretty sad…down in the dumps most days." He paused. I could hear him drinking something then puffing on something, inhaling and exhaling. *Most likely a cigarette or weed*, I thought. He continued after a loud swallow, "I feel shitty most of the time. I'm disabled…that's no big deal, but I feel trapped sometimes…that sucks; nothing to do, nowhere to go, no one to visit or talk to. What kind of life is this?" He stopped talking abruptly. I heard nothing…then another sound in the background, a shuffling or something moving. I could hear what sounded like the truck door closing.

"Hello, Rick? Hey, buddy, are you there?" Nothing but a daunting silence. "Talk to me, Rick…hello?" *What is happening?* I thought. *Why did he leave so quickly? Did he get out of his truck? He said nothing. The phone line is still open; where did he go?* I waited. I sat with my elbows on the desk, head held in my hands, eyes looking straight down at my yellow notepad. I looked up, adjusting my headset and glancing in the direction of the health techs—our most valuable support team. They were looking in my direction, as they do sometimes, on alert for a rescue. I had no reason to dispatch a rescue at this point in my discussion with Rick. I looked back down at my notepad. I doodled around my notes. I had written a few things as I was talking to Rick: "Suicidal?" I jotted down another note: "Mixing alcohol with prescription drugs…big problem!!" I wrote with big, double exclamation marks and circled. *This can be more serious than Rick even realizes: possible overdose, non-intentional suicide. Mixing drugs for depression and anxiety with the depressive effects of alcohol is not a good thing. Where is he? He probably would have hung up the phone if the call was over. Would he think to hang up the phone in his present state of mind, depressed and possibly suicidal? What's going on?*

The common psychological denominator in nearly all suicides is depression, the miserable mood, the "anomie that bleaches the color from life." Chronically depressed individuals who have "never known a day of happiness" live with an inconsolable disappointment and sadness that makes existence meaningless and hopeless. Despondent veterans are convinced that they are at the mercy of unfavorable circumstances affecting their existences. On a more severe level, manic-depressive veterans in the depressed phase categorized as bipolar are a population highly vulnerable to self-destruction.

Rick appeared to be alienated from others, unable to socialize and felt unaccepted or distanced by psychological barriers from accessing support from people in the community. Rick was an alcoholic as well as abusing other substances. Victoroff explains in *The Suicidal Patient* that alcohol abuse is highly linked to suicide.[1] Rick sounded as though he was intoxicated or at the very least "high" on some mind-altering substance.

I continued listening to the open telephone line. *Where did Rick go? Why did he not say something to me if he was leaving?* I began to think in a deep and serious abstracted way. *He left so abruptly, slamming the truck door.*

All of a sudden I heard the truck door open; I sensed some sort of motion. I waited to hear a voice, Rick's voice, but all that filled the line was a continuing sense of emptiness. I couldn't imagine what was happening. *Why isn't Rick talking to me? Decision time! Do I send the police? Better safe than sorry. But I have no sound criteria that Rick is in trouble; depressed probably, but suicidal? Not sure. And I don't have a clue where he is calling from. I need more information.*

Then I heard some more commotion, a few scratches on the handset of the receiver; I assumed it was a cell phone.

"Hello," Rick broke the silence. "Are you still there?"

"I am here, Rick…still here, buddy. What is happening? Have you done anything to hurt yourself?"

"Nope…just took a leak behind a big ol' tree…hurt me?" He began. "Hurt me…well, let me see, I am buzzed on pot, drunk on booze and medicated on different colored pills for my so-called bipolar thing. What the hell. Does that sound like I am hurting myself, dude?"

"Have you ever attempted suicide, Rick?" I asked.

No answer immediately, then, "Not really, well…I think I know what is going to happen to me if I keep going on like this, I mean drinking so much…the pills, the weed. Some days I really don't want to wake up, you know…just getting tired of being sick and tired."

"Tell me more about your suicide thoughts. What has been happening in your life recently to make you want to give up?" I probed for more information.

"I told you: I have no money, just a few bucks from my lousy disability check. I am stuck here! Right here, right now." Rick was getting agitated. I decided to back off. He continued, "Every day since I got back home from the war games in the desert, haw," he retorted, "I've been homeless or living in low-life motels and cheap, cheap boarding house rooms until the money runs out. Then I sleep in my truck until the next check comes to my post office general delivery. It all started eighteen years ago, dude…now…same ol', same ol'. Nothing changes; same s—, different day." He paused to catch his breath.

"Have you tried to get more help for your situation?" I asked.

"Help from where? Hell, I was in the Battle of Medina Ridge in Desert Storm with the kick-ass 1st Armored Division that kicked Iraq's

Republican Guard's proverbial butt. Yeah, hmmm …," he paused and it sounded like he took another drink, gulping it down. "I was a part of the largest tank battle in U.S. history, dude. I was part of it. A big deal to tell my grandkids, huh? Yeah, kiddies, your grandpa was a gunner on a Bradley fighting machine in Iraq. I fought close range…lots of noise and machine guns. I watched some real blood and guts, Iraqis on fire, running, yelling; so I shot them." He paused and cleared his throat. "That's what I do as a gunner. I shoot cannons and machine guns. I am a real tough guy." Rick stopped talking; I could hear him take another swig from his bottle…*gulp, gulp.* I had nothing to say. I was transfixed on what he had just said about his grandchildren. All I could do was listen as he continued to ramble.

"Only problem is this tough guy has no family, no grandkids. When I returned home, I was twenty-four years old. My girlfriend who said she would wait for me and we could get married when I got back home…married someone else; wonderful surprise," Rick said sarcastically. "Oh, did I mention my family kicked me out of the house after a few months, because I was 'behaving strangely' they said. Imagine that— my own flesh and blood booted me out—the ultimate dagger through the heart. So here we are, dude, just you and me and I don't even know your name," he finished.

"Vic is my name, Rick. Vic Montgomery, former Marine, buddy… ooh-rah," I disclosed. "I have your back. How can I help you?"

"Jarhead, huh, Devil Dog…ooh-rah…Vic, what war were you in?" he responded as if a barrier was lifted.

"We really need to talk about how I can get you the help you need, Rick," I replied.

"Well," he slurred, the effects of the drugs and alcohol becoming more apparent, "to answer your earlier question, yes I have already been to the VA psych docs and others. I took some tests, they gave me some scripts and that was about it, end of story. I go in about every three months for refills and a five minute chat with the doc," he said antagonistically. "I have no love for some of these docs and nurses from foreign countries. Half the time I don't understand what they are saying.

I am sure they are okay guys and girls, but what the hell happened to our American doctors and nurses?" he expounded.

"What about you right now, Rick? Do you have any specific plan to kill yourself?" I asked deliberately.

"I'm doing it, brother! Right in front of you," he insisted.

"What are you doing, Rick? Have you already hurt yourself?"

"Hell, I hurt myself every day, Vic. Who the hell cares?" he said harshly.

"You're drinking?" I asked, questioning his metaphorical statement.

"I've lost my will to live, Vic. I am giving up, partner. No more, man." *Rick is beginning to bow out of this conversation,* I felt. *I think it is hitting too close to home.*

"Rick, where are you located right now? Where is the trailer park?" I insisted.

"What do you mean trailer park? How do you know that?" he questioned, somewhat paranoid.

"Earlier you said you were parked on a lot in a trailer park, living in your truck," I replied.

"Oh yeah, I forgot I told you that...it is called the Shady Oak Trailer Park...why do you want to know?" he said.

"I will tell you...because I want to send you some help to get you to the VA hospital," I responded.

"Send me help!...What, are you crazy?...First of all, this place is so small it doesn't have an address and no one will ever be able to find me out here, yo! That's why I'm here. And another thing...how do you know what I need? You are on a telephone probably hundreds or thousands of miles away," Rick challenged.

"Maybe I don't know exactly, so I am hoping you can help me help you," I suggested. "How about it, Rick? You help me understand—things like how much drinking you do. How much and how often, Rick?" I asked sincerely.

"Who's counting?" he replied quickly.

"Rick, you called the hotline, right? In a way you are asking for help, right?" I asked.

"Maybe…," he quietly remarked. I heard him take another drink from his bottle.

"So, you are drinking yourself to death; is that an accurate statement?" I questioned.

"Probably," he said.

"So, you are a suicidal veteran?" I asked.

"I guess so, now that you put it that way," he said rather reluctantly.

"Have you thought about why you are drinking yourself to death?" I asked. There was no immediate response.

"I have a lot of guilt about the killing I did in Iraq. At times I can't control my feelings. I cry out of the blue. Sometimes I can't control it or shut it off. How embarrassing is that…this tough guy, war veteran a cry baby? I don't enjoy things anymore…I can't sleep, I feel empty most of the time." Rick responded half-heartedly.

WebMD (2009) states: "The severity of the depressive and manic phases of bipolar disorder can differ from person to person and in the same person at different times." In fact, as WebMD's entry on bipolar disorder suggests, manic phases can lead to drug and alcohol abuse and, as well, depressive phases can present as crying uncontrollably, expressing feelings of hopelessness and worthlessness and thoughts of death and suicide.[2]

As I listened to Rick pour out his feelings of quiet desperation, I realized he was getting drunker and drunker as we talked and more depressed as time slipped away. I had to initiate a plan of action to get him to safety. The only way to find Rick and negotiate an emergency rescue would be for him to tell me the name of the closest city or town.

When Rick paused, I interjected calmly, "I care about you, buddy. Really do. You deserve to have a good life ahead of you. You served our country with honor and courage, Rick. Those depressive feelings of hopelessness and crying out of control you describe are treatable and there is a way out from under the dark cloud of gloom you just shared with me. I feel your pain, buddy. I have your back if you will let me help you. I know you would do the same for me…ooh-rah…wouldn't you, Rick?" I asked purposefully.

"Ooh-rah ...," came Rick's garbled response, as if he had the handset in his mouth.

"Rick, listen to me…there are professional treatment teams just for your situation that will help you work through these haunting experiences you described. You can get over this wall, Rick." I wanted so much to extend my hand to him, to pull him up through this awful time.

"Hey, Rick, I remember when I went through the Marine Corps boot camp PT course there was always a high wooden wall or two or three, looked like ten or twelve feet high, and the object was to help your squad, rifle team, climb over the wall with full packs and rifle. Remember those boot camp days, buddy?" I said hoping for some sort of response.

"Ooh-rah ...," he said more faintly now.

"Well, what a feat," I continued, "and of course it was impossible to get over the wall without help from your buddies. Right? So we offered our backs, knees and shoulders, hand in hand, anything to get over the wall." *So here I am*, I thought, *wanting to give this warrior a hand to get over his wall of discouragement. He is slipping away; I have to act quickly. Don't know if he is only intoxicated or if there are more drugs involved.*

"Rick, listen to me, buddy. I want to help you get over the wall right now. I want to send you an emergency rescue team to pick you up and take you to the closest hospital for an emergency evaluation. I fear you may have hurt yourself, buddy. We can't wait any longer. Do you hear what I am saying? Do you understand me?"

"Okay, dude ...," his tone was fainter. *I am losing him*, I thought. I quickly signaled the health techs into action. They ran over to look at my yellow pad for information on this caller as I continued to talk to Rick.

"Then we can arrange for transport to the nearest VA Medical Center, get you connected with the VA's crisis prevention coordinator and the treatment team will see to it you are referred for proper care for your depression and alcohol abuse. Which VA Medical Center do you go to, Rick? Quickly man."

"Kansas City, Missouri, VA Center…if anyone gives a s—," he spoke loudly into the telephone.

I quickly wrote what he had just told me down on my yellow pad. The health techs picked up on it immediately as I was writing—they were looking over my shoulder. The action plan now was for the health techs to call Kansas City police and sheriff departments, try and locate Shady Oak Trailer Park and get to Rick before it was too late. I gazed away for a moment, *I am worried about an accidental overdose. Rick has been drinking a lot. Many suicides happen accidentally. I know he is also prescribed anti-depressant medication and who knows what else.*

"Rick, are you still with me, buddy?" I exclaimed.

"Yeah, dude, what's happening?" he slurred.

"Rick, I need some help here. What kind of truck are you in right now?" I pleaded to him for assistance.

"Pickup with a camper shell, if you have to know," he said, sounding a bit put off and garbled, as if he had just taken another swallow of booze from his bottle. I wrote this information on my notepad and circled it with my pencil, underlining *pickup with camper shell* for the techs who were continually checking to see what new information I had gleaned. The techs handed me a note of their own telling me they were on the line with the police in Kansas City trying to find the Shady Oak Trailer Park. However, the police did not know of it in their general location nor had they figured out where it was located. The techs had contacted the local county sheriffs and they were on the hunt also. So far no one knew where Rick was parked.

"Rick," I called into the headset. No response; I spoke again, "Rick!" Silence. I mean a dead silence: no static noise, nothing. "Rick, buddy, hang in there with me. I have help on the way. Come on, Rick, you have to meet me halfway on this, buddy. Talk to me!" I said with emphasis. I was very worried. *Have I lost contact with this troubled suicidal veteran?* I asked myself. *Has his cell phone run out of juice? What is happening with Rick? Is the rescue too little too late? I should have pulled an intervention much sooner; why did I hesitate? Come on law enforcement! I can't believe no one knows the name of this trailer park. Come on, guys, give me something.*

I waited a few minutes then, getting up from my desk, I rushed to the health tech office next to mine. In the doorway I asked, "Anything?"

The tech shook his head. "Nothing yet; nobody knows where this place is. One sheriff deputy officer thought it may be in another county north of them. We have asked to be transferred and we are waiting."

"Keep up the good work, gang. Let's find this vet." I tried to motivate the tech crew, but I found little strength in my delivery. I was physically and mentally drained at this point.

The techs know how frustrating these moments in limbo can be for the crisis interventionists and the urgency of the matter. This is life and death on the line and they realize it.

I turned and returned to my desk. I couldn't sit down. I paced around the hotline room, looking up at the ever foreboding clocks on the wall locating the time zone for Rick in Missouri. *Because of the nature of what we do, unfriendly time can sometimes work against us,* I thought,

I looked up in the direction of the health tech room. I was looking for some kind of sign they had made contact with someone; any news at this point would be, at least, encouraging. I just wanted to know if the location Rick mentioned existed. *Is this a real place or did Rick steer me in the wrong direction…on purpose? Maybe he didn't want to be rescued? Maybe he just wanted someone to hear his story before he killed himself.*

I waited.

Finally the call came in to the tech team. A sheriff deputy in a rural county knew where the small, obscure trailer park was located and was en route to that location with an ambulance as they spoke. I urged the techs to communicate to the deputy that this intoxicated, suicidal veteran might be unconscious and in need of emergency medical attention. I also informed them to pass on to the deputy that this vet was already a patient at the VA Medical Center in Kansas City.

Time for a break. I took my headset off, slung it on my desk, punched the button on the phone set for "away from desk," turned and walked down the long corridor into the break room feeling satisfied we'd taken the first step to getting the vet to safety.

While in the break room I sat leaning back in a chair against the wall, briefly looking up at the wall-mounted television that was blaring some current events news show. But as I stared at the screen I realized I was not hearing or seeing anything. My mind was too involved in wondering whether the rescuers reached Rick in time. After a minute I quickly rose from my chair, threw my coffee into the sink and headed back to the hotline room. I entered the doorway and approached my desk, glancing in the direction of the health technicians' room. One of the health techs, apparently hearing me enter the room, returned my stare but did not give me any indication either way whether the rescue had been made. I sat down on the end of my desk, my phone line still in a holding pattern. I looked up at the time zone clocks on the wall; it had been at least forty-five minutes since our last contact with the sheriff deputy in route. I stood up and walked toward the health tech room, passing several hotliner desks on the way. Everyone knows when someone has a rescue in progress; the action is intense.

The team "on rescue" and in pursuit is always up and moving, handing notes and checking on data and telecom communications. Heads bob and weave in and out and around communication terminal desktops and office doorways. All designated lines are open to the sheriff's department in the suicidal veteran's geographic area. Law enforcement has always been first-rate about keeping the VA health tech team and hotliners informed on up-to-the-minute information about the rescue and particularly where they are in relation to the warrior in need.

In Rick's case, we received a call from the sheriff unit saying they had just arrived at the trailer park and were beginning to search for the pickup truck. Our health techs had passed on the information I supplied regarding Rick's name and the fact he may have passed out while talking to me due to intoxication or he may have harmed himself in a suicide attempt; either case was a real possibility. It was vital for our team to pass on to the paramedics the information that Rick may have taken other drugs as well as alcohol. It was confirmed that the sheriff was accompanied by an ambulance and paramedics at our request.

Finally, the long-awaited call came in. The sheriff deputies were approaching the camper truck from the rear. They told us they had to use extreme caution in approaching the vehicle, because they did not know if there were any weapons inside. The deputies reported no movement inside the truck. No sign of anyone sitting up in the cab or in the back camper shell. The phones went silent. The health techs waited on hold on the direct line to the sheriff. Minutes passed.

The health techs then received word the police had found Rick slumped down near the floorboards on the passenger side so it was hard to see him in the cab. The doors were unlocked and the windows open partially, so it was easy to get Rick out quickly and into the ambulance. After some time giving medical rescue to Rick, the paramedics reported he was in critical condition and had to be transported quickly to the nearest hospital. Apparently, from the medical information relayed to us, Rick may have been in an alcohol-induced coma. According to Debra Emmite, M.D., and Stanley J. Swierzewski III, M.D., excessive alcohol consumption can lead to complications requiring emergency medical attention and sometimes death. When a person consumes large amounts of alcohol in a short period of time, "the blood alcohol level rises so high and so quickly that the liver cannot metabolize the alcohol. The person may become comatose, may suffer cardiac and respiratory failure, and can die." Emergency medical attention is needed in these cases in order to save a person's life.[3]

Rick was on his way to a community hospital nearest to the trailer park location. The paramedics did not want to chance too long of a trip to get him into an emergency room intensive care unit. From there the VA crisis prevention coordinators arranged transport to the nearest VA Medical Center for further treatment and level of care follow-up.

Rick was fortunate. He was detoxified over a fourteen-day period after coming out of his coma. For many alcohol and other drug dependent veterans, detoxification is only the first step in treatment. Detoxification is more than just physical readjustment. It involves psychological readjustments as well. These psychological changes are important as the veteran continues treatment. Veterans struggling with problems that developed prior to substance dependency—for example, broken marriages, reintegration to civilian life from the military, combat trauma or psychiatric disorders—need continued care and services after detoxification to address these other problems. Detoxification without follow-up care can lead to previous mental and physical health issues going untreated and may lead to relapses or other complications.[4]

The special services that Rick had available to him included an intensive inpatient alcohol and drug treatment program for his ongoing recovery treatment planning for addictions and chemical dependency, aftercare and transitional housing referrals, Vet Center support groups for combat veterans and outpatient counseling and group therapy helping him process his war experiences as well as providing guidance to help him find balance and happiness in his personal life.

It is important to keep in mind that alcohol is a toxic substance. Abuse and even mild overuse of alcohol can have serious effects on a person's health:

- heart disease
- high blood pressure
- liver disease
- impotence
- nerve and brain damage
- sleep problems
- cancer
- damage to the stomach and kidneys[5]

### Self-Examination for Alcohol Abuse

One of the most widely used measures for assessing alcohol abuse, the Michigan Alcohol Screening Test (MAST) is a questionnaire designed to provide a rapid and effective screening for lifetime alcohol-related problems and alcoholism.[6]

Carefully read each question and decide whether your answer is yes or no based on your behavior in the past twelve months. Choose the best answer that reflects how the statement applies to you or that reflects your feelings most of the time.

Please note: This test will only be scored correctly if you answer every question. Check one response for each item.

| | YES | NO |
|---|---|---|
| 1. Do you feel you are a normal drinker? ("Normal"—drink as much or less than most other people.) | | |
| 2. Have you ever awakened the morning after some drinking the night before and found that you could not remember a part of the evening? | | |
| 3. Does any nearby relative or close friend ever worry or complain about your drinking? | | |
| 4. Can you stop drinking without difficulty after one or two drinks? | | |
| 5. Do you ever feel guilty about your drinking? | | |
| 6. Have you ever attended a meeting of Alcoholics Anonymous (AA)? | | |
| 7. Have you ever gotten into physical fights when drinking? | | |
| 8. Has drinking ever created problems between you and a nearby relative or close friend? | | |
| 9. Has any family member or close friend gone to anyone for help about your drinking? | | |
| 10. Have you ever lost friends because of your drinking? | | |
| 11. Have you ever gotten into trouble at work because of drinking? | | |
| 12. Have you ever lost a job because of drinking? | | |

|  | YES | NO |
|---|---|---|
| 13. Have you ever neglected your obligations, your family or your work for two or more days in a row because you were drinking? | | |
| 14. Do you drink before noon fairly often? | | |
| 15. Have you ever been told you have liver trouble such as cirrhosis? | | |
| 16. After heavy drinking have you ever had delirium tremens (D.T.'s), severe shaking, visual or auditory (hearing) hallucinations? | | |
| 17. Have you ever gone to anyone for help about your drinking? | | |
| 18. Have you ever been hospitalized because of drinking? | | |
| 19. Has your drinking ever resulted in your being hospitalized in a psychiatric ward? | | |
| 20. Have you ever gone to any doctor, social worker, clergyman or mental health clinic for help with any emotional problem in which drinking was part of the problem? | | |
| 21. Have you been arrested more than once for driving under the influence of alcohol? | | |
| 22. Have you ever been arrested, even for a few hours, because of other behavior while drinking? | | |

## Scoring

This self-test is scored by allocating one point to each yes answer—except for questions 1 and 4, where one point is allocated for each no answer—and totaling the responses.

- **Zero to two points: No Apparent Problem**
  Your answers suggest that you are in the normal range and at low risk of problem drinking.

- **Three to five points: Early to Middle Problem Drinker**
  Your answers suggest that you are at risk of problem drinking.

- **Six or more points: Problem Drinker**
  Your answers suggest that you are at risk of alcoholism.

This self-examination is meant only to be used as a first assessment, not as a diagnosis tool. If you now suspect that your consumption of alcohol is a problem, consult with a medical and/or mental health professional.

# Chapter 8

# A Suicide Note
# Sent to a Friend

My clinical experience suggests that at least half of potential vet suicides are veterans suffering from post-traumatic stress disorder and are coming home attempting to transition into society with many PTSD signs and symptoms. Post-traumatic stress disorder is extreme stress responses to traumatic events that threaten the veteran's safety or makes the vet feel hopeless and helpless. If a combat vet has PTSD, he or she may believe that he or she will never get over what happened or feel normal again. But with a timely intervention, a well thought-out therapeutic treatment plan and the support of loved ones, our returning warriors can overcome the symptoms, reduce the painful memories and move on with their lives. Now that's what I am talking about...ooh-rah!

If you or someone you love is in trouble, know this: America does care about you! There are tens of thousands of Americans who have called or written letters to their State Representatives or other officials demanding more suicidal veteran prevention support for our troops when they deploy home battered and dilapidated. Many veterans are emotionally distressed but say nothing to anyone.

Because veteran survivors have disturbing feelings when they feel stress or are reminded of their traumas, they often act as if they are in danger again. They might get overly concerned about staying safe in situations that are not truly perilous. For instance, a vet living in a safe neighborhood might still feel the necessity for an alarm system, double locks on the door, a locked fence and a guard dog. Traumatized combat veterans often feel like they are in harm's way even when they are not and they may be overly aggressive and lash out to protect themselves when there is no need. For example, a person who was attacked might be quick to yell at or hit someone who seems to be threatening.

There are certain signs and symptoms to look for associated with PTSD and TBI.

Remember, if you are a veteran experiencing such problems, don't attempt to treat yourself. Seek medical help immediately if these signs persist. Suicidal ideation (thoughts, intentions, plans), depression, anxiety and panic attacks are all treatable mental health conditions. Call for help! I have included telephone numbers, addresses and contact information in appendix A to provide you or someone close to you with help and resources. A checklist is provided at the end of this chapter to help you recognize in yourself or someone close to you the signs, symptoms and dangers of depression and suicidal ideation.

## Signs and Symptoms of PTSD and TBI

Here are some possible signs the veteran might be suffering:
- Intrusive thoughts recalling the traumatic experience
- Nightmares
- Efforts to avoid anything that serves as either a reminder of the traumatic event or that triggers similar feelings
- Flat emotional response; little or no affect in facial expression
- Lack of motivation
- Depression
- Feelings of guilt (survivor's guilt is believing that somehow the vet was responsible for the death of comrades or civilians)

- Easily startled
- Irritability
- Insomnia
- Panic attacks
- Intrusive memories of the traumatic event
- Bad dreams about the traumatic event
- Flashbacks or a sense of reliving the event
- Feelings of intense distress when reminded of the trauma
- Physiological stress responses to reminders of the event (pounding heart, rapid breathing, nausea, muscle tension, sweating)
- Difficulty sleeping
- Outbursts of anger
- Difficulty concentrating or thinking clearly

## Joe's Story

When the crisis line lit up, I picked up the call. "My name is Vic. How can I help you?"

Tim, the caller, is a friend of Joe, a decorated combat veteran. The caller identified himself as a retired Marine and called because he was concerned about the safety of his Marine buddy. The caller wanted to read me a farewell note he had just received over the Internet from the vet. In the note Joe stated that he had no more to live for, his wife and children had left him, he felt hopeless, emotionally numb and detached from the Marine Corps, which no longer wanted him because of his post-traumatic stress disorder and traumatic brain injury concussion suffered in the bombing of the First Battalion, 8th Marines Headquarters building in Beirut, Lebanon.

The suicide note went on to put in plain words the combat veteran's feelings of rejection and discard and his loss of interest in activities and life in general. He wrote that he had already burned his service medals, commendations and ribbons.

The alarmed caller asked me what he should do. Tim did not know where his friend was located, just the fact he was out of town. "New

Jersey, I think," he said. The former Marine did have his friend's cell phone number, but all he heard when he called the number was a voice mail message. He only knew the Marine's name, nothing more about his personal information. They had just recently become friends.

I asked Tim for the telephone number and the suicidal veteran's full name. Immediately I summoned the health technician to attempt to trace the cell phone number as I accessed my database for the interconnection to VA Medical Centers in the New Jersey area. We contacted the New Jersey police and sheriff departments. I waited. No response from law enforcement; no contact, no location determined for the veteran in crisis. *We are running out of time,* I thought. *The signs are all there for an impending suicide. He has a suicide letter, contacted his friend, burned his valuables, verbalized intent and apparently has a plan but we do not have all the details.*

*I must act quickly; we have no time to lose,* I was aware. *I must take over the intervention. We just cannot wait for the call to be traced for the location and police rescue. I must call the suicidal veteran's cellular telephone number quickly!*

I dialed the number. No one picked up, just an electronic digitized voice mail message. *Am I reaching the right phone? It isn't even a real human voice.* I was worried. "Stupid machine ...," I mumbled to myself.

I hung up, leaving no message. Up and out of my seat, I paced around my desk. I don't normally pace but the tension was higher than normal. The telephone headsets are wireless so I had some pacing room. I moved over to the health tech's work area, peering in to see if there was any word on their end of things. They reported no response yet from the cell phone company that was contacted to find the whereabouts of the vet's roaming cell number. Phone companies do have the ability to track cell phones. The health technician looked up at me and said, "No word yet, Vic. We are working on it as fast as we can...we are at the mercy of the cell phone company but have contacted the police in the area as a heads-up in hope of getting some sort of lead." *We have nothing to go on,* I thought pensively.

I felt I should not leave a message on Joe's phone; the Marine might go into hiding if I did and then we would lose our only possible contact. I decided to wait it out for few more minutes. I did, but it was a tough few minutes. *How many times can I look at the same clock on the wall,* I mused. *Idiot! The clocks have nothing to do with anything…come on, come on, Joe, where are you?* I brooded.

In a few minutes I called again. No pick up again but this time I was determined I had to say something into the recording to try and get through to speak to Joe. Time was slipping away. I felt that if I could facilitate my personal approach, heart-to-heart, buddy to buddy connection, we would have a chance to save his life. He was obviously feeling alienated. Joe had expressed feelings of rejection and abandonment. I knew if only I could talk with him it would increase his chances for a rescue and getting him to a safe environment.

I felt in my very core that if I had but a minute to communicate to Joe, I had to express my true feelings of gratitude for his service to our country and demonstrate to him through my words, from one human being to another, that I cared. Then I hoped he would respond to my plea for him to get some help.

Grabbing the receiver, I decided to leave my message on the cell phone voice mail system: "Hello, Marine…ooh-rah…*Semper Fi*. My name is Vic; thank you for serving our country, buddy. I am calling from the National Veterans Suicide Crisis hotline in upstate New York. Tim, a Marine friend of yours, called the hotline today and read me your e-mail suicide note. I hope we can talk this out, Joe. I don't want you to hurt yourself. You have too much life yet to live. I care about what happens to you right now…right here…okay?" I paused briefly, listening to the white noise in the background. Then I continued, "A lot of people care that you served our great country, Joe. I am a former Marine. We are Marine comrades. You and I know what that means. We are watching your back. We are here for you! Please call me back; I will wait for your call even if it takes all night. I want to talk to you. Please call 1-800-273-8255 and ask for me by name, Vic Montgomery." I hung up the phone. Immediately I alerted all the hotliners that I was expecting an important return phone call: a possible veteran suicide in progress needing a rescue. The wait was beginning to feel like time without end. I knew the feeling well. It is never easy when you really care about people and have the ability to unconditionally love a person even though you have never met him or her.

The call finally came in an hour or so later. I took it.

"Hello Joe. What's going on, buddy? Thanks for calling me back. Your friend and I are worried about you." I left that statement dangle for a moment and waited.

"Thanks for calling me…ooh-rah," Joe said in a quiet reserved manner. *Almost too reserved,* I thought and immediately contemplated, *Because of his calm, quiet demeanor he may be medicated or self-medicating or already overdosing or cut or something.*

"Joe, are you still thinking about suicide?" I asked him inquisitively.

"No reason to live. You probably already heard my story…no friends, kids are gone, no Corps, I'm a has-been." The proud warrior paused, cleared his throat and said, "Joe's all washed-up, time to go," he hesitated. I said nothing. Then he said, "Time to fall on my sword, as Samurai warriors would say…right, Vic?" he questioned as if he really wanted some relief from the sword idea.

"No, that's not right, Joe. You do have a purpose in life and a reason to live…your children for one, Joe; the children need their father. The grandkids will need their grandfather, too. It wouldn't be right to leave them. How old are the kids, Joe?" I asked, hoping to get him involved.

"You don't really care how old my kids are, do you? Why do you care if I live or die? What am I to you?" The veteran's voice was quivering. I listened intently. Joe continued, "The Marine Corps didn't care who I was. They sent me packing, all because of a bump on my head. All I had was a bomb blast concussion, now they're calling it TBI and post-traumatic stress disorder. Now I have nothing to show for my years of service. My family moved out, because I was acting strange, moody, hard to live with, I guess. I can barely get a good night's sleep, even after twenty-five years, tossing and turning, some flashbacks of the explosion in the barracks in Beirut. I remember feeling the growing danger in the weeks before the barracks' bombing. It was the largest single-day loss of life for Marines since the World War II Battle of Iwo Jima." Joe recalled, "Artillery shells fell on our compound. Snipers took potshots at our men. After scrambling to locate survivors, handling body bags still bothers me. I dream of body parts. We had to match the body parts with the torsos and heads.

"I couldn't handle the nightmares and sleepless nights thrashing around, so I slept in another bed away from my wife. I knew we were in trouble when that happened several years ago. Things just started getting worse…slipping away. I am jumpy, quick tempered at times and feel down in the dumps a lot. Sooo…they all left me like the Corps left me or should I say, booted me out." Joe took a deep, trembling breath, let it out, then went on, "Are you still on the line, Vic, or am I talking to myself, which I do a lot lately."

"I am here. I have listened to everything you have said and all I can say is wow, Joe. You have had a lot on your plate, buddy. Have you done anything to hurt yourself?"

"Not yet," he said mulishly.

"Joe, have you ever attempted suicide?" I questioned.

"No," he responded bluntly.

"Tell me more about your suicide thoughts. What has been happening in your life lately other than what you have just told me?" I asked frankly.

"My kids are twenty-three and twenty-six years old. The last time I saw them was a year ago and then only for a brief visit. My family has nothing to do with me. It seems no one understands what I have gone through. Vic, I am really hurting, down deep. Sometimes I feel like I am suffocating. I wake up that way sometimes. I miss my kids. I have no reason for living. Nothing is going to change. I feel like I am in a dark black hole in some other world. And it is lonely in that world, Vic, real lonely." He stopped talking. *A bit of a frog in his throat*, I figured.

"I am here for you, Joe. I won't leave you. I will stay on the line as long as you need, brother," I stated honestly.

Then Joe unleashed a salvo of excited expression, "It is like I am trapped and have no way of escape. I have had the same nightmare for years, seeing myself in a dark pit trying to crawl out, my fingers and nails worn to the bone bleeding...then I wake up shaking and sweating...I spend my days sitting, staring at the walls in my house. I don't watch much television...it's mostly trash and commercials. I cancelled my cable when the kids moved out. I have been sleeping during the day and up at night most of the time. I am on disability for my medical condition. They say I have a traumatic brain injury. I get a check in the mail. It just barely gets me by...I see the VA doctor every month or so and get a couple of scripts and come home." The veteran warrior finally stopped for air.

"What is the medication for, Joe?" I asked.

"For depression and anxiety, panic attacks and all that stuff about PTSD and oh...I forgot to add my sleeping pills...I am a freaking pharmacy," Joe quipped. He continued with a serious tone, "Actually, Vic, you are the first person I have really had a straight-talk conversation with in many years, maybe ever, and to be honest it feels pretty good. I feel people really don't want to hear what I have to say or about my problems so I just bottle it up inside. I never have talked much about my fears. I guard myself...tough guy you know...stuffing my feelings is what I have always done. We guys have to hide 'em or we're weak you know; especially us Devil Dogs.

"So now you have it all, Vic, which is why I want to stop this insanity. I can't take it another day...too much man, just too damn much." He paused for a fleeting moment. I too remained silent trying to process all of what I had just heard. Then he picked up where he left off. "That is when I e-mailed my suicide note to my vet buddy Tim and burned up all my Marine Corps stuff...medals and things."

"Joe, where are you calling from?" I asked inquisitively and an octave off-key. My voice cracks like this when I begin to get keyed up.

"I am on the Jersey shore, partner, on the boardwalk having one last fling before I check out. Yeah, Vic...there is live music down here, rocking nightclubs and dance clubs where the beat never stops, they say...and oh yes, a mix of Irish pubs, traditional saloons and sports bars you would not believe. Could you tell I'm an Irish, lad?" He did have a bit of an Irish tone. I didn't pick up on it until he mentioned it.

"Yes, Joe, now that you said something I believe you do have a slight accent," I said. And I added, "We are neighbors in the old country, lad. I am a Scotsman, and my family comes from the Scottish Highlands. In fact, Joe, I own a kilt."

"Yeah, but do you wear it? Hah," he laughed slightly and said, "That is a good one, small world really ...," and he faded off for a moment. I picked up the conversation.

"Joe, I am glad to hear you are having a good time of it...sounds like a nice getaway for you. What are your plans after the 'fling'?" I questioned enthusiastically. "Will you be heading home?"

"Home?" he questioned. "A home I don't have," he replied sharply. "I am spending all my money. And when it is all gone, I am gone."

"What do you mean 'gone'?" I grappled for those words.

"Yes, I have a plan; pretty simple really. I have picked a nice spot overlooking the shore where I will park and end it. Poof...I will be gone and no one will even care," he said with a timbre of tragedy in his voice.

"Where are you, Joe...right now?" I asked with heightened interest.

"Right now I am sitting in a motel room right near the boardwalk. Nice little place," he replied. "I am sipping on a bottle of warm ale, like they do in Ireland. Did you know, Vic, ale ferments best between sixty and seventy-two degrees Fahrenheit and therefore requires no special refrigeration or cooling."

"No, I did not know those facts, Joe. What is the name of your motel?" I inquired. Then abruptly the phone went dead.

"The phone went dead; his cell phone went dead," I ranted. I leapt up from my chair and spun around leaning on the balls of my feet, bounding forward, almost in one coordinated movement, and stepped out toward the health technicians' room, repeating, "The phone died! I have lost him...I don't believe it. What do you have for a location on my caller?" I pleaded. "Tell me you have located his calling area."

"We know where he is, Vic, but not any more specifics than you already know. He is in a shore town in New Jersey. That's it. All we can get. The cell phone company said they can't get his GPS location," the tech said downheartedly.

"Team, please…get in touch with the police department in the area where he is and tell them we have a suicidal veteran in a small motel very near the boardwalk. His name is Joseph Monaghan, about age forty-five. He may be hanging out in the Irish pubs in the area. We do not have a description of him yet. I will call Tim, his friend, back and find out what he looks like. Quick, please, we need to get to this vet."

I returned quickly to my desk and slid into my chair. I found Joe's Marine friend's phone number in my notes. I called. In a matter of a couple rings I was talking with Tim and updated him on the situation. He gave me a description. The techs immediately sent the new information to the police in New Jersey. The hunt for Joe Monaghan, decorated war veteran, father of two, was on.

In agitated times like this I have to pull myself together and focus. I began to ask myself relevant questions and weigh options: *What are the options here? How in the world do we find Joe? We can't stop trying, at all costs; we must persist in the search for the suicidal veteran. Then when we locate him, how do I motivate Joe to come home and get treatment? I have already made it clear that I care about what happens to him. But the challenge as I see it right now is to encourage him to care enough about himself. Joe isn't thinking clearly. He is overwhelmed and confused. He has a wounded soul. Joe is brokenhearted. He lost his family; he lost friends in the Beirut bombing; he lost the Corps; he has lost all hope.*

As a clinician I always have to remind myself not to get caught up in my own emotional reaction. But sometimes that is easier said than done. Therapists and counselors are taught to establish healthy boundaries, especially in times of emotional conflict. *When do I let go?* I asked myself.

I got up from my desk and went out to walk the halls as I do when there is no resolution at hand and I am waiting for something to break, anything! I resumed my thoughts. *Joe is going to kill himself when his last dollar is spent. When will that be?*

I returned to my desk a few minutes later, spun my chair around and sat down. Leaning forward, elbows planted on the desktop, I glanced down at my notes strewn around my desk. Many of the hotliners type their notes directly on the computer as they talk to the caller. Call me old-fashioned but I write with pencil and on a yellow legal pad. That works just fine for me. As I was reading my notes a thought came to me: I didn't know what method Joe was thinking about using for his suicide attempt. There was no mention of a weapon, knife or gun. *Ah, pills,* I remembered. *He has sleeping pills. Joe, what are you thinking? Where are you, buddy?* Still no word!

My shift is generally eight hours and then the next group of hotliners comes in to relieve the current shift. I glanced up to look at the clocks on the wall. *I have only a few hours left before I go home,* I thought. *What am I going to do? I can't leave him; I promised him I would stay on the line as long as it takes. But there is no open line now.*

In my mind thoughts of Joe permeated as I put my headset back on my ears, ready for another caller. I remembered reading about the incident Joe was involved with in Lebanon and the bombing of the Marine barracks in Beirut. The explosion pulverized the concrete fortress, killing over 200 U.S. service members, most of them Marines. Now, a quarter of a century, two wars with Iraq and continuing conflicts in Afghanistan have dulled the public's memory of the Beirut attack. But for Joe the effects live on.

Joe did not call back that day. I called his Marine friend and told him we had lost contact with Joe; that probably his cell phone battery went dead and maybe he did not have his battery charger with him. Or maybe he just didn't want to talk anymore. I told his friend we had the police looking for Joe and we did all that we could to bring him to safety.

Hotliners certainly don't win all the battles trying to bring suicidal vets into treatment, but fortunately, effective mental health treatments, such as those I pointed out in chapter 5, are now available for many suicidal veterans with depression, anxiety, substance abuse, post-traumatic stress disorder and several other war trauma related disorders. Unfortunately, most male and female warriors do not seek help. Many wrongly believe their symptoms are their own faults or are caused by personal weakness. They think if they try hard enough they can overcome their problems by themselves and they suffer unnecessarily.

Joe is back! A few days later I received the message that Joe had called the hotline a couple of days later and asked for me, but I was off duty for the day. The hotliner who took his call is a good friend of mine and told me Joe said he had changed his mind about suicide and returned home. He had called the hotline to see what he needed to do to get help. So, my friend on the hotline immediately connected Joe with the crisis prevention coordinator at the VA Medical Center nearest his home and arranged for Joe to stay at the medical center for a couple of days to be observed and evaluated to determine what level of care would be appropriate for this war hero. How great a feeling is that! Some people would call it luck or some would say it's not your time to go. I call it heart-to-heart resuscitation…ooh-rah!

## Warning Signs of Depression

Whether you're a depressed veteran or his or her loved one, you need to know when to ask for professional help. Learn and look for the detailed warning signs. Seek professional help if any of the following warning signs is severe or long lasting.

- **Excessive anxiety.** This type of anxiety has no identifiable cause and is exaggerated for the situation. It can also manifest as a deep, continuing anxiety.
- **Clinical depression.** Severe depression is "persistent feelings of inadequacy, sadness, helplessness, hopelessness, undue pessimism, and loss of confidence" as well as changes in behavior.
- **Withdrawn.** No longer enjoying the things that formally gave pleasure, including the company of loved ones and hobbies.
- **Eating habits change.** Loss of appetite or overeating.
- **Disturbances in sleep habits.** Insomnia, an inability to stay asleep or excess sleeping.

- Low energy.
- Chronic fatigue.
- Ineffective at school, work or home.
- Decreased or no sexual interest.
- Isolation.
- Mood and behavior changes. Including gradual or abrupt, frequent or irregular changes between highs and lows. This does not include purposeful steps toward self-improvement.
- Physical symptoms. Includes headaches, nausea, tension and unexplained pains. Consult a physician to diagnose persistent symptoms and medical illness.
- Views suicide as a solution.[1]

Other resources are available to you on the Internet:
- Healthier You offers Ask the Medical Expert Archives (2000-2004) (http://www.healthieryou.com/medexpert/) and Ask the Mental Health Expert Archives (2001-2004) (http://www.healthieryou.com/mhexpert/).
- Continuing Medical Education maintains a Health Directory of reference Web sites (http://www.cmellc.com/resources/links.html).
- Sign up for a mental health newsletter. Healthier You provides a register of Mental Health Mailing Lists (http://www.healthieryou.com/connect.html).
- Use an Internet search engine to search for groups.

# PART III

# VIETNAM AND KOREA VETERANS

# Chapter 9

# Bloody Boots and Body Bags

Survivor's guilt manifests as a combat veteran's mental condition when he or she perceives to have done wrong by surviving a traumatic event. Survivor's guilt is a significant symptom of post-traumatic stress disorder and needs to be identified and treated immediately. To learn how you or someone close to you can recognize a veteran's battle with this vicious ailment, a checklist and self-exam of signs and symptoms of depression can be found at the end of this chapter.

### Erik's Story

The veteran began speaking with a loud, gruff, hoarse voice. "It smelled of diesel; it smelled like death. It just engulfed me," he said, recalling the first days he spent as a soldier in Vietnam. Since returning he had struggled with flashbacks, nightmares, PTSD and depression.

"I have nightmares about those ponchos...slippery with blood; I see my bloody boots and the body bag zippers bleeding," he said in search of a reaction from me. "You tell me, counselor, how do I keep going? Why should I keep going? How awful it makes men. I am in my fifties and have had a stroke and am trapped in my wheelchair...my legs don't work anymore...what's the use in living? Some days I feel guilty for being alive. I drink to numb my feelings and to pass out...to get some sleep; most days I don't want to wake up. You tell me—is that suicidal?"

"Erik, you are injured, partner, really hurt in the very fabric of your being. Your soul is wounded, buddy. I want to get you some help," I said, making an urgent appeal.

With no response to my plea, the Vietnam vet continued with his story. I remember thinking, *How many years has Erik endured living like this...fighting with his hideous demons? I must get him some help immediately—this is heartbreaking.*

"In the months that followed, my squad and I fought the North Vietnamese and the dense jungle undergrowth. We saw bodies lying in fields ...," Erik explained, now speaking in a lower, more dejected tone, yet with frustration in his voice. "I know firsthand the madness and violent cruelty of war in a way those in my family who have not experienced it cannot possibly know."

I responded, supporting him, "I hear you loud and clear, Erik. Let me help you." He didn't react to my offer.

Instead, he interrupted in dramatic fashion by blurting out, "I can't get the images out of my mind!" The combat veteran was now shouting angrily over the phone. "My squad was put in charge of collecting our company's dead. We were designated as the 'handling team.' When our team was notified, we carried the remains of our comrades to a collection site, downhill, downwind and out of sight of the wounded and replacements." He hesitated. "I respectfully laid the bodies on tarps to help protect them from the weather," he paused again. I heard a slight but evident sniffle.

"I'm listening, Erik," I interjected with a supporting timbre.

He continued, "And I...I took great care to help prevent the loss of their personal effects. I felt personally responsible to care for my fallen buddies. I was so angry when men of my unit just hung around making rude remarks about the lifeless, 'killed in action' bodies by names like curly-heads, kinky-hairs…or crew-cuts, balding non-coms…I felt it was shameful," Erik declared sickeningly. "I felt sick and disgusted. The images of the dead, the faces when I was putting them in the bags…haunt me to this day. I am afraid to sleep some nights…I wake up wanting to puke."

I thought, *How can a man survive this nightmare for all these years? Oh my!* He wanted to keep talking, so I allowed him the room to express his pent-up feelings.

This emotionally charged warrior cleared his throat and continued, "We then placed the KIA in the body bags by rolling the bags about halfway down the bodies…and lifted both feet, after we tied them together and pulled the green plastic bags down to their butts. Then…lowered their feet, lifted the torsos, pulled the bag up towards the shoulders and over their heads." Erik stopped abruptly. I heard a sigh, then a shuffling of papers or something similar to that in the background. I also heard the clang of something sounding like metal hitting a glass. I instantly thought, *He has a gun or knife…what is that?*

"Erik!" I tried to interrupt, "What—"

"Wait, let me finish!" he jumped in, sounding annoyed. He hesitated for a couple of seconds. "Then I closed the bags with a tie. I always made sure the zippers opened from the heads down…me and my men then carried the bags to a truck…a cargo truck usually or whatever they had at the time to transport. It normally took three or four of us to lift one body bag onto a truck." Erik paused, taking a breath. I sensed signs of a meltdown. I felt his anguish over what he had just told me. He painted such vivid, chronic pictures as I listened intently to his story; a story I have heard before. Many emotionally scarred combat warriors had been given the difficult task of filling body bags and ponchos with the remains of their comrades; some stuffing the bags and poncho liners with only body parts.

Erik came back on the line after a short break. It sounded like he was shuffling through some papers. "Are you there?" he asked, somewhat guarded.

I answered back, "Yes, Erik, I am here. I will not leave you, buddy. What are you doing right now, Erik? Are you thinking of hurting yourself?"

"Why would you say that?" he said questioning.

"I will tell you straight up; I won't mix words with you. I am concerned for your safety, Erik. You have called the suicide hotline tonight. You obviously have been upset and burdened with these things you have told me for a long time, right?"

"Yeah," he said in a bit of a jerky tone.

"Do you have a weapon in the house?" I inquired, hoping he would be honest with me.

"I do," he responded quickly.

"Have you done anything to hurt yourself tonight?" I said.

"What do you mean?" Erik said awkwardly.

"I mean, have you cut yourself or taken pills or are you planning a suicide? What is going on with you right now, Erik? Why did you call the hotline tonight?" I asked rather bluntly.

Erik replied, "I am thinking about ending it all...you are right on, compadre, but haven't done anything yet if that's your question. I can kill myself with all the things you just said. In fact, I have a .38 Smith & Wesson right here on the table; I have a pharmacy of pills in my bedroom. As a matter of fact, I have a rope in the garage and I know how to make a hangman's noose. So what. Who the hell cares? I just can't live with all the pain and nightmares anymore. I have daytime flashbacks when I watch television. I see news special reports of the troops in Iraq and Afghanistan getting hit by roadside bombs and ambushes...snipers and things, booby traps like in 'Nam. It brings back the tough times in country. I still can hear the mortar rounds of incoming Charlie sent our way relentlessly, daily, body parts flying when the hits found their marks. And the yelling...'medic, medic'...'doc, I'm hit'...all around me...still haunts me. I just can't take it. Everywhere I turn, the memories and the sounds keep coming. You would think they would go away after decades, but not for me. I can't get rid of them."

He paused. "I feel terrible most of the time when I sit here staring out at nothing, thinking that I made it out of the country alive when many of my buddies did not. I ask myself, 'Why me?' A lot of good guys,

Duke and Marshall, died over there. We went through boot together. A couple of buddies saved my skin, covered my back, then were wasted minutes later. Now, I am trapped in my own cocoon, a wheelchair, most of the time not being able to get out of the house to my appointments and get groceries. But, oh yes, big bad Erik is still alive. How is this fair? This is no way to live, all these guilty feelings. I am getting too old for this shit. No future left for me," he concluded woefully.

Unresolved and unprocessed survivor's guilt can make recovery from PTSD and depression difficult. Therapeutic assistance is a valuable step for recovery and is important for persistent, intense guilt as well as other trauma symptoms that upset a survivor's life.

As a combat veteran survivor, Erik needed to experience a renewed picture of his life. It was a matter of reframing his cognitive behavior. He needed help to change the negative thinking and unsatisfying behavior associated with depression and survivor's guilt, while at the same time teaching him how to unlearn the behavioral patterns that contributed to his illness.

For Erik, it was extremely important for him to know, even if the rest of his life seemed insignificant to him, that many people were relieved that he was alive. He needed to reassess his past and to reassess what was valuable to him, reminding him that making the best of his life can be a tribute to his survival and to those who died in Vietnam. I encouraged Erik to take the opportunity to reevaluate the meaning of his life. What was his spiritual condition, for example?

Rick Warren, author of the bestseller *The Purpose-Driven Life*, wrote: "There is nothing—absolutely nothing—more important than developing a friendship with God. It's a relationship that will last forever. Paul told Timothy, *'Some of these people have missed the most important thing in life—they don't know God'"* (1 Timothy 6:21a, Living Bible).

Dr. Warren also suggests remembering a scripture from the New Living Translation Bible, "*Draw close to God, and God will draw close to you*" (James 4:8a). [1]

It is equally important that Erik learn it is okay to take pleasure in being alive. It was as important for him to process and recognize, with therapeutic help, the reawakening of old wounds. His survival may have triggered old feelings of insignificance or dishonor. Surviving may have inflamed old messages that he received about not being worthy, about not measuring up as a combat warrior or about not counting. Erik had to learn to feel comfortable with the notion it is good to survive and it is in our nature to do so.

Erik interjected, "Hey, I have been ranting and raving for the last half hour, telling you my tales of doom and gloom and I don't even know who I am talking to. What's your name?" he asked.

"My name is Vic. Thank you for serving our great country, Erik. I really mean that...welcome home, buddy. I know when you got back home from Vietnam there was a lot of protesting going on, which was pretty ugly," I said, digressing.

Lt. Col. David Grossman, in his book *On Killing*, reflected on Vietnam veterans: "...the condemnation upon his return amplified the horror of his combat experience to result in an overwhelming degree of disgust...staggering numbers of suicide among Vietnam veterans and the tragic number of homeless who are Vietnam vets, give evidence that something has occurred that is significantly and startlingly different from that occurring after World War II or in any other war our nation has ever encountered."[2]

"I am here for you, Erik. We are very much behind our veterans and I am here tonight to get you the help you need if you will let me," I said heart-to-heart.

"Dick, huh...are you a vet, Dick?" Erik asked calming down.

"My name is Vic, as in Victor, and yes, I am a vet, Erik. And I want to help you out of the situation you are in right now. You sound down in the dumps, buddy. I have your back! I can get you to safety tonight if you are willing to go to the hospital," I said attentively.

"Victor, huh...help, huh...like what help specifically? I already see my doctors for my disability, heart and stuff and have seen mental health doctors in the past. I have PTSD they said, but I never really got caught up in the groups and treatment. I have tried to 'suck it up' myself. I have for years…toughed it out. I don't like asking for help. Never have," Erik said deliberately. "My family doesn't have much to do with me. I don't make very good company. Not very patient and fire off at little things. Not many good friends either. I am pretty much a loner and stuck here in the house my mother left me when she passed on a few years ago." He paused. "I really miss Mom." Erik went silent. I could tell this was sensitive and protected territory. I didn't push for any more information.

I sympathetically responded to his heartfelt statement about how close he was to his mother. "I am here for you, buddy. Take as much time as you need." I waited, giving him the opportunity to speak.

A few minutes went by as I shifted my headset to a more comfortable position on my ears and glanced up at the clocks on the wall. I looked around at the other hotliners hard at work on their lines, hopefully bringing other veterans to safety. The health technicians were busy running back and forth collecting information for rescues in progress.

While I was waiting for Erik to continue to open up, I asked myself, *How can I get the .38 away from this warrior? I believe he would use it. And it might be soon.*

If you or someone you care about continues to experience depressed feelings similar to what Erik was going through, don't hesitate to call a medical doctor or therapist for help. Identifying your symptoms is an important and vital step toward gaining an insightful understanding about depression, which may be what you are going though right now.

I have put together a rather simple "self-talk" test that may be helpful. Please keep in mind this is only a self-exam and is not intended to diagnosis depression or any other mental illnesses. If you find you have any of these symptoms for a couple weeks or longer and they continue for most of each day, contact your doctor or the VA hotline for assistance. A list of VA Medical Centers is located in appendix A of this book.

## Self-Talk Test

|  | YES | NO |
|---|---|---|
| Do I have continuing thoughts about death or suicide? Do I have thoughts or ideas and a plan to harm myself? Have I tried to commit suicide in the past? **Note: If you checked yes it is vital for your safety to contact the VA Suicide Prevention Hotline, 1-800-273-TALK (8255), for immediate assistance.** |  |  |
| Do I feel guilty or useless? |  |  |
| Do I feel sad or irritable? |  |  |
| Have I lost interest in activities I used to take pleasure in? |  |  |
| Do I have trouble concentrating? |  |  |
| Am I eating much *less* than I usually do and have lost weight? |  |  |
| Am I eating much *more* than I usually do and have gained weight? |  |  |
| Am I sleeping much *less* than I usually do? |  |  |
| Am I sleeping much *more* than I usually do? |  |  |
| Do I feel tired much of the time or more than usual? |  |  |
| Do I feel anxious and move around nervously? |  |  |

Total number of yes checkmarks_____

　　If you have checked five or more yes boxes, you may be experiencing major depression. Contact medical help immediately. If you checked fewer than five, you may be experiencing a mild form of depression.

These are treatable conditions. In either case, please seek medical attention and advice as soon as you are able or call the hotline for assistance.

Erik came back on the phone. "She took care of me, Vic. I feel alone
and empty now. Vic, it's over, dude…I'm a cipher; do you know what
that means?…I'm nobody, a nonentity—no one cares about me!"

"Wait! Listen to me, Erik…look at me! Look straight into my eyes,"
I exclaimed.

"Look at you? Look at you?…are you crazy, Vic? We are on the
phone, man…," he said excitedly and managed a slight laugh.

"Exactly! Was that a smile I saw for a second, Erik?" I teased.

"You're nuts, Vic. I'm talking about killing myself and you pull a
funny," Erik said in a friendly way. "I know…this reverse psychology shit,
I know. I'm not falling for it. Not for a minute," he said awkwardly.

"See, buddy, there are still things worth living for…a smile, a laugh.
You still have it in you. I care about what happens to you, Erik. Just in
this short time listening to you I can tell you have a good heart. You care
about people, which is why you took such good care of your fallen comrades over in Nam. Our country needs good men like you to help young-
sters coming back from Iraq and Afghanistan. The VA is always looking
for volunteers to help give encouragement to vets coming home. The vet
centers around the country have counselors and groups you can be part
of to share your experience, newfound strength and hope. It is your time
to shine, my man," I tried to encourage him. "I know it has been a long
time coming, but people do care about Vietnam veterans, Erik. And
many that were young hippie protesters back then now realize the mis-
takes made by not giving our Nam vets a homecoming. Let us help you
now. Your life has a purpose. It may be difficult for you to see it right
now, but happiness is around the corner for you, Erik. Brighter days are
before you. I want to help you get the help you need. Will you let me do
that for you?"

There was a silence. *What is he thinking?* I waited. Erik was quiet. I
heard no background noise at all. *Have I gone overboard making that quip?*
I thought intensely.

"Erik, I can arrange for an EMT emergency vehicle to take you to a local emergency room for a psychological evaluation tonight," I mentioned, breaking the silence. "You sound depressed and appear to be unable to make clear decisions and choices in your present condition. I can get you to safety if you give me the okay," I pleaded. "Erik, you called us. I want to help. What is your address?" I paused hoping for a response. "Erik, I need to know your location in order to get you help, buddy. I need your full name and date of birth."

"I don't think so...compadre," Erik responded in a gruff voice. Suddenly, there was some background noise. It sounded as if he was moving around.

"What's up, Erik? I hear you moving around. I need this information so I can send you some help," I continued, getting concerned about the delay on the other end of the line. Suicidal veterans are unpredictable and often act out quickly once they decide to do something. "Erik, the nightmares, flashbacks and guilt can all be a thing of the past if you are willing to work with a treatment team at the VA. You don't have to live like this anymore, buddy. Just give me the word and I will get things started for you...are you listening to me?"

"Yeah, I'm here, just thinking things over. I'm getting tired," Erik responded, sounding emotionally weary.

"Erik, will you do me a big favor right now and put the pistol away, out of your reach after you take the bullets out of the cylinder; don't forget the one in the chamber also. Will you do that?" I asked.

"Why?...I haven't done anything. No harm...it's just sitting there," he remarked.

"I would feel more comfortable with it away from you this evening, out of sight and out of reach, that's all," I concluded. "Do you have anyone who can come over and keep the weapon in safekeeping while we get you through this?

"Nope, no friends, and family doesn't come near me. It's just you and me!" Erik said defiantly.

I could see this was not going very well. I needed to change strategy, quickly. "A dog," I blurted out of nowhere. "You need a dog, Erik."

"What the hell are you talking about? A dog...what for?" he said.

"That's the answer, buddy; a companion for you...a four-legged friend to keep you company, hang out with you and look after you," I said in lifted spirits.

"What the hell...you are crazy, Vic! What am I going to do with a dog around here?" Erik said frantically, caught by surprise.

"Have you ever owned a dog before?" I asked.

"Yeah...but a long time ago," Erik said. "My family had a Springer. I haven't thought about that dog for a long time."

"What was her name?" I inquired.

"Lady," Erik replied, sounding proud to say her name.

"What happened to Lady, if I may ask?" I said.

"We had to put her down after eighteen years. She just grew old. Her back legs started giving out. I couldn't stand to see her in pain. I bought her when she was a pup," Erik shared, sounding a bit melancholy.

"Do you still have room for a dog, Erik...a fenced yard?" I tried to get him interested.

An article on CNN.com, "Dogs Chase Nightmares of War Away", discusses the increase in veterans who come home from Afghanistan and Iraq with instances of PTSD. The report goes on to explore a new program headed by Psychiatric Service Dog Society founder Dr. Joan Esnayra utilizing the service of dogs trained specifically for mental health therapy. The article explains how these dogs are conditioned to sense anxiety, panic and depression in patients. This new and unique means of therapy is being discussed with the Walter Reed Army Medical Center for inclusion into its own rehab program.[3]

Another benefit is that "caring for [an] animal forces [the] patient to overcome social isolation," which is a huge problem in suicidal depressed veterans.[4]

"I have a yard," Erik replied, sounding a bit more interested.

As for the rest of the story, Erik did put away his revolver that night. We continued with quite a lengthy discussion about dogs and what great pets they make. We both shared great experiences and stories we had about them over the years. Erik agreed to have the crisis prevention coordinator from his local VA Medical Center stop by his house the next day for a welfare check and I was told they talked in great length about getting him to the VA for a psychosocial evaluation. He also agreed to stay in the hospital a few days to go through a medical detoxification from the alcohol he had been abusing.

I called in to Erik's treatment team case manager a week or so later to check up on Erik at the hospital and found out that he was doing quite well, had completed detoxification and had been admitted to a chemical dependency rehabilitation program as well as joined a PTSD outpatient clinic veteran group. I asked the case manager to get in touch with a service dog agency and begin the process of getting Erik a best friend.

## PTSD and Depression Signs and Symptoms Checklists

Post-traumatic stress disorder (PTSD) may develop months or even years after the original war trauma and may include the following:
- Nightmares
- Flashbacks
- Efforts to avoid reminders of the traumatic event or triggers that evoke similar feelings
- Intrusive thoughts recalling the combat experience
- Lack of emotional response
- No self-motivation
- Depression (Refer to next checklist)
- Substance abuse: alcohol or other drugs, heavy drinking or drinking more than usual
- Feelings of guilt/survivor's guilt: from the false belief that one was somehow responsible for the loss of a comrade or multiple lives or civilian casualties in war
- Easily startled
- Anger, easily agitated, irritability
- Lack of concentration

- Excessive awareness of possible danger, hyper-vigilant
- Trouble sleeping—insomnia (either not getting to sleep or waking up at all hours)

The degree of your depression, which only your doctor can determine, influences how you are treated. Symptoms and indicators of depression may include:
- Low tolerance to stress
- Low self-esteem
- Feelings of hopelessness and helplessness
- Agitation, restlessness and irritability
- Feelings of worthlessness, self-hate and inappropriate guilt
- Fatigue and lack of energy
- Behaviors such as "acting out" and being impulsive
- Sudden bursts of anger (not like before the war experience)
- Trouble sleeping or excessive sleeping
- Dramatic change in appetite, often with weight gain or loss
- Extreme difficulty concentrating
- Lack of pleasure from activities that normally made the veteran happy (prior to combat)
- Inactivity and withdrawal from usual activities
- History of alcohol or substance abuse
- Family history of depression, alcohol abuse or suicide
- Recurring thoughts of death or suicide[5]

# Chapter 10

# "It Don't Mean Nothin'"

If a warrior allows emotions to seep in, he or she risks becoming a liability to the others on the mission. In the heat of battle adrenaline kicks in as well. This "bloodlust" can damage a warrior's soul for a lifetime. The guilty feelings of killing can be enormous and haunt the veteran warrior for many years after the combat experience. Many veterans express feelings of guilt, because they enjoyed the hunt and the kill.

## Dan's Story

One Sunday winter evening, for a brief moment between calls, I looked out the huge, red brick-lined window just to the left of my desk at an upstate New York winter blizzard. It was nine degrees Fahrenheit outside, snowdrifts climbed the outsides of the red brick building while desk fans blew feverishly inside, giving many of the hotliners a breath of cool air from the intrepid work they do handling life and death situations from suicidal veteran callers across the country.

As one hotliner put it, "Talking on the phone for one hour with a suicidal combat warrior is as intense and exerts as much physical and mental energy as playing a competitive game of chess with Bobby Fischer while arm wrestling a 400 pound mountain gorilla."

Suddenly, my suicide hotline lit up again. Immediately I focused away from the winter scenery and connected to the call.

"I feel like killing myself right here, right now!" The voice on the other end of the line said, wheezing heavily.

"Hello, buddy, my name is Vic. What is your name?" I asked rather apprehensively.

"Dan...the man, pretty sick in the head, I think...I've tried to hold on for all these years, Vic. I have outlasted the NVA's artillery shelling, land mines, booby traps, snipers and mortar attacks...got out of there carrying my balls on a stretcher; lived in the mountains of Colorado, Idaho and Wyoming...and for the life of me...can't remember how many years, moved around most of the United States and Canada...Mexico at times. Shit! I am tired. Just tired of living...I guess what I'm saying...it finally has whipped me. It's over...I'm dead meat...never had a home to call mine, Vic. Never had a family to welcome me back home; still have no family, no kids, no wife...oh, I had bed partners here and there...but no permanent 'ol' lady', you understand...I can't get close to nobody. I've never been right since Nam, I know it. Hell, I don't need a doctor to tell me shit!" Dan said, sounding anxious as he unloaded a pound of pent-up emotion until it sounded like he literally ran out of breath. He was obviously having a difficult time breathing.

"Dan, buddy, have you hurt yourself tonight?" I worriedly interjected.

"No," he paused. "Not yet, but I have a razor blade to do the job...just fill up some hot water and let her bleed. I have thought about that. Not afraid to cut me. Shit, in Khe Sanh we did everything, saw everything and felt nothin'. I saw guts lying out on the ground of some new recruit who stepped on a 'mouse trap' AP mine. He was still alive looking around crying out for his mommy...'it don't mean nothin'.' I didn't even know his name. He joined our team a couple of days before, real green. He looked something like my kid brother.

"He looked at me as if I could do something for him. Hell, he was laying there in his own blood and guts waiting to die. I couldn't do nothin'. He was trying to put himself back together, stuffing his own intestines back into the wound hole in his belly. I wanted to help him stuff it back in, but I knew it was only a matter of minutes, too late for a medevac. I called for a corpsman anyway...told the kid he would be alright, the doc was on his way...that's all I could do. We lie to our dying comrades every time, letting them think there is hope for them, but we know it is over. Our humanity somehow shows through this tough exterior at times like these. I still see his hazy face in my dreams," Dan agonized. "I have had to live with this since 1968...forty f—in' years, man...just too much."

I wanted to let him know someone out there cared. "Welcome home, Dan. Long time overdue, buddy, but welcome home," I said, somewhat apologizing for our country's lack of response to our returning heroes. "Thank you for serving our country," I added.

Dan did not respond. No words were spoken by either of us for a moment. I felt a burst of sadness right then. Tears welled up in my eyes as I looked down at my yellow notepad on the desk, a couple of water spots soaking into the paper, waiting for the right time to speak again. I felt for this broken, suffering suicidal vet. The lonely years of torment— he must have been in absolute misery. If only he had come in for counseling years before, who knows what his life would have been like. *A tragedy*, I thought.

Former president of the United States Herbert Hoover once said: "Older men declare war. But it is youth that must fight and die. And it is youth who must inherit the tribulation, the sorrow, and the triumphs that are the aftermath of war."

Then I heard a congested voice on the other end of the line. "Yeah, thanks Vic," Dan voiced quietly.

"Dan, we can help you now. It isn't too late for you, buddy. There is a lot of support for Nam, Iraq and Afghanistan combat vets today. The hotline is just a starting point for you. I can get you connected to a VA nearest to you, right now. There are trained counselors and therapists who can work with you and help you find solutions to overcome your feelings of hopelessness and wanting to end your life prematurely,"

I pleaded earnestly. "Will you let me get you help?"

"Too late, Vic," Dan said apologetically.

"What do mean, 'too late'?" my voice raised. "Talk to me, Dan!"

"I mean I have already made up my mind," he responded determinedly.

"Why, then, did you call the suicide hotline tonight?" I asked in an attempt to reach out to him.

"I just needed to tell someone. I am all alone and wanted someone to know I was checking out," he said sadly.

"Tell me what specifically, Dan. What do you want to tell me? I am listening, buddy; talk to me. Where is the pain?" I asked directly.

He replied softly, "I was drafted. I had no choice but to go. I have always been against brutality and feel so guilty about the killing I had to do in the war. I had to survive. I had to fight back or die. I was there; my squad was counting on me. Do you understand, Vic? I had to defend myself. I had to complete the mission." Dan spoke as if he was looking for forgiveness.

"I mean...it seems like I am numb inside all the time. I have these dreams and thoughts about some of the KIA bodies I saw: the gurgling noises from their mouths and look of their faces...at the end, all distorted. I can't forget those death stares. The scenes I saw, the destruction I witnessed. I don't think there has been a day gone by, in all these years, that I don't think about it or have nightmares...even sweats. I am tired, Vic, bone tired."

"Dan, can I ask you to do something for me?" I asked earnestly.

"What's that?" he quickly replied.

"Would you please put the razor blade away, somewhere safe and out of reach while we continue to talk about things? Is there any reason you can't do that for me, buddy?" I requested intently. No immediate response from the tired veteran. I waited, looking up at the wall clocks. *Humm, which time zone is he calling from?* I thought. *It is now early Monday morning in New York.* I glanced at the caller identification number displayed on the phone set. I looked it up on my computer database locator map; I wrote on my yellow pad: "360 area code—Vancouver, Washington." *Pacific Time*, I thought. I looked back at the clocks on the wall. *Three hours earlier than Eastern Time...it is 10:23 P.M. in Washington State.*

Quickly I signaled to the health technicians; they ran over to my desk as they have many times before. I put them in a holding pattern for the moment. I wanted to quickly evaluate all the risk factors that determine whether or not to initiate a 911 call: an emergency rescue intervention.

## Assessing Risk Factors

| | |
|---|---|
| ☐ Does the veteran have the desire to kill him or her self? | ☑ I knew Dan had the desire to kill himself. He already expressed those feelings. |
| ☐ What kind of feelings does the veteran express? Is the veteran depressed and hopeless? | ☑ Dan stated he felt hopeless and intolerably alone. He described the psychological pain, the intense misery he had to live with for so many years. |
| ☐ Does the veteran seem likely to and capable of hurting him or her self? | ☑ Dan had the capability and sense of fearlessness to make an attempt. He said, "I'm not afraid to cut me." He was also demonstrating increased anxiety. |
| ☐ Does the veteran have a specific plan and the opportunity for an attempt? | ☑ Yes, Dan had both a plan and the opportunity for a suicide attempt. |
| ☐ Has the veteran thought out the details? | ☑ Dan had acquired the means (a razor blade) to follow through on his plan. |
| ☐ Has the veteran prepared for the finality of death? Has the veteran written any notes or given away possessions? (This is a very important sign for suicide intent.) | ☐ Unknown at the time for Dan's case. |
| ☐ Does the veteran have a support system (family, friends) to connect to or is he or she alone? | ☑ Dan had explained he had no family, children or wife; that he "can't get close to nobody." |

| Does the veteran talk about plans for the future or does he or she have no plans? | ☑ Dan expressed, "I have no reason for living." |
|---|---|
| ☐ Does the veteran convey a sense of purpose? | ☑ Dan was expressing no sense of purpose. |
| ☐ Is the veteran undecided about dying? | ☑ Dan was not undecided about dying; he knew he wanted it. |

If you decided to pick up the phone and dial 911 based on the evaluation of factors for Dan, that would be the correct decision. Calling for an emergency rescue, an intervention, is exactly what we did for Dan. I gave the go-ahead for the techs to contact the Vancouver area police and sheriff's departments and collaborate on trying to locate where Dan was living. I intended to ask him for his address, but while I was waiting for Dan to speak to me I was instituting an action plan.

Eventually he began to talk. "Why should I put the blade away since I am going to use it?" he said in a somber tone.

"Wait one minute, Dan! You do have reasons to live and I will tell you why," I exclaimed.

"You tell me what this over-the-hill has-been has to offer anyone. I am worthless, Vic; haven't you been listening to a word I have been saying? Shit!...man, you don't get it, do you?" Dan recoiled.

"I get it, Dan. Now will you give me a minute and I will tell you why I think you have a reason to live. But first, where are you calling from?" I inquired.

"What do you mean where am I calling from...hell, man, Washington...Washington State," Dan replied, obviously agitated.

"I mean, what is your address; what town do you live in?" I inquired specifically.

"Vancouver," he fired back. "Where are you?"

"I am in upstate New York, in three feet of snow," I replied, sighing. "Dan, what is your street address?"

"Can't have it," he responded abruptly.

"Why not?" I questioned. I began to think, *We have to find this vet and quickly; he is not cooperating.* I signaled the techs the urgency that we were faced with by circling my right arm in the air above my head, as they were working on finding his address. The local police have the ability to track and trace phone numbers to addresses. I was hoping this would be a successful trace.

"Nobody knows my address. I like it like that," Dan said defensively.

"What do you mean when you said you can't get close to anybody?" I prompted him to respond.

"Nobody knows how I bleed inside every time I think or dream about the combat deaths and mutilation. All the carnage I saw and was part of in Vietnam still controls my thoughts, Vic."

Dan paused for a moment. I heard some commotion in the background. Then, I heard a whishing sound near the receiver. It sounded like he took a drag between his lips from a cigarette. *Humm...I wonder if he is self-medicating with cannabis weed. Is he addicted?* I wondered. *Does he take any other meds?*

Dan started talking again before I could jump in. "I feel unsafe all the time. I walk outside and loud noises from the street upset me. I never know what to expect. When I was in country, the NVA artillery barrage was pounding but at least I knew it was going to rain rockets and I always had a hole in the ground to jump into. But now I worry about protecting myself, watchin' my own back from people, noises and bad situations. So I don't go out much. I try to stay to what is familiar to me. I feel safer that way, Vic."

Dan showed signs of slowing down his conversation. *It probably is the effect of the pot,* I mused. *What is my next action plan if we can't find an address? I have to talk him down from a suicide attempt. How am I going to accomplish that? I have to stay focused and continue talking to him about the reasons he has to live.*

I looked toward the health tech room for a sign as to what was going on—did the cops find Dan's location or what? *Come on, come on...we are running out of time here,* I was beginning to feel impatient.

"Dan, do you ever get to the VA in your area?" I asked.

"Hell no, I had enough of the freakin' VA back in the '60s and '70s. They gave me nothin'. 'Take three aspirins and see me in a couple of months.' And did I have nightmares big time. Some of the veteran old timers called it 'shell shock' from all the mortars and rockets pounding us into the ground. That was tough sleddin' back then. I headed for the mountains with a couple of buddies when we got out, but could never get away from the noises in my head," Dan expounded.

"Dan, let's talk, buddy, about putting that razor blade away and letting me get you some help. I will arrange for you to talk with good people at the VA. You will be able to talk to other combat vets also from Nam and the wars in Iraq and Afghanistan—many going through the same as you. The treatment teams today are highly trained at treating combat trauma, not just medical doctors. The VA team will develop a treatment plan for you that will help you make sense of and understand your emotions and help you to get in touch with those feelings of guilt and fear," I said, arguing for his life. "We are talking about freedom, Dan. Freedom for you to be able to get out of the house and go places, meet people, make new friends and maybe find a special lady. These are just a few of the reasons why I want you to help me help you."

Dan responded, "Nope…thanks but no thanks. I can handle this."

"I care about what happens to you, buddy. *Semper Fi*. I have your back if you will let me," I pleaded, hoping he would respond in kind.

"You a leatherneck, Vic?…no shit…what the hell, you are, aren't you. *Semper Fi* back at you, bro," he replied with a level of surprise in his voice.

Suddenly the heath tech came running to my desk putting a scribbled note in front of me: "Found him. Police on the way." I gave thumbs up and a smile. I pushed my mute button and said, "Good job. Good work, team. Give the cops a heads-up that he has a razor blade with him. I will keep Dan on the phone until he lets them in—that is if he opens the door." The tech nodded in agreement turned and walked away.

I returned to the line to continue speaking with Dan. "Dan, I will give you another reason to live: your Marine buddies who died in Khe Sanh. Wouldn't they want you to live…for them, Dan…in their memory? Wouldn't they want you to help other vets from other wars recover...giving them strength and hope to overcome from their wounds?" I asked. *I have to be careful here not to transfer a burden of guilt on to Dan's shoulders but to urge a sense of purpose...encourage a mission.*

"Dan, you would have an enormous effect on these young guys coming home from Iraq and Afghanistan. Once you work through your issues and begin to get your mental and physical health back, sharing and caring is what recovery is all about," I expressed.

Dan yelled out, "Someone is at the door! I'll be right back." I heard him place the phone on some hard surface. I could barely hear his footsteps as he walked away.

The health techs had an open line to the police deputy indicating they were knocking on Dan's apartment door. We waited. Dan opened the door. The police rushed in to make sure Dan did not have the razor in hand. The cops told the health tech on the phone they had the blade in possession; it had been lying on a table. I asked the tech to give me the phone. I wanted to talk to the deputy.

"Hello, sergeant. The veteran you have right there needs to be transported to the nearest VA emergency room for a psychiatric evaluation. He has expressed suicide intentions and has the plan and desire to carry it out. Dan is a Vietnam vet. I believe an emergency medical team has come with you, is that correct?" I asked.

"Yes," the deputy replied. "What is your name, sir?"

"My name is Vic Montgomery; I am the suicide crisis hotline responder." I addressed his question and then asked, "Deputy, would you please put Dan on the line to talk to me?"

I heard in the background muffled talking, then, "What the hell are you doing to me, Vic?" Dan said obviously irritated. "The police...shit man...the police...I don't need the police in my house...what the hell, man!"

"Dan, listen to me, they are there with a medical team to transport you to safety. That's it. You are not in trouble, Dan. The police have to escort the EMTs into the house for their safety, that's all. You are not being arrested. The ambulance will take you to the emergency room at the VA; apparently there is a medical center not far from you."

"What the ...," Dan spouted.

"Let me finish," I insisted. "You will be met there by a psychiatric nurse for an evaluation and later on in the day by a crisis prevention coordinator. His name is Dr. McKenzie and he will meet with you to offer suggestions on a treatment plan and refer you to the right programs. You will have several options to fit what is best for you. Dan, this is for you, buddy. I know you don't think you want this right now, but I am truly hoping you will get the help you need and deserve. Please cooperate and go in for treatment. Will you do that?" Click, silence, dial tone.

Some of the rescue calls end like that. The veteran is very unhappy. The hotliner runs the chance of upsetting the person for the moment in order to get him or her to a safe environment. It is understandable that Dan was upset. The unannounced visit had caught him off guard. But I had to do it that way in his case, because he was in extreme lethal danger with the razor at his fingertips. If he knew beforehand I was sending help to him without his permission, he may have cut himself right there on the spot while he was on the phone with me and the rescue team would not have been able to get to him in time, especially because at one point we didn't even have his address. The health tech team of diligent, tireless men and women will follow up with the police and the VA. Did he cooperate? Did he follow through with a psychosocial evaluation and therapeutic interview? What was the outcome and diagnosis?

A generalized therapeutic model for recovery from combat trauma suggests that before Dan can begin to heal from remembering and dreaming about his feelings associated with experiences on the battlefield, he must first become more comfortable with his internal and external safety zones. Dan must come to terms and learn to process his feelings associated with his exterior environment as well as within his wounded soul. Once he finds safety in his environment and in his consciousness, he can begin to repair and rebuild the sensitive feelings and behaviors associated with his guilt. These hinge on the feelings of remorse and depression he discussed as well as the grief and anger that come with them.

Dan's story reveals the psychological harm that occurs with repressed feelings and "tough-skinned" coping mechanisms that naturally occur in battle zones. Granted, combat troops are well trained and encouraged to be thick-skinned and to restrain emotions while in combat. In fact, warriors have to learn how to "shut down" emotions in order to complete missions and stay alert. This is a highly practiced coping mechanism in battle zones.

A few days later, I found out Dan stayed on at the VA and in fact was referred to detoxification for chemical dependency. It was found in his evaluation that Dan had been smoking marijuana since his wartime service and it had become a full-blown addiction. As an expert in the field of chemical dependency, I will tell you, having a dual diagnosis, PTSD, TBI, clinical depression and other mental health or behavioral health issues mixed with a dependency on marijuana, heroin, alcohol, cocaine, methamphetamines or prescribed medications is a challenge for any veteran, but is definitely treatable; the deeper the dynamics, the longer the treatment.

Treatment planning in cases like Dan's will normally entail a three- to fourteen-day detoxification regiment, followed by inpatient treatment for twenty-eight days or more compounded with an intensive outpatient treatment program that includes transitional and readjustment counseling and aftercare. Inpatient vets, in this case Dan, begin to adjust to a safe environment, learning about the relationship with their drugs of choice and how they intertwine with their wounded souls. Cognitive behavioral therapy, biofeedback, visualization and numerous other proven techniques will be the therapeutic models used to sort out the traumatized warriors' minds.

One of the major struggles Dan brought to the forefront in our phone conversation was his inability to feel; as he put it, "it seems like I am numb inside all the time" and he was avoiding society, people and relationships.

Dr. Victor Victoroff, M.D., reveals in his book *The Suicidal Patient* how the factors contribute and one factor alone may take the lead in inciting suicide:

> The conditions that lead to suicide are like tumblers in
> a safe lock when the dial is spun at random. By chance
> they all fall into place and the lock disengages.

Similarly, the elements in a suicide bounce about, with no one factor sufficient in itself to provoke suicide.[1]

Renowned psychologist Carl Jung presented the theory that every human being wears a mask that he or she presents to the world. This persona consists of socially acceptable behaviors. However, Jung suggests, every human being also has a dark side. Present in this dark side of the persona are other socially unacceptable feelings and desires; murder is one of them.[2]

Dr. Matsakis, a psychotherapist specializing in PTSD, suggests that we have a dark side to our characters and often it is not expressed, "and when we encounter this side, we tend to experience some degree of guilt and shame."[3]

In combat, however, the dark side is not only acknowledged, but also encouraged, if not glorified. Soldiers are frequently rewarded for acting on aggressive and murderous feelings that are socially unacceptable to civilian society. Hence, unlike noncombatants, combat veterans are not only forced to recognize their dark sides, but also "given the opportunity to let it loose." The feelings of guilt, often experienced for many years, can be enormous. As a result, war can pose a spiritual or moral dilemma for many veterans. Often they feel the conflict between the warrior, who has been trained to kill and the human being, who learned that killing is morally wrong. There may be a moral pain attached to killing for some veterans, especially if those vets have a high standard of values. Traditionally, society has forgiven warriors by justifying the killing. However, in instances where society does not provide such justification for killing, the moral pain of killing can be even more intense.[4] For the Vietnam vets, at homecoming, for the most part, they were not forgiven by society for killing.

The challenge is learning how to get back in touch with your feelings. The price Dan paid for being a good warrior was the numbing effects that "toughing it out" played on his emotions long after the battles ended. For Dan, the mental battle continued and the loss of his ability to love and re-establish close relationships with family and friends became a huge problem. In fact, his battle was so huge that he felt the only alternative was to end his life. Many combat veterans with PTSD or other readjustment problems experience similar difficulties. They don't want to bond with another person, because they don't want to lose that person as they lost others as a result of war.

Vets who believe they are trapped in a situation with no possible solution and no resources to bear the mounting torment are depressed. Suicidal preoccupation soon follows such a conviction. The expression of hopelessness and self-blame are sensitive indicators of suicidal intent. Don't give up; these things can be processed with clinical supervision and are treatable.

Dan's psychosocial wounds led him to exceptionally poor social skills. Intense lack of trust in the environment may have influenced him to suicidal ideation as an escape. The most important first step to take is to call 911 or the VA Suicide Prevention Hotline if you are on the edge as Dan was.

# Chapter 11

# The Vets of Korea

The Korean War affected millions of Koreans, Chinese and Americans. Millions died in the war and tens of millions witnessed their loved ones die or experienced life or death situations in the war. Some researchers of the Korean War Era claim that more than 30 percent of those Americans who fought in Korea and are still alive today suffer from post-traumatic stress disorder.

### Ed's Story

I answered the hotline. Even before I could get my headset fully adjusted, a blistering barrage of obscenities, accusations and just plain frantic bitterness flooded into my ear. I said nothing in order to try to diffuse the outcry. Slowly the caller, Ed, began to run out of words and energy to fire them at me. I continued to remain silent, for I soon understood that this was a senior citizen war veteran struggling with anger, grief and depression.

"I am a Korean War vet but who the hell cares?" The caller added another salvo after a few moments of silence. "Who the hell remembers

the millions who died there? They say it was a 'police action' ... I say
bullshit! You probably don't even know what I am talking about, do you!
You're too young to remember. But, I will never forget...never! How can
I? I still have the memories and the nightmares."

The discrepancy of the situation in Korea was a sentiment felt by
many, especially the soldiers:

> I know they have called this just a Korean Police
> Action, but I am over here and I say this is in no way
> just a Military Police Action, this is war.[1]

"I care, Ed," I said in a controlled manner. "I understand your
outrage. You probably have stuffed these feelings for years. Am I right?"

Ed flared back saying, "You bet your young ass I have. I saw blood
and guts you can't imagine. Do you know we lost over 33,652 of our
good men over there in just three years? And another 103,000 were
wounded? People don't know that. The public didn't know it then and
they don't know about it now. Did you know we fought in below zero
weather when sometimes our rifles jammed and grenades didn't fire
because they were frozen? Yeah...I bet not...we are a forgotten breed
just like the Nam guys."

Ed paused. I continued to write notes on my yellow notepad.
I looked up at the clocks on the wall then back to the phone set's caller
ID screen to see where Ed was calling from and what time zone he lived
in.

Ed began talking again and delivered another intense outburst, which
I sensed he needed to do. "The North Korean and Chinese troops were all
over the place, piled up dead and wounded by the hundreds. They just kept
coming at us...some not even wearing boots or shoes, nothin'. Black frozen
feet wrapped in dirty, infested cloths. It was awful shit...I still see the dead
bodies. I was a young buck back then, could take a lot of abuse...but
now...it's different...I am old and tired." He stopped briefly. It seemed Ed
was running short of breath and strength to continue his fight. Yet, in a
few seconds, he picked up where he left off and continued to spew

forth from a reservoir of reserved energy, probably that same "piss and vinegar" that got him through the war.

"Our troops also had it tough...you know...a lot of injuries and sickness due to the terrible conditions." In the war journals today, Veteran Affairs calls it "unique war injuries—cold injures."

"Hell, we froze our asses off," Ed exclaimed. "Our skin stuck to the metal and weapons didn't work. A lot of men on both sides died, because they couldn't defend themselves in those conditions. I remember some Chinese were charging our foxholes and bunkers without rifles. They picked up the rifles of their dead comrades who fell in front of them and continued the charge. It was a slaughter. The place smelled of dead bodies; it was like a graveyard. We fought at close range. They kept coming, falling in front of our foxholes." Ed paused. The emotion was beginning to catch up to him. I sensed the tightness in his words.

I have been told that many Korean War survivors have nightmares of being chased and shot at, of being attacked and overrun, of hand grenades being tossed into their foxholes and the sounds of mortar rounds being launched in their direction. These nightmares often flare up twenty, forty, even sixty years later, triggering thoughts of suicide.

Jack Walker's "A Brief Account of the Korean War" describes with great insight one combat soldier's frightening account, undergoing a PFC Sheffield Clark-like traumatic experience when his unit came under attack and they had little ammunition or supplies while they were supposed to be supporting the 3rd Infantry.

In reference to these events, Walker states, "The attack was so swift that our machine gunners were killed and our own machine guns were turned against us. They captured our 105s, then captured a trainload of ammo for them. There were only twelve of us left out of my battery by the time we got back to Taejon.[2]

Ed continued to talk. He obviously needed to vent, so I listened. "We threw the bodies of our guys in shallow graves and went back later to dig 'em up. I still see images of my fallen comrades, blood and guts everywhere."

South Korea was invaded June 25, 1950, and in a few days the United States began sending men and supplies to drive back the invaders. South Korea asked the United States to step in and help defend against the invading communists.

Another revealing picture of what the hotline caller, Ed, was up against as a warrior in the Korean War is seen in memoirs Robert G. Shannon compiled for the *Korean War Educator*. It helps give a real picture of what Ed and his fellow warriors faced:

- "...so much human misery and poverty, filth and disease..."
- "At the time, in 1950, the infantry was getting slaughtered and they were sending cooks, clerks and the likes to fill in the front lines."[3]

Many of our eighty- and ninety-year-old Korean War post-traumatic stress victims have difficulty sleeping. Some have experienced someone else's suicide; perhaps that of an aging veteran buddy. Others have a history of violence or substance abuse problems. In many cases, the veteran is out of touch with reality or is seen as having increased anxiety and recent dramatic mood changes. Many Korean War vets have turned to self-medication in the form of alcohol and other drugs as a way to forget haunting memories of the past. Some have become permanent residents of a veteran's hospital or nursing home waiting out the time until death. Many have shattered marriages because the veterans are suicidal and emotionally unstable. You may find yourself or your combat veteran expressing suicidal ideation by saying things like, "I have no reason for living; I am just a burden."

My experience reveals post-traumatic stress disorder and traumatic grief victims of the Korean War avoid getting too personally involved with other people. They have difficulty establishing lasting relationships. Many of these older veteran warriors are suicidal and emotionally unpredictable; even minor incidents cause them to explode. Some combat warriors withdraw and become loners, seldom or never again making friends or keeping close relationships. Some express extreme anger and others are inclined to hide their emotions. Survivors of traumatic events can experience acute symptoms of distress including intense agitation, self-accusations, high-risk behaviors, suicidal ideation and intense outbursts of anger. Delaying grief may well postpone problems that can become chronic symptoms weeks, months and years later. Older veterans who have developed post-traumatic stress disorder and/or depression may well be masking their grief symptoms.

As a result, many veteran warriors are unable to enjoy happy family lives in their "golden years." Spouses and children leave or abandon the veterans, because they do not know what to expect from their loved ones or what to do to comfort them. Families feel helpless. At this point in their lives, many senior citizen veterans feel alone, abandoned and angry.

Understanding these feelings, I reached out to the veteran now calling the hotline. "Ed, my name is Vic," I interrupted. "Are you thinking about suicide?" I asked gently.

"Suicide! What suicide?" Ed fired back.

"Ed," I quickly responded, "this is a suicide crisis hotline you called. Have you thought about suicide in the last two months?" I inquired quietly.

"I never thought about killing myself. God will do that for me, young man," Ed said, sounding calmer although a bit put-off. "I received a letter from the VA a month or so ago and thought I would call the number to see what all the fuss was about. Hell, I have some of these things they talk about…but killing myself isn't one of them. Hey, thousands of Chinese tried to kill me at Unsan when I was a young buck and couldn't get the job done so why on God's green earth would I want to do their job for them? I might be screwed up in my head, my family thinks I'm nuts and they don't come around much anymore, but I'm not going to shoot myself, if that's what you are thinking."

"Ed, may I arrange for you to have an appointment with the Mental Health Department in the VA nearest to you? Would you do that?" I asked.

Ed did not answer immediately. He cleared his throat and breathed heavily. Sensing how much he needed my concern, I waited.

"I'm okay," he finally said despondently. I was not convinced. *He has too much going on*, I thought. *I want to get him in for an evaluation and hopefully some counseling. He could be wrestling with some grief issues and certainly loneliness and depression. He also seems stressed. Isolation and loneliness are not good for anyone, especially a combat war veteran growing old with nightmares.*

"Ed, I can arrange for a crisis prevention coordinator to come by your place tomorrow and visit with you for a checkup…just to see if you need anything. Can I do that for you?" I requested.

"Nah, I will get by," Ed hesitated. "What was your name again?"

"Vic…Vic Montgomery, Ed," I replied immediately. "Ed, how are you getting along? Where are you living?"

"Well…let me see." He paused for a moment. "Where am I living? I'm living in my run-down old house on a small farm my folks and George— that's my dead older brother, George—left me out here in West Virginia, in the sticks. Yeah, when George died, he couldn't remember my name or anything like that. I took care of him up to the end," Ed said sadly. "I miss George."

"Who is taking care of you? Who comes around to check up on you?" I asked inquisitively.

"They tried to take me to an old age place or something a few years back," Ed replied with some indignation. "They try to give me pills for this and that but I don't take them anymore."

"Who are they?" I questioned.

"Oh…I have a daughter. She is a good girl, but I don't need her help. She comes out here every Saturday to bring me stuff…food, pictures of my grand-kids, things like that. I don't mix well with the family, you know…so she sees me by herself. I feel alone most of the time now with my brother George gone," Ed said. I felt a pang of pain there.

"Ed, can you tell me where your pain is? What hurts you the most, Ed; is it in your heart, your mind or is it your body hurting?" I asked, truly trying to find out what had finally prompted the phone call.

For a few moments I heard nothing on the other end of the phone line. Then an outpouring of anguish and a tear-filled reply came over the receiver, "I'm tired, Vic…tired and alone. I don't know anymore. I just sit staring some days…tears start rolling down my face…and the nightmares…so real…I don't know; just plain don't know what to do sometimes. Ya know?…sometimes I feel trapped out here. I don't drive anymore. And what about death? Where do I go? What happens to me? Will I ever see my brother George again or my war buddies, my mother?"

"What about death, Ed?" I questioned.

"I mean, is there a heaven and hell? Will I go to hell for all the killing?" Ed challenged.

"I don't have the answers to that. What is your spiritual condition, Ed?" I asked him. "What do you believe will happen to you after death?"

"What do you mean my condition?" Ed said, sounding somewhat puzzled, a bit annoyed.

"I mean, do you believe there is a higher power greater than you?" I asked.

"If you are asking me do I believe in God…the answer is yes. I was taught by my mother about the Bible stories…when I was a kid, but I don't go to church or anything like that," Ed responded.

In his article "What happens after we die?" for the Ontario Consultants on Religious Tolerance, B.A. Robinson writes about his ideas on the fear of and life after death and reflects on why and how religions were developed to comfort people in times of natural disasters, war and widespread disease:

> Religions answered these fears with a belief that
> somehow a person's personality, memories, talents, and
> consciousness survived death in a new form.[4]

"Ed, if I were to convey to you that it is my belief that you have a wounded soul, would you understand what I meant?" I asked.

"Wounded soul?" Ed questioned as if thinking out loud.

"Yes, wounded soul," I responded back. The line went quiet. I sensed he was really internalizing the question. I waited. *Not an easy question*, I thought.

"I guess that makes sense. I never thought of it like that. I always thought of wounds as physical, not what you just said. I guess you are right. I think of my life gone by and the people who were in it and have died. I get lonely just thinking about things like that and my brother George who took care of me for so many years after the war. I start thinking about where he is right now and if I can see him again. I think about his soul. I get confused. I don't even know what a soul is. How do I know what a soul is, Vic?"

"I can't answer that for you. And who knows, if I tried to answer that question my answer may be wrong. So, Ed, do you still have a Holy Bible around the house?" I asked.

"Yes, my mother's. She wanted me to have it. But to be honest I never read two lines in it," he replied apologetically.

"Ed, there are many beliefs and religions in the world about who God is and about the soul, Heaven and Hell, what they mean and where we go after death; the Bible is one of the sources for this kind of information," I suggested. "Look in your Bible in the New Testament—that's in the second half, Ed—in the Book of John. Read that book and the answers you are searching for may be in there, particularly in chapter 3. Read verse 16."

"It's too late for me, Vic. I am too old now, just wasting away," Ed said sorrowfully.

"It is never too late," I responded unequivocally. "Ed, how about you see that crisis coordinator from the VA I suggested earlier. He will come to your house for a visit."

"I guess that wouldn't hurt. I may have some questions. I haven't been in there very much lately," he said, sounding a bit remorseful.

"All right then, good for you. This is a good decision, Ed. Now, I just need some personal information from you: your full name, address, phone number and date of birth, and I will make an appointment for Dr. Bender to come by and talk with you, say tomorrow at 10 A.M....alright, Ed?" I asked

"Now, who is this again?" Ed questioned.

"Dr. Bender is a VA therapist, a combat veteran specialist in the areas of geriatrics and war related disorders, like PTSD, depression and anxiety disorders," I responded. "This is a routine visit just to make sure you are getting everything you need," I urged. "I will call Dr. Bender right after we hang up and he will call you to confirm the appointment to meet with you...alright, Ed?"

"Hey, what the hell. I don't have anything to lose that I haven't lost already. I will give it a try," Ed said.

"Ed, I wish you the very best life has to offer, partner. You are a good man. Thank you for serving our country. And, Ed, don't forget to look up those verses in the Bible, particularly John 3:16. You follow up with that and you will begin to know what I am talking about when I asked you about your spiritual condition. You will find it, keep looking." There was silence. I heard a gentle sobbing in the background. "Ed, you take care of yourself, buddy."

Ed was an eighty-five-year-old Korean War veteran who was questioning his mental health and possibly had thoughts about ending his life, although he would not admit to it. If you or someone you care about has similar feelings about suicide, loneliness or overwhelming grief, contact your VA immediately. You can either go in for a psychosocial evaluation or call the crisis hotline for a referral to a crisis prevention coordinator.

Aging vets, you must learn how to ask for help. It takes the courage of a warrior to ask for help. Don't let another day go by suffering alone. You do not have to allow your suicidal thoughts and depressed feelings of loneliness go unexpressed or unattended. Remember that grief, stress, depression and suicidal ideations are treatable mental health conditions. You owe yourself the right to arrange for a VA consultation with a professional clinician to assess whether or not you have clinical depression as a result of prolonged or untreated post-traumatic stress disorder or other war-related physical and psychological stresses.

I made a phone call to Dr. Bender and arranged a consultation.

When I followed up to see how Ed was doing, I found out that Ed was visited by the crisis prevention coordinator and the senior citizen veteran agreed to go into the VA medical center for further evaluation to determine the level of care he needed.

It appears that Ed may have experienced years of suffering from PTSD coupled with depression, anxiety and, after his brother died, grief.

Ed was offered ongoing mental health and physical primary care and his treatment team discussed the possibility of a permanent move for Ed into a small community housing program the VA offers. This would bring Ed out of isolation and into a nurturing environment. The VA recently launched a medical foster home program that enables veterans to live in small facilities with a home-like environment.

An insightful article by Susan C. Hedrick, Ph.D., Marylou Guihan, Ph.D., and Michael Chapko, Ph.D., in the VA health publication *Forum* discusses the alternatives of assisted living and adult family homes:

> These programs offer the promise of serving persons
> needing long-term care in settings that can meet their
> needs while maximizing autonomy and privacy in a
> home-like setting.[5]

Today, Ed is benefiting from this pilot program. He is also receiving long overdue cognitive behavioral therapy for PTSD and grief counseling for the loss of his beloved brother, George. Ed is finally beginning to enjoy his "golden years" with visits from his family, his grandchildren and great-grandchildren he had never met.

Thank you to those 1.8 million who served during the three years of hostilities in the Korean War Era over half a century ago. Of these warriors, 997,000 also served during World War II, 347,000 during the Vietnam War and 291,000 during all three wars.[6]

What tried and true warriors you are, as are those who served in the MASH units and behind the scenes. Ooh-rah! Today you are our senior citizen veterans. I want to send this message straight to you, up close and personal, from one vet to another: Suicide is not the answer. I know many of you or someone close to you may be struggling, right now, with post-traumatic stress disorder (PTSD) or depression, "which is associated with substantial suffering, disability, suicide risk, and decreased health-related quality of life",[7] or both. Don't give up! Please believe that most of these mental and behavioral health disorders are treatable.

Korean War Era vets, wherever you are now, I salute you! We as a nation salute you! Welcome Home!

## Aging Veteran Resources

James F. Burris, M.D., explains the additional services now offered at VA Medical Centers in his article "VA Responds to the Needs of Aging Veterans". Among the services he discusses are: adult day care centers, skilled caretakers and aides, home-based primary and palliative care, hospices and care for disabled veterans.[8]

Look in appendix A for a VA Medical Center located near you to take advantage of these and other services for veterans.

# Chapter 12

# The Tide Within

Sergeant Jake Storm's story gives an extraordinary perspective on a war fought forty years ago that continues to plague the consciousness of some aging combat veterans. Jake Storm is a sixty-three-year-old Vietnam veteran in crisis. They don't make men any tougher than Jake. However, even the toughest of warriors are human and after time may become vulnerable and concede defeat to thoughts and plans of suicide.

Jake had already been diagnosed and treated for post-traumatic stress disorder. But after years of treatment and medications, Jake continued to struggle with his own identity, insomnia, continuing nightmares, flashbacks and suicide ideation. This honorable and courageous man is not unlike many other combat veterans returning home from Iraq and Afghanistan. Wherever the war or conflict is fought, be it the jungles and rice paddies of Vietnam, the deserts of Iraq or the mountains and caves of Korea and Afghanistan, it does not change the enormity of the human cruelty and tragic events seen and experienced that are beyond many veterans' abilities to cope. Jake's story takes you on his journey to hell and back, insanity to recovery. It conveys the perseverance needed to get help even if it has been a long time coming.

## Sergeant Jake Storm's Story

In his mind, the sun had just broken through the early morning fog bank along the beach breakwater of the Marine Corps Base Camp, Pendleton, California. The waves broke on the reef rocks in front of Sergeant Jake Storm, casting a fine mist onto his graying, whiskered face. The brackish seawater mist joined the salt from the tears rolling down his cheeks. The tide was rolling in. As he gazed from his furrowed facial features looking deep into the ocean water's sudsy edge, in his mind's eye he carefully observed the tide action in the ocean's surf. He was always fascinated by the vastness of the ocean. The Vietnam Marine veteran stood with amazed admiration as he watched the tide's effects on the ocean and its habitation. He closed his eyes, face catching the breeze as clouds began to swallow his mind.

Jake Storm's thoughts continued to wander. He seemed to constantly be playing back tapes that seemed to run on and on, disappearing into the mist. He visualized large old-fashioned metal reels spinning in a never ending loop.

Jake's lessons began at an early age; not so pleasant at times. Jake's parents divorced when he was about four years old. He couldn't remember being held or nurtured by his mother or father. No ball games with Dad. A small voice in his head often told him to suck it up and get over it. He questioned his thinking. His room at home and in the military boarding school always seemed cold, empty and void of feeling. Something or someone was missing; no selective bonding. The pain of abandonment dominated his soul. The tide was out most of the time in his early childhood, empty and shallow; forever retreating like the water's edge from the sand. He felt deformed and detached most of the time growing up. *Whose child am I anyway?* he often reflected.

Jake had no early connectedness. His thoughts became distant when he tried to identify with connectedness between human beings. He remembered no attachments. He considered the scene of nature returning to his mind. *Do not the dolphin and her calf create a secure bond, improving the calf's chances for survival?* he deliberated. Reflecting on the notion, he accepted the wisdom the baby instinctually knows the caregiver is dependable, which seems to create a secure base for the calf then to explore. This baby calf knows its parent will provide comfort and reassurance, so it is comfortable seeking it out in times of need. As the seasoned Vietnam vet looked off into the vastness of the blue skies, he thought about how the naturalistic imagery of this type of in-the-wild relationship impresses him as evoking the strength of nature. The former Marine scuba diver imagined the baby dolphin as it swims close to its mother and is carried in the mother's slip stream, the hydrodynamic wake that the mother creates as she swims. *Did I ever have a dynamic wake to guide me as a child?* He thought about this question in a distant, deeply abstracted way.

Jake's initial voyage of discovery and emotional development began as a big disappointment. He began to think of the maternal deprivation of childhood as he watched the seagulls soaring above him. *How nice the birds seemed, flocking together as a family and gliding together up, down and around one another, landing on the soft sandy beachhead together in groups,* he thought to himself. *There is something warm and peaceful about this image.* As he was inspired for the moment, he managed a smile. In fact, he began to speak bird-talk to the swarming seagulls as if they could understand his gibberish. On occasion Jake brought a bag full of bread crumbs down to the beach to feed the seagulls out of his hand. He liked the rare natural moments of feeding birds in the wild. Jake would not go to the zoo; he despised people who caged any form of wildlife.

Caught in the layers of memories, Jake's mind moved to another moment of his past. Sergeant Storm remained living in country when he and several of his buddies were honorably discharged from the service. Most were decorated combat veterans. The term "in country," in this case, was not the jungles of Vietnam anymore, but the hills and mountain ranges of the Sierra Nevada. Sarge, as he was called then, walked out of the El Toro Marine Corp Air Station in California a free man, but one angry veteran. The day he and his friends left the main gate of the base they were greeted by anti-war protestors. Most were chanting and holding signs of negative propaganda and demeaning slogans like "U.S. Imperialism" and "Get out of Vietnam." This was about the time of the huge twenty- to thirty-thousand-person-staged "Human Be-In" anti-war event that took place in Golden

Gate Park, San Francisco. The discharged Marines were told about possible protestors, but never expected such a negative homecoming. Sarge and his Marine Corps buddies felt abandoned. The men were outraged and demoralized and wanted nothing to do with civilians, so they set up a survival tent camp located at about 9000 feet at the North Fork of the Kings River about 100 miles east of Fresno, California. There they constructed a camouflage fabric-sheltered camp and lived off the land, finally settling in for several years near Big Pine Creek.

Jake's foggy memories and flashbacks began to gather again, and the scene of him at the seashore watching the birds flowed back. He sat alone, hair and beard showing signs of gray, enveloped in his own indulgent self-pity. As he scanned the distant horizon for fishing boats, his imagination traveled without destination. He found himself wiping the tears intermittently undulating down his face from his slightly swollen, wrinkled eye sockets, thinking about life gone by.

Jake watched the seagulls play in the sky as the salty sea mist cooled his face. Another memory came to mind. He always enjoyed the moment when his grandfather asked his awkward, young grandson to assist him in putting on his wooden leg. In the early years of Jake's life, he lived with his grandparents quite often while his parents were in the throes of a divorce.

Jake recalled putting on the large, soft, cotton stocking that covered his grandfather's stump. Then, Jake went over to the chair beside his grandpa's bed and carried his shiny, polished wooden leg to him. He helped him slip it on and strap it to his thigh and waist. Then Jake went over to the dresser drawer that he knew so well and picked out a set of socks for his grandpa to wear that day. He put the socks on his grandpa's feet: both the wooden foot and his natural one. Grandpa patted his oldest grandson on the head and smiled. Each time Jake felt his love even though he couldn't remember his grandfather ever telling him he loved him. Jake just knew it.

Yet another memory slipped into his thoughts. The whirlpools, down the slope in front of Jake, swirled among the rocky reef as if for a moment the marine life was caught up in a washing machine spin cycle. The tall, broad-shouldered, aging Marine just had to take a closer look. He rose up slowly from the weather-beaten, rough, stony place where he had been sitting and started down the trail to the beach. As he approached the tidal waters among the rocky shore, a hermit crab scampered across the light brownish-colored sand between the rocks, seemingly to seek shelter under crusty stones covered with small marine invertebrate animals enclosed inside spherical shells. He carefully kneeled down to join their world. As Jake was kneeling in the salty, foamy seawater, he couldn't help but notice the beautiful colors illuminating from the reef rocks around him. The purple spine sea urchins clustered about the stones and rocks. *There must be hundreds of them,* he thought. He gently put his rather large, thick finger in the center of one of them. The soft, slimy, spherical sea animal welcomed Jake into its world with a soft squeeze closing in on his index finger. He grinned, feeling a simple pleasure of life, if for only a moment of relief.

As Jake began to settle in, his strong muscular knees sank into the wet, swirling sand; with the keen sense of a sniper's eye, he watched the sea creatures' world and began to notice other interesting wildlife floating about in their busy little space.

He wondered how a wounded dolphin may feel knowing it is vulnerable prey to predators on the hunt at any moment. Or how an aging tortoise feels, swirling, stiff and slow, caught up in the surf coming to shore for rest, in a weak position and exposed. Jake's stalwart, sturdy body began to relax into the sand. *Do they sense these things of desperation?* he thought. *Is it the freedom in the ocean's deep abyss that releases them from such bondage?* He wondered whether or not animals commit suicide when they have had too much pain and abandonment, left alone feeling aged and wounded. *Why do dolphins and seals and whales intentionally beach themselves? Or do they? Have they had enough of life? Why do we, as the species of bipedal primates to which modern humans belong, struggle and endure a troubled life?* Jake's thoughts wandered. *What is my purpose here on earth?* Jake asked himself again and again.

Jake's swirling memory took him back to another time. Sarge was always troubled by those small voices in his head. The doctors at the Naval Hospital at Camp Pendleton Marine Base suggested that he suffered from post-traumatic stress disorder (PTSD). Sometimes Sarge felt that he had heavy emotional and personal problems. Other times he thought about his difficulties controlling his emotions and poor social skills. Jake couldn't keep a job. He had many. He often wondered about his persistent sadness, negative thoughts and disturbing ideas about suicide.

No counseling or therapy was mandated at the time when Sergeant Storm returned home from the war in Vietnam. He voiced concern about his changes in self-perception but only after years of suffering from feelings of helplessness, guilt and a sense of being completely different from other human beings. He felt isolated and like a loner most of the time. For years he had been experiencing alterations in relations with others, including distrust of almost anyone. Sudden loud noises—any number of things other people don't even notice—acted as a trigger back to his intense war experiences.

Nam took a lot out of this giant of a man. He was barely twenty years old when his Marine Company first arrived on the beachhead of Red Beach in Vietnam in 1965. He and his other Marine buddies were told their sole purpose was to provide protection to the American air base at Da Nang. In fact, the official directive was: "The U.S. Marine force will not engage in day-to-day actions against the Vietcong." However, as the U. S. expanded its build-up with additional bases south at Chu Lai and north at Phu Bai, these rules of limited engagement became increasingly difficult to maintain. Jake was a combat Marine. He was a "grunt" rifleman, rated expert on the range in Camp Matthews, trained to kill. He wanted and waited to use his keenly honed skills. Jake spent many hours cleaning and maintaining his battle equipment. He spent endless hours with his finely grained sedimentary rock used as a whetstone for sharpening razors and other cutting tools. He favored his eleven-inch, black carbon USMC Fighting Knife, which he had strapped to his leg bindings in its leather sheath. Jake was so proficient with this weapon he could throw and hit a marker on a tree twenty feet away.

The Vietcong set up strongholds in neighboring villages from where they launched attacks against Jake and his "search and destroy" unit. His command soon recognized that in order to protect the American bases, these pockets of resistance needed to be flushed out.

The former high school football all-American and graduate from Advanced Infantry Training at Camp Pendleton had waited patiently for this opportunity to demonstrate his leatherneck reputation.

The South Vietnamese Army had the responsibility of securing the countryside, but it was soon apparent they were not able to do so without assistance of American forces. Jake's company commander received word that the initial directive was expanded to allow Marines to work with the RVN soldiers but only in areas that were critical to U. S. security. Jake and his buddies knew that meant action was coming. The Marines were given permission to run offensive operations in areas that were critical to the security of their bases. Though these "search and destroy" missions did produce a limited amount of success, it was soon clear that this was not enough to ensure protection for the American troops and equipment in Vietnam. The Vietcong had a talent for vanishing into the hills, only to return after an area was declared secure.

In the Vietnam War, intelligence reports were never precise; Jake's company landed right in the middle of the Vietcong 60$^{th}$ Battalion and found itself surrounded. The VC let the first helicopters land without incident, then opened up on succeeding waves, a tactic they had used successfully against the South Vietnamese's Army. Three U.S. Army UH-1B helicopter gun ships were called in to strafe the VC stronghold: a small knoll called Hill 34. Meanwhile, Jake's patrol teams protected the landing zones until the full company had landed. The company commander ordered an assault on the hill by one platoon, but it quickly stalled. Regrouping his men, his platoon leader realized that he had happened upon a heavy concentration of Vietcong, ordered in strikes against Hill 34 and then assaulted it with all three of his platoons. Reinforced by close air support, Jake's rifle squads overran the enemy position, claiming six VC killed in action at one machine-gun position alone. Hill 34 was taken. It was here Jake received his first experience of how to kill. He was awarded a field promotion to the rank of Sergeant E-5. By the end of March 1965, the 9$^{th}$ Battalion numbered nearly 5,000 Marines at Da Nang, including two infantry battalions, two helicopter squadrons and supporting units. And so Sarge's combat legacy began.

Another memory came. In it, the fog at the beach had lifted and the ocean tides seemed peaceful and quiet. Jake often told the story of his yellow Labrador retriever. He had to put his dog to sleep after sixteen years of his daily sacrificial devotion. His dog died in his arms in a veterinarian's examining room. In many ways, he had a fonder affection toward the animal than toward anyone he knew. When his dog died, Jake was unable to function for days; he didn't speak or eat. At night he slumped in a rocking chair in the dark. He was paralyzed with grief. Jake had no tears left. There was no fanfare or wake or funeral procession for his closest buddy. His heart was broken beyond description once again.

Jake refocused on life as he'd seen it in the tide pool. In the memory he realized the red reef hermit crab had nestled along his leg, testing his skin softly with fire engine red pinchers. He began to wonder what she could be thinking. She was beautiful and feminine gliding in the surf, looking up at him with protruding yellow eyestalks. Most species of hermit crabs have long soft abdomens that are protected from predators by the adaptation of carrying around a salvaged empty seashell, into which the whole crab's body can retract. Most frequently hermit crabs utilize the shells of sea snails. This habit of living in a secondhand shell is what gave rise to the popular name "hermit crab," which is a reference to the idea of a hermit living alone in a small cave. Jake began to deliberate the notion that his life had been lived in a cave. *Sometimes I feel I am incapable of understanding the feelings of loneliness*, he thought. As he continued watching the hermit crab retreat to her cave, he reached out to gently touch her shell. *When am I going to stop running and come out of hiding?* he thought, as the tidal currents pulled on his body kneeling in the surf.

Suddenly, the muscles in his stomach started to tighten. Jake's teeth began to clench and his throat started to ache. He had to restrain himself from bellowing out. His body was fighting back, but somehow the war-torn veteran managed to suppress those sensitive feelings that were burning to escape the pain of so many years. Again and again, he continued to push down the feelings deep within. Jake had a major battle going on inside himself. His mind was reeling now. *I feel friendless! I feel alone in this battle. Who could care enough to really understand me? If I killed myself no one would miss me. It would end my pain. I will never forget the devastating agony and helplessness I felt the day my Marine buddy was killed by a sniper's bullet, blood gurgling out of his neck and down his face from his nose; my first smell of blood; the touch of hot fluid running through my fingers as I tried to stick my finger in the wound to stop the flow.*

Jake had been so young in battle, so confused and alone. His body was filled with fear, anger and rage. *Who wouldn't want to kill themselves?* he thought, remembering the American protesters. *It is all one can do to live with the memories of war from combat and now a battle must be fought back home against those I served and protected.* "Ooh-rah...that's bullshit!" Jake had moaned out loud, still remembering the hippie protesters four decades before.

Jake returned to his vision of the sea creatures. His tears had begun to run again, dripping off his nose into the tide pool. The turbulence within him began to hurt beyond description. He fought back again. He could hear the upheaval and expression of grief in his abdomen. For a brief moment this resilient Marine considered running from this peaceful place where the hermit crab lived. His depression deepened unbearably, and finally it seemed as though he was at the very bottom of the pit. His face distorted with anguish as he plunged his head into the tide pool. He opened his eyes under the salty seawater for a moment in the swirling current. Jake's eyes began to sting, but he didn't notice. He was focused on the thought of death and began to wonder what it would be like to hold his head and body under water and float away with the tide.

He sat up and pulled his head out of the water, still kneeling and sinking into the sandy beach around the rocks. Jake's head was drenched in salt water as he gasped for air and rose from the outgoing tide exclaiming, "I am a coward!" Thoughts raced through his head: *I am still alive, not allowing the retreating tide to engulf me and carry me out to sea to freedom's welcoming arms. Where are my Marine buddies? Why was it not me who took the sniper's bullets that pierced my best friend's neck?* Guilt permeated his heart and soul. "I have no need to live another day. Oh God, take me!" he screamed out. The echo of his words jumped between the rolling waves. He paused looking out over the ocean, wiping his eyes with the backs of his huge, age-marked hands.

Jake had felt himself shiver as a gust of cool, ocean spray seemed to swallow his thoughts when it covered his half-naked body kneeling in the surf. He watched the currents come and go. He quivered again for a moment as his thoughts returned to the empty, cold feelings of abandonment, rejection, shame and guilt drenching his life, entrenched in his mind. He began to remember how his heart was splintered into fragments as an adolescent growing up. Jake felt alone in this struggle. At the time, as the veteran squinted into the sunlight's glaring rays and stinging reflection from water's edge of the Pacific Ocean, he had stood up from the tide pool and turned to look over his shoulder, as if he was startled by a noise. Then he moved quickly down the beach.

Jake Storm considered his war trauma with caution, with its periods of mental disturbances reflecting his abnormal behavior and reoccurring evidence of post-traumatic stress disorder symptoms. He was told that to be true and he believed it to be so. Jake constantly wrestled with sequences of flashback images that appeared involuntarily, often a mixture of real and imaginary characters, places and events.

Much of Jake's knowledge and understanding about his psychological trauma came from the arena of war and rehabilitation recovery at the Naval Hospital at Camp Pendleton and the Veterans Administration Medical Center in Fresno, California, several years after he returned from his military tour in Southeast Asia. More corroboration came later from other sources and events such as civilian disasters; for instance, the foreign strike on American soil in New York City, 8:47 A.M. on Tuesday, September 11, 2001.

Jake mumbled to himself, his upper lip quivering, holding back emotion as he remembered wanting to suit up, boot up and go fight the enemy. Feelings from his war experience resurfaced. Some years back, Jake began drinking heavily. Whiskey helped him sleep. He knew he was warned about mixing some of his medications with booze, but he did it anyway. That traumatic day in September he drank until he passed out.

Jake had continued walking down the sloping, soft, sandy beach, still a bit unsettled by his revolving thoughts. He hesitated for a moment, crouched down and lunged toward an elongated stem-like structure. Aggressively he began stomping on the gas-filled bladders of sea kelp.

Under the weight of his huge feet, the bladders began to "pop" like gunshots. This seemed to amuse Jake. He managed a smile; he knew from instinct the enemy was close at hand.

Then Jake's face winced. He closed his eyes briefly as his thoughts of the past consumed him. The day had slipped away. For Jake, time had no meaning. An orange palate reflecting from the sun sent fiery rays skipping over the vast Pacific. As the sun slowly disappeared, an eerie fog bank had crept in and hovered near the shoreline, masking the colorful brightness. Jake kicked at a broken seashell lying lifeless on the sand and began walking farther down the beach. He disappeared into the misty fog bank, his strides somewhat crouched with heightened alertness. His pace quickened. Jake began to run, sprinting like a wild man, yelling to the fullness of his lungs until his throat burned. When he finally stopped he fell forward on his knees with outstretched arms, clutching at the sand with his beefy hands. He began to sob. His head lowered in anguish as his face settled into the sand; the powerful current of his hot breath blew a hollow cavity under his opened mouth into the sand. His teeth bit at the shore's coarse granules.

He rolled over on his back, spitting the sand out of his mouth. Jake quickly rolled back over into the prone position. His head suddenly tilted up slightly. His face penetrated the fog...elbows dug in. He quieted his breathing. He was Sarge again and his body became tense, perched like a cat ready to strike. Jake heard foreign voices approaching; he began hearing attack screams all too familiar. Sarge tilted his head again with his ear in the direction of the sounds. Almost as if in slow-motion, familiar looking Vietcong faces began to pop out of the fog bank. One appeared from the right flank, another from the left, coming right at him firing an AK-47. Sarge ducked, desperately searching for his weapon and for cover. He tried frantically to stand up and defend himself. He looked for his buddies for backup; he was alone.

Jake woke up. It was mid-afternoon. He was in his small apartment, dripping wet with perspiration, his body shaking. He found himself crouching on all fours under the top sheet and blanket of his bed covers. The heap of white sheets appeared as a large bundle lumped on his mattress. Suddenly he felt suffocated, trapped, held down by the weight of the covers. He panicked, tearing and tackling at the sheet with his brawny shoulders and arms. He lost his balance and rolled off the bed, hitting the wood-paneled floor. For a moment, Jake lost all sense of where he was. He labored to breathe. After a few moments, he rolled on his side and began looking around his small apartment. He shook his head trying to make sense out of what he had just experienced. *That same nightmare, again and again*, he thought. "Just too real, too much to take. I'm tired," he muttered to himself, shaking his head again and again as if to release the nightmarish dream from his mind. Still on his side, leaning limply on his right elbow, his head partly raised, Jake began scanning the apartment as if he was looking for something familiar.

His eyes suddenly focused in on his side table, next to the bed. Anxiously he began pushing and kicking the sheet covers away and off his naked legs. He scooted himself across the lacquer-polished floorboards, then Jake reached up and opened the table drawer. He extended his long arm into the drawer, shuffling around with his hand. He paused; his arm stopped moving as if he had found what he was looking for.

The raw cold metal was in his grip. Jake pulled the heavy misty-gray, single-action, semi-automatic pistol from the side table drawer. His cold steel weapon was a standard-issue sidearm for the United States armed forces. Jake knew it well. In fact, he could tear it down and reassemble it blindfolded in under a minute. In Vietnam, he wore it as a sidearm every day even when he was sleeping. During the war, Jake, when he was called Sarge, had carried it cradled in a well-linseed-oiled, cowhide-leather shoulder holster hanging under his left arm. His weapon had saved his life and others' lives during several firefights and close combat encounters on Hill 34.

Jake was still sitting on the floor leaning against his bed. He stared at his weapon resting in his lap. The custom leather-wrapped pistol grip was indenting and creasing into his thigh, the barrel pointing between his bare legs. He knew its exact weight and length. He mumbled out loud, "2.437 pounds empty, without the magazine in it and 8.25 inches in length including the 5.03 inch barrel." He grinned realizing it had been many years since he learned all about this weapon and he still could recall the information. He grunted, "Ooh-rah, *Semper Fi*, good buddies." Jake's eyes rolled back under his eyelids as his head tilted backward, face toward the ceiling. Once again tears began rolling over his chiseled cheekbones, repelling down his beard. He tightened his grip on his weapon until his hands turned white, bloodless, throbbing with emotion in his veins. Then, with blurry eyes, he looked down and pushed the clip release on his weapon, dropping the clip into his hand as he intently studied it on the way down. Jake's head jerked to the right abruptly and he looked at the apartment's misty, dirt-stained window. The window was glowing with sunlight. He thought he saw a shadow passing by the window. Jake startled easily from offbeat sounds and rapid movements around him. His mind drifted off for a moment as he recalled the day he was told that he had post-traumatic stress disorder and that these types of reactions and reflexes may stay with him his entire lifetime. He made a half-nasal, deep sound in his throat as if he were annoyed and dismissed the thought as unimportant. *Seven rounds,* he contemplated as if taking a quick ammo count before a firefight in country. *Standard-capacity magazine, muzzle velocity 800 feet per second; effective range seventy-five yards on a good day. Today is a good day to die,* he thought.

Jake raised the full clip in front of his face and studied the single round protruding like a torpedo ready for launch at the top of the casing. Then he quickly jammed the magazine clip back into the pistol handle, pulled back the slide sending the bullet into the chamber, cocked the weapon and released the safety all in a two-second motion. The tired, confused warrior slowly closed his eyes and rested his head back against the bed mattress. Jake sat there leaning against his bed for several minutes. His eyes remained closed tightly. Methodically, Jake slowly lifted his cold steel .45 pistol up toward his head, bringing the gray barrel upward under his chin and moving it rhythmically back-and-forth from his whiskered chin to his throat. Tears began again to trickle from his eyes. He pushed the barrel up under his chin as his index finger danced around the trigger, grazing it slightly. Jake slowly began to position his knees up against his chest, resting his right forearm on his right knee. The weapon was in place. His breathing became rapid; his entrenched hand began to quiver. Time passed. And then suddenly, for no apparent reason, he began to relax his position. Jake lowered his sidearm to the floor still loaded and ready to fire. He exhaled and yelled out, "If there is a God I need you now…not tomorrow, not next year…right now, God!" Jake dropped his head between his elevated knees and began to cry feverously.

After several heart-wrenching moments Jake paused, his eyes swollen and barely open. Suddenly he began to perk up, sitting alert and poised as if waiting for a sign or someone. There was nothing. No words, no sign, no one. He waited and sat on the floor against his bed for hours until the sun's streaking rays disappeared from the misty window. Darkness once again fell upon Jake's small apartment. Another day had passed.

Jake struggled to stand up. He grabbed the bedpost for balance. His legs were weak and numb from sitting for hours in awkward positions on the floor. He stumbled toward the bathroom to find the light switch. He carried the loaded weapon in his right hand, arm hanging straight down along his side. He swiped at the wall with his large hand then slapped for the light switch several times. Finally the light went on. As he pivoted through the bathroom doorway the sink mirror loomed ominous. Jake grabbed the sink basin and pulled himself closer to stare directly into his own bloodshot eyes. His face was only inches from the mirror. His breath ricocheting off the mirror smelled of stale whiskey. He leaned forward touching his nose to the glass, pushing harder and harder. His nose began to flatten out. The force he exerted also began to flatten his lips. The reflection of his eyes came together and centered on his nose. He froze in that position for several minutes and closed his eyes tightly.

Suddenly, his eyes opened forcefully. Jake pushed himself arm's length from the mirror fixedly staring at him. Slowly but deliberately he raised his loaded weapon and pushed the muzzle against the glass right between his eyes. "Who are you?" he screamed. "Don't look at me like that! I did everything I could to save him; and the others …," he gritted his teeth. He spit at himself in the mirror. His speech garbled, he said, "Why am I alive? You torture me!"

Early on in Jake Storm's initial days of PTSD discovery and treatment planning, he received many hours of therapy and group counseling for survivor's guilt as well as for the flashbacks and nightmares he experienced from the ugly, dehumanizing trauma seen in combat ambushes and firefights. The bloodcurdling screams of the fatally wounded—"Doc, over here. I'm hit, I'm hit"—the smell of diesel, the whistle of incoming missiles, the "pop" of a sniper's bullet, the smell and stench of death all haunted Jake. Several times in treatment he was asked about suicide ideation. At the time he felt immune to the possibility of taking his own life; but, years had passed.

Jake, still leaning on the sink basin in front of the mirror, heard a solid, hard knuckle knock on the apartment's wood-paneled door. His head jerked wildly to the left to look out the bathroom door into the bedroom. He paused. The noise startled Jake who rarely had visitors at this hour or at any time for that matter. He quickly shuffled sidestep across the bedroom as if guarding a dribbling basketball player and then crouched to look around the corner and out the slightly opened bedroom door toward the front door. Jake still had his cocked and loaded weapon in his right hand. He waited. Jake tilted his head and ear in the direction of the noise to pick up any slight movement coming from outside the doorway.

A second knock came accompanied by a familiar voice, "Sarge? Sarge, it's Corporal Rodriquez. I am in your men's group at the veteran's center. Remember I fought with you in Nam?" An eerie silence filled the air. Jake continued to glare hypnotically at the front door with beaming eyes as if he could see through it. "Sarge," the corporal continued, "I haven't seen you in group for weeks. I came over tonight to see if you are alright." Jake moved cautiously toward the front door raising his weapon behind his back with his right hand and tucking the barrel of the .45 into the waistband of his skivvies.

Jake put his head against the door. "Rodriquez, what's up?" The door remained closed. "Sarge, may I come in for a minute? I have something I want to give you." Jake slowly opened the door with his left hand. The corporal was standing in the hallway and had what appeared to be an envelope in his hand. Jake opened the door only slightly to look out, standing behind it.

"Hey, Sarge, *Semper Fi!* I received this letter in the mail from Veteran Affairs last week and thought you may want to take a look at it." Jake looked at him, searching for something to say. Nothing came to mind. Then, he looked down at the envelope in the corporal's hand. Rodriquez raised the envelope up to his former Marine rifle team squad leader. Jake took the envelope and looked back at him with an empty stare.

"I have your back, Sarge. I owe you my life...ooh-rah!" The corporal saw it was not a good time for his Marine buddy. He turned and began to walk away. Ever so slightly and under his breath, Jake managed, "Ooh-rah, Rodriquez, *Semper Fi.*" The corporal heard Sarge's words, but never turned around. Tears began to well in Rodriquez's eyes as he walked away down the hall. Jake closed the door with the weight of his large body leaning against it and his forehead touching the panels. Jake pounded his forehead into the back of the door several times, then his balled fist.

Sergeant Jake Storm was at a crossroads. He turned away from the door pulling the .45 he was squeezing in his right hand from inside the elastic waistband of his boxers and found the closest chair and flopped down. Jake was exhausted. He stared at the loaded pistol in his hand for a couple of minutes and set it on the table next to the chair. The white envelope rested on his lap. Jake rested his aching head back against the upholstered chair. *What was Rodriquez thinking?* he thought. Tired of fighting his demons, Jake closed his eyes and fell asleep.

The next morning, still slumped in his chair, Jake opened the envelope and read the one-page letter inside:

Department of Veteran Affairs
Under Secretary for Health
Washington, DC 20420

Dear Veteran,

If you're experiencing an emotional crisis and need to talk with a trained VA professional, the **National Suicide**

Prevention toll-free hotline number, 1-800-273-TALK
(8255), is now available twenty-four hours a day, seven
days a week. You will be immediately connected with a
qualified and caring provider who can help.

<u>Here are some suicide warning signs:</u>

1. Threatening to hurt or kill yourself
2. Looking for ways to kill yourself
3. Seeking access to pills, weapons and other self
   destructive behavior
4. Talking about death, dying or suicide

*The presence of these signs requires immediate attention.* If
you or a veteran you care about has been showing any of
these signs, do not hesitate to call and ask for help!

<u>Additional warning signs may include:</u>

1. Hopelessness
2. Rage, anger, seeking revenge
3. Acting reckless or engaging in risky activities,
   seemingly without thinking
4. Increasing alcohol or drug abuse
5. Feeling trapped—like there's no way out
6. Withdrawing from friends and family
7. Anxiety, agitation, inability to sleep—or, excessive
   sleepiness
8. Dramatic mood swings
9. Feeling there is no reason for living, no sense of
   purpose in life

Please call the **toll-free hotline number, 1-800-273-TALK
(8255)** if you experience any of these warning signs.

We'll get you the help and assistance you need right
away!

Sincerely yours,
Michael J. Kussman, MD, MS, MACP


Jake's eyes scanned the letter quickly top to bottom. *What was
Rodriquez thinking?* he repeated. *Why did he give me this letter?* He
mused. Gazing thoughtfully back to the beginning of the letter, he began
to read it out loud to himself. He hesitated at several points. When he had
finished reading the letter a second time, his hands grasping the sides of
the paper dropped onto his lap. Jake clenched his teeth. He was trying to
endure the message he was getting loud and clear. *Get help, Sergeant
Storm. Get help now before it is too late.*

A month earlier Jake's youngest sister, Samantha, came by to visit
and check up on her big brother. She visited from time to time, inviting
him to church and wanting to talk about their good childhood memories
and the Bible. She left spiritual tracks and booklets for him to read. He
never could bring himself to open them up. He threw them in the bottom drawer of his dresser. Jake remembered her saying, "I am not talking
about religious doctrines or affiliations, Jake. I am talking about a personal relationship. There is a huge difference. There is hope and healing in
Jesus." Jake never really understood what she meant by a personal relationship with Jesus. He knew his sister meant well and shrugged it off.

Jake's sister Samantha was his favorite. He came from a family with
three sisters and a younger half brother. His youngest sister always looked up
to him. From the time she began to walk and talk, her big brother meant
everything to her. When they were growing up, Jake always gave her a lot of
attention and took her with him everywhere. He will never forget the time
when he first retuned home from boot camp Marine Corps Recruiting
Depot in San Diego, head shaven and starving to be treated to something
special. His kid sister ran into the kitchen and came out with a plate piled
high with bologna sandwiches, his favorite. Sam was the only family member

who kept in touch with him over the years, always tracking him down and trying to look after her brother. She knew he was still struggling to adapt in the painful years after he returned from Vietnam. In fact, it was Sam who was the prime factor that led to Jake coming out of the mountains.

Jake rejected the notion of religion. Oh, he always said he believed in God. Certainly most combat warriors he served with including himself had foxhole religion when the heat was on in a firefight or incoming motor rounds were blazing and shells were exploding and sending hot chucks of steel everywhere around them. Yet for Sarge and so many other seasoned combat veterans, believing in something unseen, something or someone they can't touch or hear or trust is difficult at best. They are survivors of the killing fields. Most had to rely on their own skills and strength to get through the bloody battles. For many, anything spiritual was a foreign thought.

Jake's sister told him, "Jake, it is a matter of faith and belief that you could begin to realize God's forgiving Grace talked about in the New and Old Testaments. The Bible says in the book of Romans 10:17, 'So then faith cometh by hearing, and hearing by the word of God.'"

Each time she visited her brother, Sam read to him from the Bible. Another Bible verse she read her brother many times was from the Old Testament, Book of Isaiah, 41:13, "For I the Lord thy God will hold thy right hand, saying unto thee, Fear not; I will help thee."

Samantha had left her brother a Bible many years before, with his name inscribed in the lower right corner of the front cover. It also found its place in the bottom drawer of the dresser, never opened. It wasn't that Jake didn't want to open the bottom drawer, read the book and discover what his sister was talking about. He trusted her more than any human being. Her love was unquestionable. She was always there for him; but, he was stuck. Spiritually he felt empty. Psychologically he wasn't able to function without help from antidepressants and doctors. After time, alcohol became his crutch.

Jake's apartment was near an old, ivy-covered stone church building on a corner. Every Sunday morning he could hear the ring of the bells coming from the church bell tower across the street. Jake seldom paid much attention to it. He had adapted to his environment. *Just another disturbing noise*, he thought, an *agonizing loud sound too early in the morning.*

On two occasions in the three years he had lived in the neighborhood, Jake found himself walking across the street to the church on
Sunday morning looking into the sanctuary out of curiosity. He found it
to be a beautiful place filled with colorful stained glass windows. *Not so
threatening*, he thought, but left anyway. This occurred coincidently only
days after his sister's visits. One Sunday morning, he found the courage
to sit in a pew at the very back of the church hoping to go unnoticed.
He listened to the music and choir singing, even stayed for the sermon.
He watched what others were doing: when they stood up and when they
sat. He followed along to fit in.

Picking up the Veteran Affairs letter again, Jake studied it well into
the hour. He read the words "If you're experiencing an emotional crisis and
need to talk" over and over again. His eyes zeroed in on sentences:
"Threatening to hurt or kill yourself", "Looking for ways to kill yourself",
"seeking access to pills, weapons and other self-destructive behavior." The
words "The presence of these signs requires immediate attention" jumped
off the page. He glanced over and for a brief minute studied his loaded .45
still sitting on the end table, left untouched from the night before.

Jake never really opened up and shared his true feelings with anyone in all the years he attended veteran groups and therapy. He felt there
was no use. He felt safer keeping the emotions to himself. Jake never was
one to believe in shrinks. Not even nice ones. He went to all these things
not necessarily because he wanted to, but because he had to in order to
receive his sleeping pills and pain relievers. And besides, he had promised
his sister that he would keep going. Jake didn't want his little sis to worry
about him, but she did anyway.

As Jake's eyes continued down the VA letter, once again he read out
loud with heightened emphasis, picking out only certain words that
caught his attention: "hopelessness"…"feeling trapped"…"withdrawing
from friends and family"…"feeling there is no reason for living, no sense
of purpose in life." He squinted his eyes in deep thought.

It happened to be another Sunday morning. Jake lifted himself up out
of the chair and walked over to the window. He looked around the studio
apartment, simple and modest. He couldn't afford to pay much out of his

100 percent disability check. The apartment faced the same street the church was on. He leaned forward a bit to get a better look down the street. *Humm…some people are gathering in front of the main door of the church*, he thought. He looked back at the clock on the wall; it was 8:37 A.M. Jake knew the church bells would ring at 9 A.M. He paused. Turning slightly he looked out the window again, then looked back at the clock on the wall; it read 8:41 A.M. Suddenly, Jake decided he would go to the church service.

Approaching the church grounds, Jake began feeling unsettled inside. His heart began to ache, his stomach twisted. Jake arrived at the church just in time for the tower bells to ring. After a few minutes he proceeded to make his way to the rear of the church. He looked around. He picked out a pew bench that looked safe; his back would be to the outer wall. Jake still could not sit in public places unless his back was against a wall. He felt safer sitting that way. He sat down. The church began to fill up. Jake had wished many times he could tell a minister about his pain, but he was afraid. Instead he went to church a couple of times and sat in the back to look from a safe distance.

As he waited for the opening hymn, he began looking high above the altar. A very large white cross hung suspended diagonally from the ceiling. *It is beautiful*, he thought. As he stared up at the cross, the organist began to play. Jake's eyes began to fill uncontrollably with tears. *What is going on here?* he thought, a bit concerned. He had experienced some tears during the last visit to this church. *Surely this is nothing new or out of the ordinary.* In the past, Jake remembered having had a comfortable feeling when entering the doors of this church. *So what is the big deal now?*

The church for Jake felt like a safe haven—a sanctuary away from the maddening crowds of people and fast-paced society that tore at his soul. It seemed the pressures and troubles of the world faded away while he sat there. He could not quite understand that peaceful feeling.

The choir was singing now. Jake looked around, carefully and guarded, so no one nearby could see the tears he was fighting back. The hymns were upbeat, full of praise and worship. He searched through his blurry vision trying desperately to find another's teary eyes; however, he could not. *So why am I crying?* he asked himself.

Suddenly, the muscles in Jake's stomach began to tense up. His teeth tightened down on one another. Jake had to restrain from shouting out. He bullishly fought back, somehow managing to suppress those sensitive feelings that were fervently trying to escape; the years of suppressed pain were overwhelming. Again and again, Jake continued to push down the eruption ready to happen. The church service continued.

Jake Storm had a major battle going on inside himself. *What is happening to me?* he asked himself in desperation. *I cannot ever remember feeling this torn up. I feel alone in this battle—abandoned. Who could care enough to really understand me? Men died on my watch in Vietnam; how do I live with that? Who cares about the abandonment and rejection I received when I was a child or the abuse and cruelty of being separated and sent away from my family when I was seven years old? I am fatherless. Who could possibly forgive an alcoholic who used and abused so many people for so many years? How could I ever forget the devastating pain and helplessness I felt the day the sheriff came and took my boys away from me, because I was too drunk and out of control to be allowed to be their father? Who could love or forgive such a man?*

The tears continued to run. The turbulence within him began to churn. He fought back again. This proud warrior felt the throbbing of grief in his heart. *I can go on no longer,* he thought.

For a brief moment Jake considered running out of the church as the pastor was preaching his sermon. He was crying out from inside, *Oh God, help me. I need you.*

The sermon seemed to take forever. Jake was waiting for something to happen. He needed something to happen. Then he remembered the letter he was given by Corporal Rodriquez. He now understood he needed help. And he needed help from God.

The pastor issued an invitation to come to the altar for those who wanted God in their lives, his forgiveness and eternal salvation. Jake began thinking ahead. *The moment has arrived. This is the moment my little sis has been talking about all these years. The time is now. This must be it. The sign from God has come to me. I feel it.*

As the pastor's invitation rang out among the congregation, Jake hesitated. He looked around. No one had come forward. A million thoughts raced through Jake's confused brain. *What will everyone think about me—that I'm weak, less than a man? Look at that big combat-hardened Marine vet, Devil Dog, leatherneck, macho man on his knees at the altar, crying like a baby?* Time was passing. Jake's feet would not move. He began leaning in the direction of the aisle, hoping his feet would follow to the altar. They did not. He felt numb all over. The man who fought so many firefights and had so many kills could not move an inch. He was frozen in place. Tears streamed down his cheeks.

The church service ended. The congregation began to file out. Jake quickly wiped his tearstained eyes on his shirtsleeves. His mind raced. *I must regain my composure on the way out. What will everyone think of my eyes all puffy and red? They will know I was crying. Not the manly thing to do.*

Slowly moving out of the main sanctuary into the foyer, Jake's tears returned. This time he was far too weak to fight them off again. The emotion was too much; he quickly turned on his heel to escape attention and hurriedly headed toward a small door twenty feet away.

Just as his hand landed on the door handle, the volcano began to erupt from deep within Jake's body and soul. He opened the door not knowing what to expect and quickly shut the door behind him. No one was there. He had entered a prayer chapel.

The chapel was a small, dimly lit room with a dozen wooden pews and a short aisle to the modest altar. The cross on the wall seemed larger than life and beamed with a radiance that Jake will never forget. His eyes were swollen with tears. His legs became weak. He could not move another inch—not even the short distance to the altar. Jake fell to the floor on his knees and crawled the rest of the way.

Driven to his knees in front of the radiant cross, Jake cried out with a burst of emotion, "God forgive me. Please forgive me, oh God, forgive me. I need you in my life, I am a killer of men; worthless and not worthy to live another day." Jake began rocking back and forth on his knees, almost out of control. The floodgates continued to spew forth both tears and his prayers for help. He was emotionally spent. Nevertheless, Jake sensed something felt different around him. A quiet calm began to come over him.

Stopping his prayers out loud, Jake was silent. The only noise in the room was Jake's occasional sighs from exhaustion. Jake remained on his knees in the same position where it all began several minutes earlier in what seemed like a lifetime.

Jake's gruff, bearded chin was still resting on his chest, his hands remaining clasped in prayer and his body slumped on the floor. His knees could no longer hold up his six-foot-four-inch, 250-pound frame. He tried to get up, but nothing worked. His legs had no strength; they would not move. Jake leaned over to the nearest pew and began pulling himself up onto the seat. He rested for a moment. An unspeakable burden was removed from his shoulders that day.

Finally, Jake left the little chapel in the church and walked back to his apartment. As he opened his door, he glanced down the hallway as if looking for Corporal Rodriquez and thinking about the last words he had said to him as he walked away, *I have your back, Sarge.*

Entering his apartment, Jake looked around surveying the front room. His eyes focused on the weapon on the side table and the opened letter and envelope sitting right next to it. He studied the scene for a moment then walked into the bathroom. As he passed the mirror over the sink, he hesitated and looked at himself facing slightly sideways, turning his head. He managed a weak smile and rubbed his bearded chin with his hand.

Still in the bathroom, Jake cooled his face with water. He walked into the small kitchen; typical of a bachelor's pad, there were a few unwashed dishes in the sink. Sitting on his kitchenette table was an empty whiskey bottle. The wall telephone was unplugged and the wall jack hung loosely from the wall mounting. He opened up the refrigerator. *Not much in there,* he thought. *Have to get to the market.* He pulled out a half-opened package of lunch meat and threw it on the table. A loaf of white bread was sitting in the corner cabinet. Jake had lost his appetite through much of his ordeal. Normally Jake was a big eater, but not in recent weeks. He found eating interfered with his drinking. At this point, though, he felt hungry. Jake sat down at the table and threw together a bologna sandwich. As he began to chow down the sandwich, his first meal in several days, he thought about his sister Sam. *She would have wanted to be with me this morning. I owe her my life.*

After Jake finished the sandwich, he got up from the table and went into the other room to get the letter from the VA. As he picked it up from the table he bumped the custom grip of the .45, spinning it around. He noticed the hammer remained back and ready to fire. The safety was off. Jake reached down to retrieve his weapon. He carefully uncocked the hammer with his right thumb and put the safety in place. He walked into his bedroom, opened the drawer to the side table and placed the revolver back where he normally kept it.

Then he walked away, back to the kitchen table. Once again he began to read the letter from the Veteran Affairs Department. "Dear Veteran"...*that would be me*, he thought sarcastically. Jake looked over the letter again from top to bottom bouncing back and forth from one section to the next but always stopping at "Please call the toll-free hotline number 1-800-273-TALK( 8255)." He was curious now. *How can they help me? I am already on meds and see a VA doc for five minutes every other month. What more can I need?* Jake suddenly got serious and thought for a minute. *I do have many of these symptoms and warning signs laid out in this letter. Who walks around with a loaded gun to his head...drinking himself to death?*

Jake turned a bit in his kitchen chair and looked at the telephone hanging loosely on the wall. He just sat there and stared at it for what seemed the longest time. His mind began to flash back. Jake began thinking about the times as a young man he spent with his grandparents. His granddad had a rather large garden in the backyard of his house and kept thin, green bamboo sticks for his potted plants. Jake was alone most of the time, so he had a huge make-believe world and the run of the backyard. He used the sticks as swords and bows and arrows, pretending to be a great warrior. Little did he know at the time he was in training for more serious battles.

His mind came back to the present. Jake moved over and reached for the telephone on the kitchen wall. With the other hand he pushed the modular plug into the wall jack. He clicked the phone switch a couple of times and put the receiver to his ear...dial tone.

Then Sergeant Jake Storm made the call: 1-800-273-TALK. The phone rang at the other end. Jake suddenly felt some fear. *What will I say? How can I trust this person I have never seen?*

"Hello, you have reached the National Veterans Suicide Prevention Hotline. My name is Kevin. How may I help you today?... Hello?... Hello?"

Jake hit the switch and disconnected the call. He hung up the phone. "Shit!" he said shaking his head radically left and right. He put his head in his hands, elbows on the table. "Shit, shit, shit!" *How tough is this?* he thought. *Well, Sergeant, you can't shoot yourself...now you can't even make a phone call...pretty pathetic! And you call yourself a warrior. Get real! F— me!*

Jake settled down in the next minutes, walked into the bathroom again to take a break. Then he went back into the living room and sat down in the chair. He switched on the television with the remote control, flipped through the channels and looked at them with a blank stare. He turned it off. "I can do this," he said. "I can do it for Sam...hell, for me." Jake made the call again: 1-800-273-TALK. There was ringing. *What if it's the same guy, Kevin or whatever his name was?*

"Hello, you have reached the National Veterans Suicide Prevention Hotline. My name is Susan. How may I help you?...Hello?"

Jake began to speak. "I am a disabled Vietnam vet."

"What is your first name?" Susan asked.

"Why do you need to know that?" Jake responded quickly and somewhat agitated.

"Because I told you mine—is that fair?" she said.

"Jake is my name."

"Well, Jake, how may I help you today?"

"I don't know exactly. I am thinking some strange things the last few days. I have nightmares...can't sleep much," Jake shared.

"Are you thinking about suicide?" the hotliner responded.

"I was last night," Jake answered.

"Have you done anything to hurt yourself today?" Susan replied.

"No," said Jake.

"What has changed since last night?" Susan asked inquisitively.

"Church," Jake replied. "I went to church this morning."

"Will you tell me about church, Jake? What happened at church this morning?" the hotline responder asked.

"I had a good conversation with God, that is what happened," Jake replied.

"How are you feeling right now? Are you drinking alcohol or taking any other drugs?" Susan asked.

"No booze today. As for the pills…just taking my antidepressants and anxiety pills that don't seem to work anymore. That's for my PTSD stuff," Jake replied.

"Do you have a gun?" Susan asked.

"Yes," Jake said responding quickly.

"Where is the gun right now, Jake?" Susan continued.

"In my bedroom side table drawer," Jake said.

"Where are the bullets kept?" Susan continued the inquiry.

"In the clip of my .45, which is in my weapon," Jake replied.

"Have you ever attempted suicide?" the hotline responder asked.

"No, but I think about giving up. Last night I almost did it. I have no reason for living. I have nothing to live for. I am just a burden to society and my sister. She worries about me, I know. She always has. She is the most important person in my life. If I am not around she won't have to worry about her big brother," Jake responded.

"Jake, is there any way someone can come over and take your gun somewhere else, out of your hands, just for awhile until I can get you some help? A neighbor or relative perhaps?" Susan asked.

"No, just my sister, but she lives an hour away," Jake replied. "I wouldn't want to involve her in this. She has a family. She would really be sick with worry if she knew about this. I can't do that to her."

"Our conversations and records are all very private and confidential. Your sister won't be involved unless you want her to be," Susan said. "But you would kill yourself? You don't think that would devastate your sister, Jake?" Susan was getting a little testy. Jake was silent. Susan decided to back off.

"Tell me more about your suicide thoughts, Jake…what's been happening in your life to make you feel this way?" Susan asked.

"I'm just tired of living. I have trouble sleeping; I have nightmares and flashbacks about things that happened decades ago in Nam. The only way I can get to sleep is by filling up with pills and booze…I have a VA psych doc, but he only has time to see me every other month and then for just a few minutes. He gives me more pills or ups the dosages and sends me home. I'm not blaming him. He is a nice guy. All the docs over the years have been the same. They are medical doctors who hand out pills; psychiatrists. What the hell do they know about the stink of body decay and death and emotional pain of watching a buddy die in my arms? But for all the years I have been coming to the VA for so-called treatment, nobody seems to really care, I mean really care about what happens to me. Back in the 1960s, '70s and even '80s, we Vietnam vets got the short end of the stick. Today, we old guys get stuck in a group with a bunch of younger vets and all of them talk about their war stories. I am sick of war stories…sick of them!"

"Tell me more about the men's groups you have been in lately, Jake," Susan said emphatically.

"You want to hear it, Susan? Really hear it?" Jake's voice elevated.

"Yes," Susan responded. "But, Jake, we can talk about it only with the understanding that you don't get all worked up and upset. Slow down and just talk to me; don't yell. I am trying to understand how I can get you the help you need right now. Okay? Jake, just talk to me."

"Susan, I don't need to hear about those people in Iraq or Afghanistan; I have my own stories and memories about Victor Charlie and the gooks of Vietnam. Hell, I was killing gooks before some of those guys were born. How about someone helping me get rid of some of these demons I carry around with me day in and day out. That's what is driving me up a wall. I can't stop the damn dreams and flashbacks—the lit-up faces and lifeless eyes. That's just the beginning, Susan," Jake said.

"Jake, where are you living right now?" the responder inquired.

"You mean my address?" Jake seemed annoyed.

"No, Jake, what is your living situation? Do you have money to have a place to live?" she asked caringly.

"Yes, I am on 100 percent disability," Jake said. "Not much money but enough to keep me off the streets, for now anyway."

"Jake, I want to get you some help today, right now. I can have you transported to a safe environment in ten minutes if you will give me some information like your address and phone number and date of birth. Will you do that?" Susan asked.

"No way, Susan! I can get around on my own. No EMTs for me. Thanks but no thanks," Jake said insistently. "I'm okay today. The gun is in the drawer; I'm not going to kill myself. I am feeling much better after church this morning. I just called to talk to someone and find out what this suicide crisis hotline was all about. A buddy gave me this letter saying to call the hotline if I need help. Well, I need help but not an ambulance."

"Okay, Jake. I am very glad to hear you are feeling better. But I would like to refer you to a suicide crisis prevention coordinator—Bill Elliott, a VA Medical Center psychologist. He is a specialist in war trauma and PTSD treatment planning. I can arrange for him to contact you if you will give me your phone number and address. He can make arrangements with you to come by your place for a visit and talk with you about some of your concerns. Can we do that?" Susan asked.

"That sounds alright, Susan. I will agree to do that...but no ambulance," Jake requested.

"No ambulance, I promise, Jake. Now I need your address, phone number and date of birth and I will have Dr. Elliott get in touch with you in twenty-four hours or less. Sound good?"

"That's alright. Thanks for your help, Susan," Jake responded.

"Jake, please always remember, if you ever need help and support in the future, don't hesitate to call us again, any time 24/7. We are here for you. Welcome home!"

Jake connected with Bill Elliott the next day. Today, Jake is reunited with his family. He has happily discovered he is a grandfather. Jake spends countess hours each week at the Veterans Center helping and counseling other veterans, old and young alike. He shares with them his experience, strength and hope.

Sergeant Jake Storm continues to address his PTSD and alcohol dependency recovery and treatment at the VA, but now he sees his treatment in a different light. He is beginning to understand that living life is a matter of balance and his spiritual condition is as big a part of that as his physical and mental development. He is not running away from anything today—he is running toward new experiences.

Jake has joined a newly formed Vietnam Vets group at his local Veterans Center. He chooses to attend 12-step meetings for his alcohol dependency. Sarge has been spending time reconnecting with Corporal Rodriquez and meeting his family for the first time.

Jake has returned to that small church across the street from his apartment. He is now an usher and greeter at Sunday church services. When the bells toll at 9 A.M. a whole new meaning comes with that sound for Jake—the sound of hope. In fact, this once suicidal veteran with the wounded soul has asked the church pastor to be in charge of ringing the bells on Sunday mornings.

# Chapter 13

# The Psychological Wounds of War

What is happening to our combat veterans? Extremely disturbing experiences that cause severe emotional shock confront many competent, healthy, stalwart, honorable veterans. When enlisting to fight for his or her country, no one can completely guarantee to protect him or her from traumatic combat experiences or the psychological wounds that may result from such exposure.

Many veterans have ongoing psychological and physiological difficulties following exposure to combat. Veterans who react to war traumas are not going mad. They are experiencing symptoms and difficulties that are connected with having been in emotionally charged situations. Witnessing the death and destruction of people, places and things is something that has serious effects on the psyche. Our troops are not trained or prepared in boot camp for such severe psychological impact. Having critical symptoms after a traumatic event is not a sign of personal weakness. Many psychologically well-adjusted and physically healthy veterans develop PTSD. Many people develop post-traumatic stress after being exposed to severe traumas.

When you or someone you care about can recognize trauma symptoms, you can become less fearful and better able to manage the symptoms. By understanding the effects of the emotional shock and knowing more about symptoms, a combat warrior is better able to decide to get treatment.

If you or someone close to you is a returning combat veteran having difficulty readjusting to civilian life, you may be concerned and wondering what's going on. *Why am I angry all the time? Why am I feeling detached and isolated? No one understands me. I feel hopeless and alone. At least in combat I had my squad; my buddies had my back. They are all gone now. I feel empty and hopeless.*

The critical distinction is between a veteran's thoughts regarding death and suicide and actually wanting to die. When I hear from a veteran that he or she wants to die, I refer to these thoughts as suicidal ideation and divide them into two categories:

- Suicidal ideation can be active and involve a current desire and plan to die.
- Suicidal ideation can be passive and involve a desire to die, but without a plan to bring about one's death.

Suicide ideation may involve thoughts, contemplations, fantasies and obsessions in which you or someone you care about invents themes and stories with his or her suicidal death. A strong feeling without a realistic basis that death is going to happen or anxious feelings of dying does not satisfy the definition. An example of such a situation may include the veteran provoking an act of violent behavior or acting like he or she has been stricken with a life-threatening disease.

A veteran's concerned friend or partner should inquire directly about thoughts of suicide. Contrary to predictable sensitivity, asking about suicidal thoughts or plans does not put the idea in another's mind. If you are concerned that your veteran loved one may be depressed or suicidal, then ask in a direct and caring manner. You might simply say, "You seem very down to me and I'm concerned. Is everything all right?

Are you experiencing thoughts about death or suicide?" If you recognize symptoms of depression or suicide in yourself, confide in a trusted person who will assist you in finding help or consult your physician who can recommend treatment.

Suicidal thoughts can be very disturbing, especially when accompanied by depression, other mental illnesses, alcohol or drug abuse or plans to take one's life. This situation demands immediate attention. These thoughts can indicate serious mental illness.

One example of an active desire and plan to die is depicted in Joe's story in chapter 8. Joe's friend called the hotline, because Joe had sent him a farewell note, in which Joe stated he had nothing left to live for. Joe suffered from PTSD and TBI and felt rejected and worthless. Joe's note explained his desire to die and that he had already burned his medals, commendations and ribbons.

Several military media reports and other medical research suggests that about 30 percent of soldiers who have returned home from combat in Iraq and Afghanistan have shown signs of post-traumatic stress disorder and, in many cases, traumatic brain injury.

Unlike previous wars, few of our warriors have been shot. As I've indicated earlier, the primary weapon of the Iraq War—the improvised explosive device (IED)—has left a signature wound: traumatic brain injury, better known as TBI. Soldiers hit in the head or knocked out by blasts often don't display visible wounds, but a murkiness of the war experience in their minds. They can be confused, muddled or irritable; depressed and unaware they are impaired.

A recent study of incoming wounded troops at Walter Reed Army Medical Center revealed a high number of brain injuries. The report indicated only a limited number of brain injury cases have been treated, but doctors think many less obvious cases have gone undetected. Subtle brain damage afflicting soldiers on active duty is often overlooked when the soldiers are treated for more visible wounds. In addition, reports indicate "half of those wounded in action returned to duty within 72 hours, before some brain injuries may have been apparent."

For the active and returning Iraq and Afghanistan warriors, mental health problems are greatly imminent. Already, reports on returning Iraq troops show "[troops receiving counseling] were diagnosed with a problem."[1]

Suicide ideation as a result of PTSD and TBI continues to be a growing and significant problem that as a nation we must address by providing resources for our veterans.

It is my experience as a crisis interventionist that many veterans from present and past wars and conflicts clearly are having PTSD problems complicated by trauma-induced bipolar disorder. Today, more than ever, Vietnam veterans are regularly coming out of solitary and self-proclaimed reclusion. Their combat experiences in the marshes, jungles and killing fields of Southeast Asia continue to haunt them forty years later; many suffer from nightmares, flashbacks, sleeplessness, alcohol abuse, addictions and chemical dependency. Veterans report counseling and therapy is in short supply. Suicide hotline callers complain they are seen by psychiatrists or other mental health professionals for less than fifteen minutes at a time, given medication and told to return in a month or two. Though help has been scarce, the good news is more help is on its way. Recent media reports indicate Veteran Affairs and Congress are stepping up their efforts to increase staffing and other resources in order to be able to handle the enormous task of providing healthcare for the thousands of psychologically wounded warriors returning home from the battle zones. Reliable sources suggest that the expanding war zones and the need for additional second-, third- and fourth-tour troops, many being redeployed from Iraq to Afghanistan, are going to increase in coming years.

My experience and personal contact with the VA healthcare system from 1980 to today reveals that veteran support has improved by leaps and bounds in recent years (e.g. the addition of the National Suicide Prevention Hotline and the network of suicide prevention coordinators located at each of the 153 VA Medical Centers). However, I continue to be very much concerned there are not enough combat veteran services or personnel who are trained and educated in this suicidal prevention specialty, especially in light of the increasing numbers of veteran suicides.

My experience while working on crisis hotlines in the VA system and other law enforcement agencies in the civilian sector suggests that at least half of the veteran suicide callers had an original diagnosis of PTSD and were receiving medication and medical treatment at the time.

In his article "New post clinics to fight dual threat: PTSD, TBI", Jake Lowary explains that "concussions are...a large factor for TBI." Yet in the majority of cases, to get TBI a veteran has also experienced something horrific, which is the basis to why both PTSD and TBI often appear in conjunction. PTSD and TBI are not new conditions for soldiers, but they previously weren't recognized as unique disabilities. Lowary goes on to give important statistics regarding TBI: "The Department of Defense estimates about 10 percent of the 1.5 million troops that were deployed to Iraq and Afghanistan could have some form of TBI. More than 60 percent of soldiers wounded in Operation Iraqi Freedom sustain blast injuries [improvised explosive devices or roadside blasts], a major cause of TBI"; other causes of TBI include falls or military vehicle rollovers.[2]

Many vets literally hide out in fear of harming others with whom they may come in contact. One of the scars from trauma caused by combat experiences is the constant state of hyper-vigilance and increased arousal to the extent some veteran combat warriors actually look at ordinary people walking in the park at home and see the faces of the enemy.

David Wilkerson, author of *Have You Felt Like Giving Up Lately?*, explores the pain of those traumatized as time passes:

> Pain is layered over pain. A broken heart is usually a
> tender, fragile one. It is easily broken because it is not
> protected by a hard shell.[3]

If a veteran has an actual desire to die, he or she or a caring friend must seek immediate medical attention. The vet, a family member or friend should call the VA hotline for an immediate intervention and rescue. Telephone the National Veterans Suicide Prevention Hotline toll-free at 1-800-273-TALK (8255). A professionally trained responder is on duty twenty-four hours a day, seven days a week to help you or call your local emergency services at 911.

Some symptoms connected to veterans' suicidal thoughts may be:
- Depression: Suicidal thoughts may be present if a veteran is experiencing depression. Most veterans who are depressed appear to be "down" or upset.
- Sleep disturbances: Either the inability to properly fall asleep or the inability to sleep through the night.
- Rapid weight gain or weight loss.
- Feeling hopeless or helpless. Depressed veterans seem unable to experience any feelings of happiness, even when participating in family activities they normally enjoy.
- Inattentiveness: Performance at work or around the house may suffer.
- Appearing listless and even complaining of feeling "down" or depressed.
- Survivor's guilt: To an outside observer, this guilt often seems unwarranted, but to the combat veteran, it seems deserved. Survivor's guilt many times will accompany suicidal ideation that can be passive, involving a desire to die but without a plan to bring about one's death.

An example of such symptoms was reported in the article "Veterans' Group Emphasizes Suicide Risks" by Jennifer Kerr. She describes a Marine's difficult transition home from Iraq. He suffered from a mixture of insomnia, nightmares, weight loss, depression and numbness. After he promised his wife that he would get help for his issues, he tragically killed himself.[4]

Other signs of suicidal ideation may include:
- Alcohol or drug addiction: If a veteran has an ongoing problem with an alcohol or drug addiction, he or she is at increased risk to become

actively suicidal. Drug and alcohol problems generate other circumstances in a veteran's life, which may worsen depression.

- A veteran's impending divorce or separation, loss of job, legal trouble and financial and housing difficulties often grow from a dependence on alcohol or drugs and can bring about thoughts of suicide.
- Mental health: For a veteran who is diagnosed with mental health disorders such as post-traumatic stress disorder (PTSD), bipolar, schizophrenia or head trauma injuries such as Traumatic Brain Injury (TBI) or for someone who has attempted suicide in the past, thoughts of suicide take on a new height of importance.

When should a veteran or a veteran's worried friend or family member become involved and seek medical care?

A call to the VA National Suicide Prevention Hotline, 1-800-273-TALK (8255), should be the first step in order to properly assess and evaluate a suicidal or potentially suicidal situation. Or a call to 911, if the veteran does not want to have any contact with the VA, is warranted when he or she admits to thoughts of suicide. That is, if the vet actively wishes or threatens his or her own death, then evaluation by a medical professional is absolutely essential. Do not delay! Any form of suicidal ideation should prompt immediate action and psychiatric evaluation. Don't be misled by "time will heal"; in the aftermath of combat trauma, it doesn't. Get help! By the time the veteran admits to having a thought or plan to end his or her life, the vet already may have initiated the plan. Call the VA suicide hotline or 911 immediately for a rescue.

It is not uncommon for a veteran with suicidal ideation to be treated in the emergency department as having taken an overdose but told no one. Guessing about a person's true intentions when suicidal ideation is a concern is dangerous. Professionals often speak of a "suicidal gesture." This occurs when a veteran harms him or her self in such a way as to bring sympathy and attention but not death. Even if you believe the veteran is doing it just for attention, you must not rely on this feeling.

Many people make gestures that are unintentionally lethal.

It is not your job as a concerned friend or family member to evaluate the intent of the veteran with suicidal ideation. Your job is to get the warrior to the local community hospital or VA Medical Center quickly.

Be vigilant, informed and aware of the vet's condition. Here are some suggestions that may assist you in recognizing key questions to ask regarding the veteran's present mental health condition:
- "Are you thinking about suicide?"
  Answers at <u>high risk</u> include but are not limited to:
  - "I have no reason for living."
  - "I don't want to wake up in the morning."
  - "I wish to die."
  - "I wish I was killed with my buddies."
  - "I don't deserve to live."
  - "I want to end it all. Everyone would be better off without me."
  - "I feel trapped." (Feels there is no other escape.)
  - "I feel alone."
- If the veteran indicates feeling helpless or hopeless or describes psychological pain (hurt, anguish, misery).
- If the answer is <u>yes</u>, follow up the question by asking: "Have you done anything to hurt yourself?"
- If <u>yes</u>, ask the vet, "What did you do?" Find out the severity of the situation.
- Reduce the immediate threat by taking away knives, guns, pills and car keys on or around his/her person.
- Get the veteran to safety! Call 911 or call the National Veterans Suicide Prevention Hotline, 1-800-273-TALK (8255).

If the answers are no and you are still deeply concerned about the well-being of the veteran, work towards developing a plan of action. First, call the VA hotline and ask the professional for next-step assistance. They will be able to refer the vet to a crisis prevention coordinator at the VA

Medical Center nearest to the vet. In turn, the coordinator will be able to get the veteran an appointment with a healthcare treatment team immediately. The VA hotline responder and the crisis coordinator's number one job responsibility is to get you or the person you care about immediately to safety if the risk is high.

Other questions and behaviors that are extremely important to inquire about and observe:
- **Suicide Desire**: "Tell me more about your suicide thoughts."
  - Hopelessness
  - Helplessness
  - Perceives self as burden to others
- **Suicide Capability**: Do you or someone close to you have a sense of boldness to make an actual attempt and a sense of know-how to follow through with the attempt?
- **Suicidal Intent**: Have you or someone close to you expressed intent to die, accessibility of means to and opportunity for an attempt, detailed plan, preparations for an attempt or preparatory behaviors (giving away possessions, writing a note)?
- **Attempt in Progress**: "Have you already done something to end your life?"
- **Suicide Plan**:
  - Method chosen? If so, what?
  - Specific details thought out?
  - Available means?
  - Expressed intent to die?

If you are one of our proud warriors who is experiencing symptoms of depression or suicide ideation, please get some professional help. Your life is worth saving and your condition is treatable. Ooh-rah! You may think, *Who cares whether I live or die?* For one, your country cares. I care! That is why I wrote this book—for YOU.

Veterans presenting evidence of suicidal ideation pose many challenges to those who attempt to work with them in clinical settings and on suicide crisis hotlines and lifelines. Their personal traumas and factual accounts frequently contain painful stories of events that altered their inner senses of self, giving rise to vulnerable scars and unhealed wounds on the heart of their uniqueness. To recover from the various emotional injuries caused by war trauma, the veteran requires a supportive safe haven that is experienced as a safe and constantly secure place where the work of counselors and therapists who can help the vet cope with the adaptation and affirmation of the combat experience can occur. Considering this, the healthcare provider's task of creating a therapeutic structure is never an easy one. The clinician not only confronts the pain and personal struggle of the traumatized veteran but must do so with the capability of unceasing empathy. I call this ability to counsel with compassion "heart-to-heart resuscitation". This is a different therapeutic approach than most traditional models of therapy. My experiences suggest that when working with psychologically wounded combat veterans, showing signs of caring and a sincere heart-to-heart attitude is monumentally important.

For many veterans, the emotional wounds of traumatic brain injury and post-traumatic stress disorder symbolize a giving up of something valuable in their own lives for somebody else considered to be of more value—given up as a sacrifice. So it is in the Iraq, Afghanistan and other wars.

In the poem "Purple Heart" by E. Everett McFall, a veteran medic, conveys the sacrifice and emotional wounds he feels:

They are all evidence and plain to see,
Except the scars in my mind called PTSD.[5]


The article "Concussions Occurring Among Our Soldiers Deployed in Iraq" (*Walter Reed Army Institute of Research*) summarizes the findings presented by Charles Hoge, et. al., ("Mild Traumatic Brain Injury in U.S. Soldiers Returning from Iraq," *New England Journal of Medicine*, 31 January 2008) on an anonymous survey conducted in 2006 on over 2,500 soldiers approximately three to four months after returning home after a one-year deployment to Iraq.

The survey results showed a link between mild traumatic brain injury with loss of consciousness and an increase in post-traumatic stress disorder. Soldiers with superficial injuries or no injuries did not show this increase in PTSD. The article explores how 85 percent of soldiers healing from mild cases of TBI or concussions enjoy quick recoveries, but more serious brain injuries take more time and may not even completely heal. In regards to the connection between brain injuries, PTSD and depression, the article goes on to explain that "'post concussive symptoms'" can be related to PTSD and depression may cause surprise but are promising in that PTSD and depression are better known and treated than the less well defined condition referred to as "post concussive syndrome."[6]

These signature wounds are a connection that binds all veterans from all wars and conflicts together in a somber unwritten pledge of allegiance to the United States of America. In fact, many veterans report feeling as though they are letting themselves and their units down if they seek outside help. I have received calls for help from veterans in such diverse places as the Philippines, Guam, American Samoa, Juneau, Alaska, Arizona, California and Florida. The list of veterans or loved ones asking for help is a long one. Hotliners, responders and counselors hear many variations of veterans' life experiences, socioeconomic conditions and wounds of war when these men and women come into clinics and recovery centers or call the hotlines and lifelines. Veterans of all sizes and shapes, races and beliefs, suffering from all types of psychological disorders and discomforts, come home from the war zones feeling broken down, spiritually bankrupt, discarded and abandoned. The *Times* reported that "194,254 homeless people on any given night were veterans."[7]

It is natural for you or someone close to you to push aside agonizing memories just as it is instinctive to avoid dangerous scenes in actuality. This natural tendency to discard the stressful or the dreadful is especially well-defined in veterans whose capacity and strength of resistance have been reduced by the long-continued strains of combat firefights, second and third tours or other war incidents. If you were left to your own plans, most would naturally make every effort to forget terrible memories and thoughts. If you are a veteran, there is a natural tendency to be encouraged to recount these events by your relatives and friends. Nothing upsets a combat veteran more than the continual inquiries of his relatives and friends about his experiences in the war zone, not only because it awakens painful memories, but also because of the noticeable pointlessness of most questions and the hopelessness of bringing the truth about the brutal realities to those who listen.

When veterans realize the impossibility of forgetting their combat experiences and have recognized the hopeless and debilitating nature of trying to repress these memories, they may be more open to treatment planning. I usually tell my demoralized veterans that in order to heal they should attempt to banish all thoughts of war from their minds. In some cases, such as in clinic settings, all conversation between vets about the wars in which they've fought is strictly forbidden. I instruct my clients to guide their thoughts to other topics, to serene surroundings and other pleasant aspects of calming experiences.

I firmly believe first in encouraging traumatized combat veterans to visualize pleasant thoughts, search for spiritual meaning to their lives and learn breathing exercises, systemic desensitization, positive thinking and story-telling. Later they can revisit the significant event or events that have negatively impacted them, but only under the careful direction and guidance of trained client-centered therapists or counselors in clinical environments. Just a side note: sometimes I find a walk in the park on a sunny day or sitting on the beach watching the waves break on the shore helps my veteran client tell his or her story.

Every professional crisis interventionist who has ever had to answer the ring of a suicide hotline has encountered chronic cases of combat obsession. Especially when confronted with that form of neurosis dependent on anxiety, the responder has to face the critical challenge of providing poignant advice concerning the all-important attitude that the caller should adopt towards his or her war experience.

A trained crisis line responder's primary goal is not to provide veterans in crisis with psychotherapy or tele-psychiatry. Rather, each and every call should be handled with extreme priority, which includes individualistic and immediate advice, applicable crisis intervention counseling as well as motivational interviewing. The veteran caller is then stabilized or, in fact, literally rescued by their local police or fire department paramedics, when summoned by the crisis counselor, and physically rescued on the spot. A consultative follow-up and assignment to a behavioral health treatment team at a nearby Veteran Affairs Medical Center are standard.

Veterans and their families must be cautious during the early stages of medication treatment, because normal energy levels and the ability to take action often return before mood improves. At this critical time, when decisions are easier to make but anxiety and depression are still severe, the risk of suicide may temporarily increase.

The gathering together of a group of men or women veterans in a hospital or outpatient clinic or veteran center with little in common except their war experiences naturally leads their conversations far too frequently to this topic; even among those whose memories are not especially distressing it tends to enhance the condition for which the term despondent seems to be the universal designation.

It is, however, one thing that those who are suffering from the shock and grief of warfare should dwell continually on their war experience or be subjected to unrelenting inquiries; it is quite another to attempt to banish such experience from their minds altogether.

An example of this problem is shown by an urgent call I received from one veteran who expressed to me her physical pain from fibromyalgia syndrome tearing at her body. Carol, a veteran Army nurse, was crying and wanted to end the body pain. I spent the first twenty-five minutes of the call listening to her sobs, restricted breathing and incoherent, muffled speech. My immediate reaction suggested, *This is a suicide ready to happen. I can sense the urgency.* I could feel and sense her physical and psychological misery. The despair was too much for her. The veteran nurse had a plan and the means to kill herself. She described how she felt trapped within her broken illness-riddled body, helpless and hopeless, isolated and lonely. She was experiencing intense pain head to toe, tossing and turning throughout the night, unable to sleep. Carol said she was never a big drinker of alcohol, until returning home. But she felt she was becoming addicted to it. She felt she had to drink vodka to get to sleep at night. "Medications aren't working," she said emphatically. Carol went on to explain how she woke up to pain and a foggy brain most mornings. The *DSM-IV* suggests these as common symptoms experienced by fibromyalgia syndrome (FMS) and chronic fatigue syndrome (CFS) patients. Two and a half hours after we first began to talk, we worked out an action plan for her.

The rescue ensued. We had her transported via ambulance to a local community hospital psychiatric doctor in the emergency room and then I connected the former Army nurse with a crisis prevention coordinator at the closest VA Medical Center near to where she lived. She was safe from harm and agreed to begin a new approach for her physical as well as psychological treatment.

Working as mental health professionals, our oath and duty to these veterans and their families crying out for help is to listen intently and empathetically and to stay with them until help arrives. We must always keep the thought in the forefront of our minds: *Get the veteran to safety!*

In Hebrew law and discussion, the significance of saving a life is expressed by the Talmudic admonition: "He who saves one life, it is as though he has saved the world."

# Chapter 14

# Heart-to-Heart
# Resuscitation

Heart-to-heart resuscitation is about the present. It is about you or someone close to you. My mission as a teacher and therapist, whether I am face-to-face with a suicidal veteran in my clinic or talking with one on a crisis hotline, is to create an immediate atmosphere of being present "right here, right now" to help the suffering veteran rediscover his or her own humanity and find the starting place of personal happiness.

I teach the "Montgomery Model of Heart-to-Heart Resuscitation," which embraces a more personal approach to therapy and counseling. The application of my approach eclipses most conventional therapeutic theories and codes of behavior in that it focuses on the suicidal veterans' special needs and dynamics that most civilian client clinicians do not encounter in a lifetime. The facts really present themselves that not many Veteran Affairs doctors, social workers or nurses specialize in combat veteran psychological trauma. In fact, most have never looked deep into the eyes or heard the cries of the wounded souls. I have been present with them and will tell you it is enough to tear your heart out. If you or someone close to you gets this message, I want you to know you are not alone.

Foundations of trust and a caring attitude are truly the most fundamental of human needs suicidal vets require and want from their healthcare providers. A simple, genuine direct statement such as "Welcome home" or "Thank you for serving our country" said face-to-face in an emergency room or over a hotline to any combat warrior is a meaningful way to begin an encouraging, caring therapeutic relationship. I will tell you firsthand that those words are very important and have bought tears to the eyes of many combat-seasoned veterans who hear them spoken. The need to reconnect is vital for a successful recovery from depression. The need to feel normal is their mantra. Simply processing post-traumatic stressed combat warriors through the revolving doors at the VA, as they do cattle in the stockyards heading for slaughter, is not the level of mental health care they need or deserve.

Major Robert H. Stretch, Ph.D., states in the *Textbook of Military Medicine: War Psychiatry*: "After wars' end, soldiers once again become civilians and return to their families to try to pick up where they left off. It is this process of readjustment that has more often than not been ignored by society."

Ilona Meagher, editor of the Web site PTSD Combat, gathered these facts on Army mental health and suicides in her article "OEF/OIF Veteran Suicide Toll". She relates that CBS News reported on the 40 percent of veterans whose doctors prescribed them medications for depression and PTSD. She also discusses the fact that many had been declared unfit for combat and were seen by mental health providers one month prior to their suicides.[1]

The core principle of the "Montgomery Model of Heart-to-Heart Resuscitation" is to convey the power of a genuine caring heart and the sharing of ideas for change until its wisdom can be integrated and applied to helping the veteran to make new healthy life choices and develop an action plan to help get the treatment plan started. Throughout this book I have included examples of action plans and treatment planning.

The "Montgomery Model of Heart-to-Heart Resuscitation" for veteran rescues offers a much more empathetic method than usually taught. I have found that combat veterans come to us in extreme, highly emotional, aroused states of mind. Many are abandoned by the military, their family and friends and are broken-hearted. Dr. Edward Tick says it best: "Their souls are wounded." I agree emphatically and say their souls desperately need revival. The vets need to know they are loved and someone cares about them.

Numerous warriors have psychological issues stemming from lingering childhood and adolescent experiences. I believe crisis intervention for these veterans is really all about the integration of theology and psychology: spirituality and cognitive behavioral therapy.

The process of heart-to-heart resuscitation is active listening, responding with empathy, encouraging, motivating and mentoring the veterans from the heart, not the head. It is all about building trust and genuine caring. The buddy system is what kept them alive in the war. So ideally, the buddy system has a better chance of keeping them alive through their present suicidal ideation conditions. I don't necessarily believe that only service connected veteran counselors and therapists can do the job, but I do advocate that veterans counseling veterans and clean and sober recovering alcoholics counseling or sponsoring alcoholics will result in more successful outcomes. I do not possess a scientific method or peer reviewed study to give to you the facts and figures about outcome data, but I do have over twenty years' experience helping veterans and others find their ways. And to the best of my knowledge and resources, I have not lost one person to suicide.

Please do not misunderstand me. Much credit for recovery must be given to dedicated social workers, nurses, therapists and caregivers within the VA system, but I believe we need to define what it is that warriors need, not what we think is applicable. We must think out of the box when dealing with combat traumatized veterans. I feel heart-to-heart resuscitation is what most wounded souls want and need to hear. Most combat warriors have been emotionally torn, tattered, battered and stressed beyond belief waiting for their vehicles to be hit by roadside blasts or booby traps to explode when kicking in doors of suspected insurgents' hideouts. Many veterans in war zones wear audio headsets in their helmets blasting metal and rap music to motivate them into firefights and seek and destroy missions. The high-volume music seems to desensitize the moment. In reality, most vets are tough and well-trained, but scared when preparing for combat.

It is my belief and experience that wholly effective and genuine substance abuse counselors, nurses, licensed clinical social workers, addiction therapists and treatment team psychologists are born, not made. However, we all can learn from one another's experiences and research. Counselors and therapists choosing to use my model in the treatment of suicidal veterans first and foremost must learn to express genuineness and honesty and demonstrate the ability to actively listen, not intellectually pontificate.

I believe that in order for crisis interventionists and crisis line responders to have the greatest success in veterans' rescues, they must own the ability and willingness to feel what the veteran callers feel and accept every veteran in crisis with unconditional positive regard, a term from the Humanist school of psychology. By showing acceptance and unconditional positive regard, a counselor provides the best conditions for a client's personal growth.

Theorist Carl Rogers incorporated unconditional positive regard in his "belief that all people have the internal resources required for personal growth. Rogers' theory encourage[s] other psychiatrists and clinicians to suspend judgment, and to listen to a person with an attitude that the client has within himself the ability to change, without actually changing who he is." If the crisis interventionist does not show these qualities, the veteran's realization for a rescue will be minimal, no matter how many "pre-assessment and therapeutic techniques" are used.[2]

Heart-to-heart resuscitation is all about reflective caring. Rogers suggests reflection is the mirroring of emotional communication. "Reflection must come from the heart—it must be genuine, congruent," he has written.

Counselors must use reflective responses carefully. They must respond with feeling and empathy, not just "parroting" and repeating the phrases the veterans say. In considering the use of heart-to-heart resuscitation, counselors must remember to apply client-centered reflective listening in therapy relationships.[3]

*Healing Suicidal Veterans* is not a clinical study or exposition about PTSD, TBI and mood disorders relating to suicide. I have written this book to introduce the veteran or someone close to a rather unusual therapeutic approach to help overcome suicidal thoughts and the intent to harm one's self. The investigative reports released in the media almost weekly and other research data indicating what is now being done to help distressed veterans and their families simply is not enough and is not working. I am an advocate for change in the VA healthcare delivery system for this specific tragedy of veterans killing themselves or thinking about it at an alarming rate. The number of deaths as a direct result of suicides exceeds the number of deaths caused by wounds of war.

In this book I have tried to express the human mindset and suicide ideologies I have experienced firsthand in talking to, researching and counseling veteran combatants who have fought for the United States of America. Many of these vets who call hotlines and lifelines or seek aid around the country are in dangerous and disturbing crises. Remember, vets have relied on their buddies in war and need undying support in their depressed states.

During the initial stages of an intervention, especially in a hotline telephone conversation, and contrary to therapeutic schooling and what is deemed to be a proper and acceptable therapeutic relationship, I become their ooh-rah buddy. My extremely important role at this point is not as their therapist or rescuer. Simply said, "I have their backs!" They trust me and I get them to safety. In this book I hope I have conveyed the signs to look for and the means by which a veteran's loved ones or the veteran who is in danger of suicide can be saved.

# Conclusion

Roughly twenty-five million military veterans are living today in the United States of America. Approximately 1.6 million of those have served our great country boldly and loyally during the "thunder and lightning" of the Desert Storm ground invasion and air campaigns in 1991 on through to the conflicts in Iraq and Afghanistan. Tens of thousands are alive who served in wars and conflicts fifty to sixty years ago, including World War II, the Korean War and the Vietnam War. And the need for healthcare isn't going away. It is mounting, especially because of the thousands of depressed, suicidal veterans who have been in hiding for too many years and are now seeking help.

Because of the pressure of the American people, especially many families living with troubled veterans and a more positive and proactive congress, more money and resources are being sent to the Department of Veterans Affairs to help these American heroes. We are beginning to see the results.

The establishment of the National Veteran's Suicide Prevention Hotline is one example of action taken. Another is a huge effort to offer

OEF/OIF, Iraq and Afghanistan combat veterans an accelerated assessment and evaluation process by the on-site crisis prevention coordinators at each of the 153 VA Medical Centers. These coordinators are psychologists, psychiatrists, therapists, medical doctors and other highly trained healthcare team members who receive referrals directly from the National Hotline. The hotline's primary function and goal is to get suicidal veterans to safety and the CPC will provide further referrals, treatment planning and other treatment team support contacts at one of the Medical Centers.

President Obama has authorized 17,000 more troops to be deployed to Afghanistan, doubling the number of troops in that area. In one interview, a prominent politician stated that 30,000 new troops have been requested and declared needed in order to help stabilize the areas around Pakistan and Afghanistan.

Because of the buildup of a military presence in these and other parts of the world, our regular and reservist troops will continue to serve second, third and fourth tours in combat zones. I feel healthcare providers and veterans' families will also continue to see an increase in veteran suicides proportionately. The fact that men and women are sent into battle over and over again raises many serious issues. One *Time* magazine article, "America's Medicated Army", states another ominous reality: "For the first time in history a sizable and growing number of U.S. combat troops are taking daily doses of antidepressants to calm nerves strained by repeated and lengthy tours."[1]

It is important to be aware of these facts, because well-documented statistics indicate that tens of thousand of our combat veterans will be returning home suffering from a piling-on, adding layer after layer, tour after tour of PTSD symptoms. Many will find themselves struggling to transition back into society or becoming incapable of it altogether. This puts them at a higher risk of suicide. Studies from 2008 indicate that the probability for a combat warrior exhibiting signs of PTSD increases about 12 percent with each additional tour. Major depression and hopelessness, a significant sign in PTSD patients, have been implicated in 75 percent of all completed suicides. It is this hopelessness, constant bombardment of flashbacks and unrelenting nightmares with no end in sight that magnifies despair and substantially increases the risk of lethal behavior.

Even if there is no suicide ideation, you or a vet close to you may be experiencing other crises: unrelenting mental and physical pain, feelings of helplessness and hopelessness, substance abuse, addictions, feeling out of control or in need of anger management and family counseling. Many disabled vets feel trapped with no escape. These are just a few reasons to call for help and why we should care.

The pattern of those veterans coming home but seldom reporting any mental health problems is also growing. In this book, I have shared with you some personal stories and captured moments when these vets or their family and friends called the hotline or came to outpatient clinics and emergency rooms crying out for help. I have pointed out certain signs and symptoms that indicate when to ask for assistance. Remember, if you are a veteran, seeking help is not a sign of weakness or something to be ashamed of—it is your right to seek help. As I've said previously and what is stated on that iconic poster, "It takes the courage and strength of a warrior to ask for help."

Please remember, if you find yourself or someone close to you increasingly depressed and despondent, you are not alone. It is important you know that feeling suicidal is a serious but treatable condition. Depression is a treatable disorder as well, with the proper care.

We have gone over how to recognize what defines a veteran's suicidal ideation, what signs to look for and what to do when you discover them. Utilize the resource sections and checklists in this book so you or someone close to you can better recognize signs and symptoms of alcohol abuse and chemical dependency, post-traumatic stress disorder, depression and other emotional trauma you or your loved one is going through.

I have shared with you how extremely disturbing experiences cause severe emotional shock, which happens to many competent, robust and rugged veterans. I sincerely hope I have conveyed the message and the facts that having such symptoms after serving in combat's traumatic events are not signs of personal weakness. Many formerly psychologically well-adjusted and physically healthy veterans develop PTSD as a result of the severe traumas to which they have been exposed.

Earlier in this book we discussed how veterans who react to war traumas in such ways often feel depressed, out of control and perhaps

even feel they are losing their minds, but these physiological and psychological problems are treatable. The first important step to recovery is to
educate combat warriors and their families so they can recognize the
effects of emotional shock and know when and how to seek help.

I know that suicidal thoughts can be agonizing, especially when
accompanied by depression, other mental health conditions, alcohol
or other drug abuse. The most important thing I hope to convey is that
this situation demands immediate attention. These thoughts can indicate
serious illness.

The up close and personal stories and information in this book will,
I hope, help you realize the impact depression and suicidal thoughts have
had on the very souls of other veterans. The men and women veterans in
this book are real people with whom I have talked and counseled. I
hope reading of their experiences will inspire you to recognize that you
can recover from being stuck in what may seem to you at this point an
endless, hopeless pit of darkness. I want to encourage you to plant your
feet firmly on the ground and put one foot in front of the other. Step
forward. Reach out. Test the waters of healing. You can do this. Your life
is very much worth saving.

# Appendix A

# Veteran Support and Healthcare Eligibility

Do you or someone close to you have thoughts or signs of suicide? Call toll-free the National Veterans Suicide Prevention Hotline: 1-800-273-TALK (8255). Here is information about some additional organizations and places you can get in touch with to find help.

The following contact information was gathered from http://www.ptsdcombat.blogspot.com.

**Gulf Coast VA Med Center Hot Line**
1-800-507-4571

**Miles Foundation**
1-877-570-0688

**Military OneSource—DOD contracted**
1-800-342-9647 (24/7)

**Nat'l Coalition for Homeless Vets**
1-800-VET-HELP

**Nat'l Veterans Foundation Helpline**
1-888-777-4443 (M-F, 9-9 Pacific)

**NY/NJ Veterans VA Nurses Helpline**
1-800-877-6976

**Suicide Help Online**
http://www.hopeline.com
http://www.spanusa.org

**Suicide Hotlines** 1-888-649-1366
1-800-SUICIDE (784-2433)

**Veteran Crisis Hotline**
with veteran-to-veteran counseling
1-877-VET2VET
(838-2838)

**Veterans Affairs Suicide Prevention Hotline**
part of the National Suicide Prevention Lifeline
1-800-273-TALK (8255)

**Veterans of the Vietnam War**
1-800-843-8626

**Wounded Soldier and Family Hotline**
1-800-984-8523

*National Service Organizations*
Here is information collected from http://www.ptsdsupport.net on service
groups that offer assistance during the process of filing a claim with the
Department of Veterans Affairs. They will be your representative before any
review committee that will determine what rating of disability you will have if
your claim is approved.

**The American Legion**
Nat'l Veterans Affairs &
Rehabilitation Division
1608 K St., NW
Washington, DC 20006
Phone: 317-630-1200
Toll-free: 1-800-433-3318
www.legion.org

**AMVETS National Headquarters**
4647 Forbes Boulevard
Lanham, MD 20706-4380
Phone: 301-459-9600
Toll-free: 1-877-726-8387
Fax: 301-459-7924
http://amvets.org/

**Disabled American Veterans**
3725 Alexandria Pike
Cold Springs , KY 41076
Phone: 606-441-7300
http://www.dav.org

**Military Order of the Purple Heart of
the U.S.A.**
5413-B Backlick Road
Springfield ,VA 22151
Phone: 703-642-5360
Fax: 703-642-2054
www.purpleheart.org

**Veterans of Foreign War**
National Headquarters
406 West 34th Street
Kansas City, Missouri 64111
Phone: 816-756-3390
Fax: 816-968-1149
www.vfw.org

**Vietnam Veterans of America**
1224 M Street, N.W.
Washington, DC 20005-5183
Phone: 202-628-2700
Fax: 202-628-5880
www.vva.org

### Veterans Integrated Service Networks (VISNs)

The Veterans Health Administration of the Department of Veterans Affairs is divided geographically into health system networks, called Veterans Integrated Service Networks (VISNs). Each medical center has points of contact to work with veterans from Operations Enduring Freedom and Iraqi Freedom. I hope this section will be helpful in locating a suicide crisis coordinator nearest to where you live in the United States. Further information on each network can be found at www.vacareers.va.gov/networks.cfm.

**VISN 1: VA New England Healthcare System**
Togus, Maine; Manchester, New Hampshire; White River Junction, Vermont; Providence, Rhode Island; VA Connecticut HCS (West Haven and Newington campuses); Bedford, Boston (Brockton, Jamaica Plain, West Roxbury campuses); Northampton, Massachusetts; over thirty-five Community Based Outpatient Clinics
200 Springs Road Building 61
Bedford, MA 01730
Phone: 781-687-4821
Fax: 781-687-3470

**VISN 2: VA Healthcare Network Upstate New York**
Albany, Bath, Canandaigua, Syracuse and the Western New York Health Care System (Buffalo and Batavia) plus twenty-nine Community Based Outpatient Clinics
113 Holland Ave. Building 7
Albany, NY 12208-340
Phone: 518-626-7300
Fax: 518-626-7333

**VISN 3: VA NY/NJ Veterans Healthcare Network**
New York and New Jersey
Building 16, 130 W. Kingsbridge Road
Bronx, NY 10468
Phone: 718-741-4110
Fax: 718-741-4141

**VISN 4: VA Healthcare**
Pennsylvania, Delaware, West Virginia, Ohio, New Jersey and New York
323 North Shore Drive, Suite 400
Pittsburgh, PA 15212
Phone: 412-822-3316
Fax: 412-822-3275

**VISN 5: VA Capitol Health Care Network**
Maryland, Virginia, West Virginia and District of Columbia
849 International Drive, Suite 275
Linthicum, MD 21090
Phone: 410-691-1131
Fax: 410-684-3189

VISN 6: VA Mid-Atlantic Health
Care Network
West Virginia, Virginia, North
Carolina, Charlotte and Winston-
Salem, North Carolina
300 West Morgan Street, Suite 1402
Durham, NC 27701
Phone: 919-956-5541
Fax: 919-956-7152

VISN 7: VA Southeast Network
Alabama, Georgia, South Carolina
3700 Crestwood Parkway, NW, Suite
500
Duluth, GA 30096-5585
Phone: 678-924-5700
Fax: 678-924-5757

VISN 8: VA Sunshine Healthcare
Network
Florida, Southern Georgia, Puerto
Rico, U.S. Virgin Islands
P.O. Box 406
Bay Pines, FL 33744
Phone: 727-319-1125
Fax: 727-319-1135

VISN 9: VA Mid South Healthcare
Network
Lexington and Louisville, Kentucky;
Memphis, Mountain Home,
Murfreesboro and Nashville,
Tennessee; Huntington, West Virginia
1801 West End Ave., Suite 1100
Nashville, TN 37203
Phone: 615-695-2200
Fax: 615-695-2210

VISN 10: VA Healthcare System of
Ohio
Ohio, Northern Kentucky,
Southeastern Indiana
11500 Northlake Drive, Suite 200
Cincinnati, OH 45249
Phone: 513-247-4621
Fax: 513-247-4620

VISN 11: Veterans In Partnership
Central Illinois, Indiana, Michigan,
Northwest Ohio
P.O. Box 134002
Ann Arbor, MI 48113-4002
Phone: 734-222-4300
Fax: 734-222-4340

VISN 12: VA Great Lakes Health
Care System
Northwestern Indiana, Northern
Illinois, Wisconsin, Upper Peninsula of
Michigan
P.O. Box 5000, Building 18
Hines, IL 60141-5000
Phone: 708-202-8400
Fax: 708-202-8424

VISN 23 (VISN 13 and 14 integra-
tion): VA Midwest Health Care
Network
Minnesota, North Dakota, South
Dakota, Iowa, Nebraska, Western
Wisconsin, Western Illinois, Wyoming,
Kansas, Missouri
5445 Minnehaha Avenue
Minneapolis, MN 55417
Phone: 612-725-1968
Fax: 612-467-5967

**VISN 15: Heartland Network**
Kansas, Missouri, Illinois, Indiana,
Kentucky, Arkansas
1201 Walnut St, Suite 800
Kansas City, MO 64106
Phone: 816-701-3000
Fax: 816-221-0930
Veterans Crisis Intervention Hotline:
1-888-899-9377

**VISN 16: South Central VA Health Care Network**
Oklahoma, Arkansas, Louisiana,
Mississippi, Texas, Missouri, Alabama,
Florida
1600 East Woodrow Wilson
3rd Floor, Suite A
Jackson, MS 39216
Phone: 601-364-7900
Fax: 601-364-7996

**VISN 17: Heart of Texas Health Care Network**
Oklahoma border to the Lower Rio
Grande Valley of Texas, Dallas/Fort
Worth Central and South Texas, San
Antonio, Austin, Bonham, Kerrville
Lower Rio Grande Valley
2301 East Lamar Blvd., Suite 650
Arlington, TX 76006
Phone: 817-652-1111
Fax: 817-385-3700

**VISN 18: VA Southwest Health Care Network**
Arizona, New Mexico, western
portion of Texas, bordering counties
in Colorado, Kansas, Oklahoma
6950 E. Williams Field Road
Mesa, AZ 85212-6033
Phone: 602-222-2681
Fax: 602-222-2686

**VISN 19 VA Rocky Mountain Network**
Utah, Montana, Wyoming, Colorado,
portions of Idaho, Kansas, Nebraska,
Nevada, North Dakota
4100 E. Mississippi Ave
Suite 510
Glendale CO, 80246
Phone: 303-756-9279
Toll-free: 1-866-301-9626
Fax: 303-756-9243

**VISN 20 Northwest Health Network**
Alaska, Washington, Oregon, Idaho,
one county each in Montana and
California
P.O. Box 1035
Portland, OR 97207
Phone: 360-619-5925
Fax: 360-737-1405

**VISN 21 VA Sierra Pacific Network**
Northern and central California,
Northern Nevada, Hawaii,
Philippines, Pacific Islands, Guam,
American Samoa
201 Walnut Avenue
Mare Island, CA 94592
Phone: 707-562-8350
Fax: 707-562-8369

**VISN 22: Desert Pacific Healthcare Network**
Southern California and Southern
Nevada
5901 E. 7th Street
Long Beach, CA 90822
Phone: 562-826-5963
Fax: 562-826-5987

*Combat Veteran Health Care*
The following information on healthcare eligibility, enrollment and women
veterans is from the Web site of the Department of Veterans Affairs. Please refer
to their Web site (www.va.gov) for the most up-to-date information.

### Enhanced Eligibility For Health Care Benefits
The National Defense Authorization Act of 2008
Veterans of Operation Enduring Freedom/Operation Iraqi Freedom (OEF/OIF)
Under the "Combat Veteran" authority, the Department of Veterans Affairs (VA)
provides cost-free health care services and nursing home care for conditions
possibly related to military service and enrollment in Priority Group 6, unless
eligible for enrollment in a higher priority to:
- **Currently enrolled veterans and new enrollees who were discharged from
  active duty on or after January 28, 2003**, are eligible for the enhanced benefits, for 5 years post discharge.
- **Veterans discharged from active duty before January 28, 2003, who apply
  for enrollment on or after January 28, 2008**, are eligible for the enhanced
  benefit until January 27, 2011.

### Who's Eligible?
Veterans, including activated Reservists and members of the National Guard, are
eligible if they served on active duty in a theater of combat operations after
November 11, 1998, and have been discharged under other than dishonorable
conditions.

### Documentation Used To Determine Service In A Theater Of Combat
Operations
- Military service documentation that reflects service and the combat theater,
  or
- receipt of combat service medals and/or,
- receipt of eminent danger or hostile fire pay or tax benefits.

### Health Benefits Under The "Combat Veteran" Authority
- Cost-free care and medications provided for conditions potentially related to
  combat service.
- Enrollment in Priority Group 6 unless eligible for enrollment in a higher pri-
  ority group.
- Full access to the VA's Medical Benefits Package.

**What Happens After The Enhanced Eligibility Period Expires?**
Veterans who enroll with VA under this authority will continue to be enrolled even after their enhanced eligibility period ends. At the end of their enhanced eligibility period, veterans enrolled in Priority Group 6 may be shifted to Priority Group 7 or 8, depending on their income level, and required to make applicable co-pays.

**What About Combat Veterans Who Do Not Enroll During Their Enhanced Authority Period?**
For those veterans who do not enroll during their enhanced eligibility period, eligibility for enrollment and subsequent care is based on other factors such as: a compensable service-connected disability, VA pension status, catastrophic disability determination, or the veteran's financial circumstances.

IMPORTANT: For this reason, combat veterans are strongly encouraged to apply for enrollment within their enhanced eligibility period, even if no medical care is currently needed.

**Enrollment Guidelines**
- Currently enrolled combat veterans will have their enhancement enrollment period automatically extended to 5 years from their most recent date of discharge.
- New enrollees discharged from active duty on or after January 28, 2008, are eligible for this enhanced enrollment health benefit for 5 years after the date of their most recent discharge from active duty.
- Combat veterans who never enrolled and were discharged from active duty between November 11, 1998 and January 27, 2003, may apply for this enhanced enrollment opportunity through January 27, 2011.
- Combat veterans who applied for enrollment after January 16, 2003, but were not accepted for enrollment based on the application being outside the previous post-discharge two year window will be automatically reviewed and notified of the enrollment decision under this new authority: National Defense Authorization Act of 2008.

**Additional Information Regarding Combat Veteran Benefits**
Additional information is available at your nearest VA facility or Veterans Service Center and by calling toll-free 1-800-827-1000 or 1-877-222-8387.

**National Resource Directory Offers Veterans One-Stop Info and Access to
Myriad Health, Employment Services**
The Department of Defense launched the National Resource Directory, a
collaborative effort between the departments of Defense, Labor and Veterans
Affairs.

The directory is a Web-based network of care coordinators, providers and
support partners with resources for wounded, ill and injured service members,
veterans, their families, families of the fallen and those who support them.

"The directory is the visible demonstration of our national will and
commitment to make the journey from 'survive to thrive' a reality for those who
have given so much. As new links are added each day by providers and partners,
coverage from coast to coast will grow even greater ensuring that no part of that
journey will ever be made alone," said Lynda C. Davis, Ph.D., deputy under
secretary of defense for military community and family policy.

Located at www.nationalresourcedirectory.org, the directory offers more
than 10,000 medical and non-medical services and resources to help service
members and veterans achieve personal and professional goals along their
journey from recovery through rehabilitation to community reintegration.

**Disabled Veterans**
Veterans who are 50 percent or more disabled from service-connected conditions, unemployable due to service-connected conditions, or receiving care for
a service-connected disability receive priority in scheduling of hospital or outpatient medical appointments.

**How do I get my disability compensation claim reevaluated?**
You may request a reevaluation of your claim anytime that you believe your
condition has changed or worsened. Submit the request to reopen or reevaluate
your claim to the VA Regional Office in either letter or statement form or on VA
Form 21-4138 (Statement in Support of Claim).
(http://www.vba.va.gov/pubs/forms/21-4138x.pdf) Request should include the
following information:
- Name
- Claim number or Social Security Number
- Day and evening contact information
- Current address
- Statement explaining change requested
- Any new and pertinent medical evidence that supports your request

**Homeless Veterans**
VA offers a wide array of special programs and initiatives specifically designed to help homeless veterans live as self-sufficiently and independently as possible. In fact, VA is the only Federal agency that provides substantial hands-on assistance directly to homeless persons. Although limited to veterans and their dependents, VA's major homeless-specific programs constitute the largest integrated network of homeless treatment and assistance services in the country.

VA's specialized homeless veterans treatment programs have grown and developed since they were first authorized in 1987. The programs strive to offer a continuum of services that include:

- Aggressive outreach to those veterans living on streets and in shelters who otherwise would not seek assistance;
- Clinical assessment and referral to needed medical treatment for physical and psychiatric disorders, including substance abuse;
- Long-term sheltered transitional assistance, case management and rehabilitation;
- Employment assistance and linkage with available income supports; and
- Supported permanent housing.

**How do I contact a coordinator for options for women veterans who are homeless with children?**
Contact the local VA homeless coordinator (or point of contact), Social Work Services department or Women Veterans Coordinator at your local VAMC. There are homeless women veterans and homeless women veterans with children pilot programs located at eleven designated VA facilities as well, and the Women Veterans Coordinator can discuss what options are available in your area.

*Women in Uniform*
**VA Successes for Women Veterans**
The Department of Veterans Affairs has experienced a number of successes for women veterans. These successes include:

- Legislative gains in the areas of military sexual trauma, homeless women veterans programs, special monthly compensation for women veterans who lose a breast as a result of a service-connected disability (final regulation effective March 18, 2002), maternity and infertility services and studies indicating negative reproductive outcomes in women veterans who served in-country in Viet Nam.
- Receipt of the 2000 Wyeth-Ayerst Bronze HERA Award in recognition of Veteran Health Administration's demonstrated leadership in women health.

- Guidance in the assessment and treatment of infertility in both women and men.
- Women Veteran Program Managers (WVPM) at every VA Medical Center and Women Veterans Coordinators at every regional office.
- Increased coordination and expert consultation through the appointment of a Lead Women Veteran Program Managers in all twenty-one networks.
- Establishment of specialized and frequently separate women's health clinics in nearly two-thirds of VA medical centers, as well as women's health providers or teams within primary care practices.
- Migration of Women Veterans Health and Military Sexual Trauma Software with Computerized Patient Record System.
- Gains in the number of corrective actions taken relative to women veterans' privacy deficiencies.
- In April 2002, the Women's Health Program sponsored a national women veterans coordinators (WVCs) conference bringing together WVCs nationwide from both Veterans Health Administration and Veterans Benefits Administration to discuss women veterans issues and network so that services to women veterans with benefits and health issues can now be accomplished more smoothly.

For more information, contact the Center for Women Veterans, 202-273-6193.

**Where are the special PTSD treatment centers?**
Women Veteran Stress Disorder Treatment Programs have been established at the following VA sites (see the VISN listing for telephone numbers):
Boston, MA
Brecksville, OH
Loma Linda, CA
New Orleans, LA

**Where can I get Military Sexual Trauma treatment?**
You may enroll and receive counseling and treatment for any emotional or physical condition experienced, as a result of sexual trauma experienced while on active duty, at any VA health care facility or Rehabilitation Counseling Center (Vet Center) in the continental United States without regard for your service-connected rating or length of military service through December 31, 2004.

**Where can I get inpatient psychiatric care as a woman veteran?**
Most VA Medical Centers have inpatient mental health programs. Contact your VA Primary Care Provider or the local Mental Health Program office for

assistance. If you already have a therapist and need inpatient care, please discuss your concerns with your therapist.

If you have urgent or emergency needs, you can contact your local VA health care facility telephone care program or urgent care clinic.

**Where are the designated Clinical Programs of Excellence in Women's Health?**
(See VISN listings for phone numbers)
Women Veterans Health Care Program, Alexandria VAMC
Women Veterans Comprehensive Health, Durham VAMC
Women Veterans Health Program, Boston VAMC, VA New England HCS
Women Veterans Health Program, Bay Pines VAMC
Women Veterans Health Program, VA Pittsburgh Healthcare System
Women Veterans Health Program, South Texas Veterans Health Care System

**Pet Therapy**
Canine Helpers for the Handicapped, Inc. is a non-profit organization dedicated to training dogs to assist individuals with disabilities to lead more independent and secure lives. This organization provides custom-trained assistance service dogs for mobility, hearing impaired, PTSD and therapy.
Canine Helpers for the Handicapped, Inc.
5699 Ridge Road (RT. 104)
Lockport, New York 14094
716-433-4035/ Fax 716-439-0822
Email: CHHDogs@aol.com
Web site: http://www.caninehelpers.org/

# Appendix B

# Veteran Resources

**PTSD References**

Allen, S.N. "Psychological assessment of post-traumatic stress disorder. Psychometrics, current trends, and future directions." *Psychiatric Clinics of North America* 17, no. 2 (1994): 327-349.

American Psychiatric Association. *Diagnostic and Statistical Manual of Mental Disorders: DSM-IV-TR.* 4th ed., Text Revision. Washington, D.C.: American Psychiatric Pub, 2000.

Beers, Mark H. and Robert Berkow, eds. *The Merck Manual of Diagnosis and Therapy.* 17th ed. Whitehouse Station, NJ: Merck Research Laboratories, 1999.

Blank, A.S. "Clinical detection, diagnosis, and differential diagnosis of post traumatic stress disorder." *Psychiatric Clinics of North America* 17, no. 2 (1994):351-383.

Brenner, David. *Care of Souls.* Grand Rapids, MI: Baker Books, 1998.

Brom, D, R.J. Kleber and P.B. Defares. "Brief psychotherapy for post-traumatic stress disorders." *Journal of Consulting and Clinical Psychology* 57 no. 5 (1989): 607-612.

Cantrell, Bridget and Chuck Dean. *Once a Warrior: Wired for life.* Seattle: WordSmith Books, 2007.

Choy, T and F. de Bosset. "Post-traumatic stress disorder: an overview." *Canadian Journal of Psychiatry* 37 no. 8 (1992): 578-583.

Daniels, Linda. *Healing Journeys: How Trauma Survivors Learn to Live Again.* Far Hills, NJ: New Horizon Press, 2004.

Davidson, J. "Drug therapy of post-traumatic stress disorder." *British Journal of Psychiatry* 160 (1992): 309-314.

Dawe, Bruce. "Homecoming." In *Sometimes Gladness,* ed. V. Bernard, South Melbourne: Pearson Education Australia, 2000: 95

D'Souza D. "Post-traumatic stress disorder: a scar for life." *British Journal of Clinical Practice* 49 no. 6 (1995): 309-313.

Finnegan, AP. "Clinical assessment for post-traumatic stress disorder." *British Journal of Nursing* 7 no. 4 (1998): 212-218.

Grossman, Dave. *On Killing: The Psychological Cost of Learning to Kill in War and Society.* NY: Back Bay Books, 1995.

Jacobs, W.J. and C. Dalenberg. "Subtle presentations of post-traumatic stress disorder. Diagnostic issues." *Psychiatric Clinics of North America* 21 no. 4 (1998): 835-845.

Lundin, T. "The treatment of acute trauma. Post-traumatic stress disorder prevention." *Psychiatric Clinics of North America* 17 no. 2 (1994): 385-391.

Mason, S. and A. Rowlands. "Post-traumatic stress disorder." *Journal of Accident & Emergency Medicine* 14 no. 6 (1997): 387-391.

Matsakis, Aphrodite. *Back from the Front: Combat Trauma, Love, and the Family.* Baltimore, MD: Sidran Institute Press, 2007.

Matsakis, Aphrodite. *I can't get over it: Handbook for trauma survivors.* Oakland, CA: New Harbinger Publications, Inc., 1992.

McFall, Everett E. *I can still hear their cries.* Denver, CO: Outskirts Press, 2007.

Medley, I. "Post-traumatic stress disorder." *British Journal of Hospital Medicine* 55 no. 9 (1996): 567-70.

Peniston, E.G. "EMG biofeedback-assisted desensitization treatment for Vietnam combat veterans post-traumatic stress disorder." *Clinical Biofeedback and Health* 9 no. 1 (1986): 35-41.

Pitman, R.K, S.P. Orr, A.Y. Shalev, L.J. Metzger and T.A. Mellman. "Psychophysiological alterations in post-traumatic stress disorder." *Seminars in Clinical Neuropsychiatry* 4 no. 4 (1999): 234-241.

Shapiro, F. "Efficacy of the eye movement desensitization procedure in the treatment of traumatic memories." *Journal of Trauma Stress* 2 (1989): 199-223.

Sherman, J.J. "Effects of psychotherapeutic treatments for PTSD: a meta-analysis of controlled clinical trials." *Journal of Trauma Stress* 11 no. 3 (1998): 413-435.

Spragg, G.S. "Post-traumatic stress disorder." *Medical Journal of Australia* 156 no. 10 (1992): 731-733.

Symes, L. "Post traumatic stress disorder: an evolving concept." *Archives of Psychiatric Nursing* 9 no. 4 (1995): 195-202.

Tarrier, N., C. Sommerfield, H. Pilgrim and L. Humphreys. "Cognitive therapy or imaginal exposure in the treatment of post-traumatic stress disorder. Twelve month follow- up." *British Journal of Psychiatry* 175 (1999): 571-575.

Tick, Edward. *War and the Soul: Healing Our Nation's Veterans from Post-Traumatic Stress Disorder.* Wheaton, IL: Quest Books, 2005.

Turnbull, G.J. "A review of post-traumatic stress disorder. Part II: Treatment." *Injury* 29 no. 3 (1998): 169-175.

Vargas, M.A. and J. Davidson. Post-traumatic stress disorder. *Psychiatric Clinics of North America* 16 no. 4 (1993): 737-748.

Victoroff, Victor M. *The Suicidal Patient: Recognition, Intervention, Management.* Oradell, NJ: Medical Economics Book, 1983.

Watson, C.G., J.R. Tuorila, K.S. Vickers, L.P. Gearhart and C.M. Mendez. "The efficacies of three relaxation regimens in the treatment of PTSD in Vietnam War veterans." *Journal of Clinical Psychology* 53 no. 8 (1997): 917-923.

Wessely, S, S. Rose and J. Bisson. "Brief psychological interventions ('debriefing') for trauma-related symptoms and the prevention of post traumatic stress disorder." *Psychotherapy and Psychosomatics* (2000) in Cochrane database of systematic reviews. http://www.cochrane.org/.

Witt, P.H., D.P. Greenfield and J. Steinberg. "Evaluation and treatment of post-traumatic stress disorder." *New Jersey Medicine* 90 no. 6 (1993): 464-467.

Zivin K, et al. "Suicide Mortality Among Individuals Receiving Treatment for Depression in the Veterans Affairs Health System: Associations with Patient and Treatment Setting Characteristics." *American Journal of Public Health* 97 no. 12 (2007): 2193-8.

**Korean War References**

Alexander, Bevin. *Korea: The First War We Lost.* New York: Hippocrene Books, 1986.

Badsey, Stephen. *Korean War.* New York: Gallery Books, 1990.

Clair, Clay. *The Forgotten War.* New York: Time Books, 1987.

Goulden, Joseph. *Korea: The Untold Story of the War.* New York: Time Books, 1982.

Halliday, Jon and Bruce Cummings. *Korea: The Unknown War.* New York: Pantheon Books, 1988.

Hastings, Max. *The Korean War.* New York: Simon & Shuster, 1987.

Hedrick, Susan, et al. "Characteristics of Residents and Providers in the Assisted Living Pilot Program." *Gerontologist* 47 (2007): 365-77.

Hedrick, Susan, et al. "Resident Outcomes of Medicaid-Funded Community Residential Care." *Gerontologist* 43 (2003): 473-482.

Kim, Chum-kon. *The Korean War 1950-53.* Seoul: Kwangmyong Publishing Company, 1973.

MacDonald, Callum A. *Korea: The War before Vietnam.* New York: Macmillan, 1986.

Matloff, Maurice, ed. *American Military History.* Washington: Center of Military History, 1969.

Paschall, Rod. *Witness to War, Korea.* New York: Perigee, 1995.

Pratt, Sherman W. *Decisive Battles of the Korean War.* New York: Vantage Press, 1992.

Principi A.J. Letter to Arlen Specter, Chairman, Committee on Veterans' Affairs, United States Senate, 23 November 2004.

Ridgway, Matthew B. *The Korean War.* New York: Doubleday, 1967.

Russ, Martin. *The Last Parallel.* New York: Kensington, 1957.

Stokesbury, James L. *A Short History of the Korean War.* New York: Wm. Morrow & Co., 1988.

Summers, Harry G., Jr. *Korean War Almanac.* New York: Facts on File, 1990.

**Veteran Internet References**

"An Abstract Bibliograophy: Journal Articles." In Diagnosis and Treatment of Combat Related Post-Traumatic Stress Disorder.
http://www.crdamc.amedd.army.mil/library_med/PTSD_Bibliography.pdf.

Addiction Medicine, http://www.Addiction-medicine.org.
The America's Intelligence Wire: Desert Storm, www.navy.mil.
Ballas, Christos, ed. "Suicide and Suicidal Behavior." *The New York Times: Health Guide*. http://health.nytimes.com/health/guides/disease/suicide-and-suicidal-behavior/overview.html?inline=nyt-classifier.
CMPMedica, LLC. Healthier You. http://www.healthieryou.com/index.html.
EHow Relationships & Family Editor. "How to Talk to a Suicidal Friend." eHow.com. http://www.ehow.com/how_2071390_talk-suicidalfriend.html?ref=fuel&utm_source=yahoo&utm_medium=ssp&utm_ca mpaign=yssp_art.
Everyday Health Network. "Depression Checklist." Waterfront Media, Inc. http://www.everydayhealth.com/publicsite/index.aspx?puid=0512F6BA-8101-4877-B11D-3E99973800D4&p=2.
Fibromyalgia Network. http://www.fmnetnews.com.
Foong, Whyetatt. "Analysis of 'Homecoming' by Bruce Dawe." LiteratureClassics.com. http://literatureclassics.com/essays/408/.
Fort Campbell Crisis Assistance. http://www.campbell.army.mil/crisis/index.html.
Harvard Health Publications. "What Is Depression?" Harvard Health Publications Special Health Report. Everyday Health. http://www.everydayhealth.com/depression/understanding/what-is-depression.aspx.
Integrative Medicine Communications. "Post-Traumatic Stress Disorder." Integrative Medicine Access. http://www.gardenoflight.net/Site2/Research_Center/library/ConsConditions/Print/PosttraumaticStressDisordercc.html.
KIA Collection Sites, http://usacac.army.mil/CAC2/index.asp.
Lee, Scott. PTSD, A Soldier's Perspective. http://ptsdasoldiersperspective.blogspot.com.
Mayo Foundation for Medical Education and Research. "Psychotherapy: An Overview of the Types of Therapy. Revolution Health. http://www.revolution-health.com/conditions/mental-behavioral-health/depression/therapy/index.
Meagher, Ilona, ed. PTSD Combat: Winning the War Within. http://ptsdcombat.blogspot.com.
Mundell, E.J. "Younger Veteran at Greater Suicide Risk." *U.S. News and World Report*. 10 October 2007. http://health.usnews.com/usnews/health/health-day/071030/younger-veterans-at-greater-suicide-risk.htm.
PTSD Support Services. http://www.ptsdsupport.net.
Reinberg, Steven. "With Depression Vets Face Higher Suicide Risk." HealthDay (Jan. 12, 2009) http://www.healthday.com/Article.asp?AID=622964.
Salmon, K. Poetry of Bruce Dawe. (2000) http://www.ozseek.com.au/English2UGen/PracticePapers/00301a.shtml.
Scott, Larry, ed. VA Watchdog. http://www.vawatchdog.org.

Segal, Jeanne, ed. Helpguide. http://www.helpguide.org/.
Shields, John. "Suicidal Thoughts." eMedicine Health. http://www.emedicine-health.com/suicidal_thoughts/article_em.htm.
WGBH educational foundation. "The War Briefing." *Frontline.* PBS.
http://www.pbs.org/wgbh/pages/frontline/warbriefing/.
Wikipedia. "Casualties of the Iraq War." Wikipedia.
http://www.crdamc.amedd.army.mil/library_med/PTSD_Bibliography.pdf.
Wood, Starr A. "Crisis Intervention."
http://www.albany.edu/~sawood/crisis%20intervention.htm.

**Suggested Reading**
*The Old Man and the Sea* by Ernest Hemmingway.
*The Red Badge of Courage* by Stephan Crane.
*The Hiding Place* by Corrie Ten Boom.

# Acknowledgments

A ll my love and appreciation and a huge thank you goes to my wife and steadfast partner, Diane Joy Montgomery, for all the hours enthusiastically sustaining me and praying for this book to be published in order to feed hope and encouragement to our nation's veterans, their families and friends experiencing the quandary of suicide.

To my good friends, staff and co-workers in counseling centers around Southern California: Liz Hagaman, Lauren, Lynn & Larry Vaughan, Neil Sommer and Marianne Abulone for all the years of camaraderie and working together each day with a positive treatment team spirit. Thank you!

To my friends, confidants and ministers: Russ & Carol Milnes, Rev. Powell Lemons, Chaplain Glen Davis, the late Rev. Eric & Gladys Johnson and Rev. Dr. Al Vom Steeg…my brothers and sisters in ministry.

To my colleagues: Bill Cerveny, Terry Taylor and Roger Cheney for their continuing support and engaging encouragement for me to publish this book.

And finally, a special thanks to Dr. Joan Dunphy, Publisher of New Horizon Press, for her belief in me and in the cause of spreading hope and support to our nation's suicidal veterans and for the editorial assistance to write and publish stories about the hearts, minds and souls of our great American warriors and their families.

# Notes

**Preface**
1 Alexandra Marks, "Back from Iraq—and suddenly out on the streets," *The Christian Science Monitor* (February 2005).
2 Ilona Meagher, ed., "OEF/OIF Veteran Suicide Toll: Nearly 15% of Overall U.S. Military Casualities Result from Suicide," PTSD Combat: Winning the War Within (September 15, 2008) http://ptsdcombat.blogspot.com/2008/09/oefoif-veteran-suicide-toll-15-of.html (accessed 2009).
3 Edward Tick, *War and the Soul: Healing Our Nation's Veterans from Post-traumatic Stress Disorder* (Wheaton, IL: Quest Books, 2005).
4 Bryan Bender, "New veterans fear repeat of Vietnam," *Boston Globe*, 30 May 2006.

**Introduction**
1 Department of Veterans Affairs, "Crisis Prevention—When to Seek Help and How," *Veterans' Wellness* (Spring 2008), http://www.visn2.va.gov/vet/wellness/spring2008/crisis.asp (accessed 2009).

**PART I: IRAQ AND AFGHANISTAN COMBAT VETERANS**
**Chapter 1: A Family in Crisis Cries Out for Help! An Iraq Vet**
1 Ilona Meagher, ed., "OEF/OIF Veteran Suicide Toll: Nearly 15% of Overall U.S. Military Casualties Result from Suicide," PTSD Combat: Winning the War Within (September 15, 2008) http://ptsdcombat.blogspot.com/2008/09/oefoif-veteran-suicide-toll-15-of.html (accessed 2009).
2 Kendra Van Wagner, "Color Psychology: How Colors Impact Moods, Feelings, and Behaviors," About.com, http://psychology.about.com/od/sensationandperception/a/colorpsych.htm.

**Chapter 2: Honoring God: A Vet's Story about Transformation**
1 Denis Waitley, *Seeds of Greatness* (New York: Pocket Books, 1988).
2 Rick Warren, *The Purpose-Driven Life: What on Earth Am I Here For?* (Grand Rapids, MI: Zondervan, 2002).
3 Og Mandino, *The Greatest Salesman in the World* (Hollywood, FL: Fredrick Fell Publishers, Inc, 1985).
4 Spencer Johnson, *The Precious Present* (New York: Doubleday, 1992).

**Chapter 3: One Combat Pilot's Struggle: The Iraq War**
[1] Victor Victoroff, *The Suicidal Patient: Recognition, Intervention, Management* (Oradell, NJ: Medical Economics Books, 1983).
[2] Prolastin, "Managing Stress," Talecris Biotherapeutics, Inc., http://www.prolastin.com/4.5.0_cons_stress.aspx
[3] Ibid.
[4] Deena Metzger, *Entering the Ghost River* (Topanga, CA: Hand to Hand, 2002).
[5] Edward Tick, *War and the Soul: Healing Our Nation's Veterans from Post-traumatic Stress Disorder* (Wheaton, IL: Quest Books, 2005).
[6] Eugene Peterson, *The Message: The Bible in Contemporary Language* (Navpress Publishing Group, 2002).

**Chapter 4: "I am a Monster": Two Tours in Al-Fallujah, Iraq**
[1] WJACTV, "Link Found Between Former Soldiers, Motorcycle Deaths," WJACTV (2006), http://www.wjactv.com/news/10325324/detail.html.
[2] Global Security, "Fallujah," Global Security (2006), http://www.globalsecurity.org/military/world/iraq/fallujah.htm (accessed August 2008).
[3] Jill Carroll, "When the war comes back home," *The Christian Science Monitor* (July 2008), http://www.csmonitor.com/2008/0712/p02s01-usmi.html.
[4] Psychiatric Association, *Diagnostic and Statistical Manual of Mental Disorders: DSM-IV-TR*, 4th ed., Text Revision (Washington, D.C.: American Psychiatric Pub., 2000).

**Chapter 5: Women in the Iraqi War Zones**
[1] Nicole P. Yuan, Mary P. Koss and Mirto Stone, "The Psychological Consequences of Sexual Trauma," National Online Resource Center on Violence Against Women (March 2006), http://new.vawnet.org/category/Main_Doc.php?docid=349 (accessed 2009).
[2] Ibid.
[3] Eve B. Carlson and Josef Ruzek, "Effects of Traumatic Experiences: A National Center for PTSD Fact Sheet," National Center for Post-Traumatic Stress Disorder (2004), http://www.ncptsd.org/facts/general/fs_effects.html (accessed 2009) (site now discontinued)
[4] Ibid.
[5] Ibid.
[6] Matthew Tull, "Military Sexual Trauma and the Iraq War," About.com, (February 2009), http://ptsd.about.com/od/ptsdandthemilitary/a/MSTOFE-FOIF.htm.
[7] Ibid.
[8] Matthew Tull, "Military Sexual Trauma and PTSD among Female Veterans," About.com (September 2007), http://ptsd.about.com/od/causesanddevelopment/a/PTSDandMST.htm.

9 Ellen Frank, ed., "NAMI Fact Sheet on Major Depression," NAMI Mercer (May 2003), http://www.namimercer.org/resource/NAMI%20Fact%20Sheet%20on%20Major%20Depression.htm (accessed 2009).
10 Christina Olenchek, "Dialectical Behavior Therapy—Treating Borderline Personality Disorder," *Social Work Today* (November/December 2008), http://www.socialworktoday.com/archive/102708p22.shtml.
11 Joan Shim, "Dogs chase nightmares of war away," CNN (January 2008), http://www.cnn.com/2008/LIVING/personal/01/29/dogs.veterans/index.html (accessed 2009).
12 Memorial Art Gallery of the University of Rochester, "MAG Exhibition Explores Healing Power of Art," Memorial Art Gallery of the University of Rochester (January 2009), http://mag.rochester.edu (accessed 2009).

**Chapter 6: Extreme Mental Hardship: Three Tours in Afghanistan**
1 Michael Craig Miller, ed., "Understanding Depression," Harvard Health Publications (2008).
2 Jim Lehrer, "The War Briefing," *News Hour*, originally aired 29 January 2009 by PBS, MacNeil/Lehrer Productions, http://www.pbs.org/newshour/bb/health/jan-june09/suicides_01-29.html.
3 National Center for PTSD, "What can I do if I think I have PTSD?" National Center for PTSD, http://www.ncptsd.va.gov/ncmain/ncdocs/fact_shts/fs_what_can_i_do.htm.
4 Department of Veterans Affairs, "Who We Are—Vet Center," United States Department of Veterans Affairs (October 2007), http://www.vetcenter.va.gov/About_US.asp.
5 Department of Veterans Affairs, "Services—Vet Center," United States Department of Veterans Affairs (October 2007), http://www.vetcenter.va.gov/Vet_Center_Services.asp.
6 Melinda Smith, Robert Segal and Jeanne Segal, "Post-traumatic Stress Disorder (PTSD): Symptoms, Treatment, and Self-Help," Help Guide (November 2008), http://www.helpguide.org/mental/post_traumatic_stress_disorder_symptoms_treatment.htm (accessed January 2009).
7 Frank Ochberg, "Partners With PTSD," Gift From Within (February 2009), http://www.giftfromwithin.org/html/partners.html.
8 Ibid.

**PART II: GULF WARS AND BEIRUT VETERANS**
**Chapter 7: Casualties of the Gulf Wars**
1 Victor Victoroff, *The Suicidal Patient: Recognition, Intervention, Management* (Oradell, NJ: Medical Economics Books, 1983).

[2] WebMD, "Bipolar Disorder Health Center," WebMD, http://www.webmd.com/bipolar-disorder/mental-health-bipolar-disorder (accessed January 2009).

[3] Debra Emmite and Stanley J. Swierzewskit III, eds, "Alcohol Abuse: Treatment, Prognosis," Healthcommunities.com, Inc. (March 2008), http://www.mentalhealthchannel.net/alcohol/treatment.shtml.

[4] D.R. Gerstein and H.J. Harwood, eds., *Treating Drug Problems: Vol. 1. A Study of the Evolution, Effectiveness, and Financing of Public and Private Drug Treatment Systems* (Washington, DC: National Academy Press, 1990).

[5] AlcoholismResources.com, "What Are the Harmful Health Effects of Alcohol?" AlcoholismResources.com (2007), http://www.alcoholismresources.com/alcohol_abuse_effects.html.

[6] Melvin L. Selzer, "The Michigan Alcoholism Screening Test: The Quest for a New Diagnostic Instrument," *The American Journal of Psychiatry* (June 1971).

**Chapter 8: A Suicide Note Sent to a Friend**
[1] Margaret Strock, ed., "You Are Not Alone," Healthier You (2009), http://www.healthieryou.com/alone.html (accessed January 2009).

**PART III: VIETNAM AND KOREA VETERANS**
**Chapter 9: Bloody Boots and Body Bags**
[1] Rick Warren, *The Purpose-Driven Life: What on Earth Am I Here For?* (Grand Rapids, MI: Zondervan, 2002).

[2] Dave Grossman, *On Killing: The Psychological Cost of Learning to Kill in War and Society* (New York: Back Bay Books, 1996).

[3] Joan Shim, "Dogs chase nightmares of war away," CNN (January 2008), http://www.cnn.com/2008/LIVING/personal/01/29/dogs.veterans/index.html (accessed 2009).

[4] Ibid.

[5] Paul Ballas, "Medical Encyclopedia: Depression," Medline Plus (January 2009), http://wwwils.nlm.nih.gov/medlineplus/ency/article/003213.htm.

**Chapter 10: "It Don't Mean Nothin"**
[1] Victor Victoroff, *The Suicidal Patient: Recognition, Intervention, Management* (Oradell, NJ: Medical Economics Books, 1983).

[2] Calvin S. Hall and Gardner Lindzey, *Theories of Personality*, 2nd ed. (New York: Wiley and Songs, Inc., 1970).

[3] Aphrodite Matsakis, *I Can't Get Over It: A Handbook for Trauma Survivors* (Oakland, CA: New Harbinger Publications, Inc., 1991), 228-337.

[4] Ibid.

## Chapter 11: The Vets of Korea

1 Luke Macauley, "Passing From Memory: An Analysis of American Servicemen's Letters: Korea 1950-1953" (Diss., University of Glasgow, 2005) 45, http://www.koreanwar-educator.org/topics/letters_warzone/macauley_dissertation.pdf.

2 Jack D. Walker, "A Brief Account of the Korean War," Korean War Educator, http://www.koreanwar-educator.org/topics/brief/brief_account_of_the_korean_war.htm.

3 Robert G. Shannon, "Veterans' Memoirs," Korean War Educator, http://www.koreanwar-educator.org/memoirs/712_trob/index.htm.

4 B.A. Robinson, "What happens after we die?" Ontario Consultants on Religious Tolerance (July 2007), http://www.religioustolerance.org/chr_deat.htm.

5 Susan C. Hedrick, Marylou Guihan and Michael Chapko, "Evaluation of the Assisted Living Pilot Program," *Forum* (April 2008), http://hsrd.research.va.gov/publications/forum/Apr08/Apr08-4.cfm.

6 Lynnita Brown, ed., "Brief Facts: Korean War Veteran Facts," Korean War Educator, http://www.koreanwar-educator.org/topics/brief/p_veteran_facts.htm.

7 Helen C. Kales and Marcia Valenstein, "Depression and Suicide in Aging Veterans: SMITREC Initiatives," *Forum* (April 2008), http://www.hsrd.research.va.gov/publications/forum/Apr08/Apr08-5.cfm.

8 James F. Burris, "VA Responds to the Needs of Aging Veterans," *Forum* (April 2008), http://www.hsrd.research.va.gov/publications/forum/Apr08/Apr08-1.cfm.

## Chapter 13: The Psychological Wounds of War

1 Bio-Medicine, "US Trying Hard to Provide Proper Treatment for Wounded Soldiers," Bio-Medicine (June 2007), http://www.bio-medicine.org/medicine-news/US-Trying-Hard-to-Provide-Proper-Treatment-for-Wounded-Soldiers-22614-1/.

2 Jake Lowary, "New post clinics to fight dual threat: PTSD,TBI," Veterans For America (January 2008), http://www.veteransforamerica.org/2008/01/25/new-post-clinics-to-fight-dual-threat-ptsd-tbi/.

3 David Wilkerson, *Have You Felt Like Giving Up Lately?* (Grand Rapids, MI: Revell, 1982).

4 Jennifer C. Kerr, "Veterans' Group Emphasizes Suicide Risks," SFGate (May 2007), http://www.sfgate.com/cgi-bin/article.cgi?f=/n/a/2007/05/28/national/w135433D60.DTL.

5 E. Everett McFall, *I Can Still Hear Their Cries: Even In My Sleep* (Denver: Outskirts Press, 2007).

6 Walter Reed Army Institute of Research, "Concussions Occurring Among Our Soldiers Deployed in Iraq," Walter Reed Army Institute of Research, http://wrair-www.army.mil/images/MildTBI.pdf.

7 Tom Baldwin, "America suffers an epidemic of suicides among traumatised army veterans," Times Online (November 2007), http://www.timesonline.co.uk/tol/news/world/us_and_americas/article2873622.

**Chapter 14: Heart-to-Heart Resuscitation**
1 Ilona Meagher, ed., "OEF/OIF Veteran Suicide Toll: Nearly 15% of Overall U.S. Military Casualties Result from Suicide," PTSD Combat: Winning the War Within (September 15, 2008) http://ptsdcombat.blogspot.com/2008/09/oefoif-veteran-suicide-toll-15-of.html (accessed 2009).

2 Wikipedia, "Unconditional positive regard," Wikipedia.org (February 2009) http://en.wikipedia.org/wiki/Unconditional_positive_regard.

3 C. George Boeree, "Carl Rogers," Personality Theories (2006) http://webspace.ship.edu/cgboer/rogers.html

**Conclusion**
1 Mark Thompson, "America Medicated Army," Time, June 5, 2008, http://www.time.com/time/nation/article/0,8599,1811858,00.html.

# Select Bibliography

Since the tragedy of suicide and the aftermath of wars are as old as empires and nations, it is impractical to offer sprawling documentation of all the works on which my book is based. This bibliography only begins to highlight the central part and collections of reading upon which I have formed many of my passions, ideals, concepts, speculation and clinical principles. I offer it as a pathway for those of you who wish to expand your knowledge further.

Armstrong, Keith, Suzanne Best, Paula Domenici and Bob Dole. *Courage After Fire: Coping Strategies for Troops Returning from Iraq and Afghanistan and Their Families.* Berkeley, CA: Ulysses Press, 2006.

Boom, Corrie Ten. *Amazing Love: True Stories of the Power of Forgiveness. I* Grand Rapids, Michigan: Baker Book House Company/Fleming H. Revell, 1953.

Coleman, Penny. *Flashback: Posttraumatic Stress Disorder, Suicide, and the Lessons of War.* Boston: Beacon Press, 2006.

Holmstedt, Kirsten. *Band of Sisters: American Women at War in Iraq.* Mechanicsburg, PA: Stackpole Books, 2007.

Matsakis, Aphrodite. *Back from the Front: Combat Trauma, Love, and the Family.* Baltimore, MD: Sidran Institute Press, 2007.

Meagher, Ilona. *Moving A Nation to Care: Post-Traumatic Stress Disorder and America's Returning Troops.* Brooklyn, NY: Ig Publishing, 2007.

Moore, Pamela R. *Life Lessons from the Hiding Place: Discovering the Heart of Corrie Ten Boom.* Grand Rapids, MI: Chosen Books, 2004.

O'Donnell, Patrick K. *We Were One: Shoulder to Shoulder with the Marines Who Took Fallujah.* Cambridge, MA: Da Capo Press, 2004.

Schirldi, Glen R. *Post-Traumatic Stress Disorder Sourcebook: A Guide to Healing, Recovery, and Growth.* Lincolnwood, IL: Lowell House, 2000.

Tick, Edward. *War and the Soul: Healing Our Nation's Veterans from Post-Traumatic Stress Disorder.* Wheaton, IL: Quest Books, 2005.

Warren, Rick. *The Purpose-Driven Life: What on Earth Am I Here For?* Grand Rapids, MI: Zondervan, 2002.

Wilkerson, David. *Have You Felt Like Giving Up Lately?* Grand Rapids, MI: Revell Books, 1982.

# NOTES

# <u>NOTES</u>